Francis Warrington Dawson and the Politics of Restoration:
South Carolina, 1874–1889

E. Culpepper Clark

The University of Alabama Press
University, Alabama

Library of Congress Cataloging in Publication Data

Clark, E. Culpepper
    Francis Warrington Dawson and the politics of
restoration : South Carolina, 1874-1889.

    Bibliography: p.
    Includes index.
    1. South Carolina—Politics and government—
1865–1950. 2. Dawson, Francis W. 3. Journalists—
South Carolina—Biography. I. Title.
F274.C5   975.7'041'0924 [B]   79-27884
ISBN 0-8173-0039-2

Contents

Contents

Acknowledgments

In making this study of Francis Warrington Dawson and the events that surround his career, I have accumulated many debts. My first obligation is to the historians who have constructed the narrative and the interpretations of South Carolina in the era of Reconstruction and Redemption. Yates Snowden, John Schreiner Reynolds, William Watts Ball, David Duncan Wallace, Francis Butler Simkins, Robert Hilliard Woody, George Brown Tindall, Joel Williamson, and William James Cooper, Jr., are representative of those historians who had the patience to seek out and to find the threads with which to fashion a tapestry of the Palmetto State in that trying and confused period of her history. My work has been made comparatively easy by their display of the scholarly virtues.

To the librarians who have given unstintingly of their time and who have endured my questions, I must also express gratitude. The staffs of the South Carolina Historical Society, the South Carolina Archives, the South Caroliniana Library, the Southern Historical Collection, the Library of Congress, and the University of Alabama Library have all been exceedingly generous. I wish to express particular thanks to Dr. Mattie Russell, Dr. Paul I. Chestnut, and the late Mrs. Virginia Gray for their friendly counsel in charting my course through the Dawson papers in the Duke University Library. I must single out Mrs. Gray, whose cataloging of the Dawson collection was a biography in itself and whose patient explanation of what I might expect to find made the search all the more rewarding.

In this respect I must also thank Mr. Samuel Frank Logan and Professor Robert Hilliard Woody, who first undertook a detailed study of Francis Dawson and whose labors led to arrangements for collecting the Dawson papers. Out of their work came a Master's thesis of exceptional quality that has been of much service to students of South Carolina's history. Dawson's grandsons, Dr. Herbert Barry, Jr., of Boston, and Stuyvesant Barry of New Hope, Pennsylvania, also made valuable contributions by illuminating the family life of their grandmother and grandfather. Their interest in my project encouraged its completion.

This book has been vastly improved by the readers who took time to save me from error and embarrassment. Joel Williamson, Peter F. Walker, Lewis Pinckney Jones, and Daniel W. Hollis were instrumental in giving me direction at various stages in the development of the manuscript. A special debt is owed George Brown Tindall who introduced me to Mr. Dawson and who, despite my wanderings in another discipline, kept faith with my ability to complete the job. Malcolm MacDonald and the staff of The University of Alabama Press should also be singled out for their role in bringing the book to completion and for taking pains to facilitate the requirements of the author and the subject. In this same regard, the patience and attention which Connie Farr gave to final preparation of the manuscript saved me both time and anxiety. The errors which survive the care of these people are clearly those of the author.

In the best southern tradition, my deepest obligations are to my family; to my mother and father and brothers who opened the door and to my sons, Culpepper and Stephen, who kept the project in perspective by figuring that when I went to the typewriter it was to work on my *A*, *B*, *Cs*. I now know why authors feel compelled to speak that which cannot be spoken. Mary has endured the crises in confidence, the threats to quit, and worse still the fleeting moments of pride in authorship, and through her, I acquired still more family, parents and sisters whose keen interest in our lives make such things as books possible. Thus, the dedication will be to our family, without whose support and encouragement of my love of history, I would have been a rich lawyer long ago.

E. C. C. February 22, 1980

Francis Warrington Dawson and the Politics of Restoration:

South Carolina, 1874–1889

A.&G.TAYLOR,   PHOTOGRAPHERS TO THE QUEEN

FRANCIS WARRINGTON DAWSON (*Manuscript Department, William R. Perkins Library, Duke University*)

Introduction

"Liberty of the press in South Carolina! There is none," complained a Georgia Republican. "The metropolitan Thunderer, the *News and Courier*, issues its Jovian mandate, and the country newspapers croak, 'Me, too; Me, too; Me, too,' like little slender frogs in the pond when some huge amphibian makes general proclamation."[1] The man behind the "Jovian mandate," against which Republicans in particular had every reason to complain, was Captain Francis Warrington Dawson, founder and editor of the powerful Charleston *News and Courier*.

What follows is a study of Captain Dawson's life in the era of South Carolina's Conservative-Democratic restoration, and while not strictly biographical in approach, it does bear out Winthrop Jordan's observation that "to contemplate any man-in-culture is to savor complexity."[2] The perspective must necessarily be that of Dawson's, for it is his letters, his writings, his life that shape the narrative, but as with all perspectives, the views of friend and foe alike are thrown into relief. It is hoped that such a "life and times" focus will yield insights into both the man and the era.

As editor of the state's leading newspaper, Dawson was in a position to exercise a strong directing influence over South Carolina's Conservative regime, and he missed no opportunity to exert himself to that end. He possessed a quick mind, a dominant personality, and a forceful pen. Foreign observers, who toured the state in the late days of Reconstruction and the early period of Redemption, were quick to note the editor's hand in the politics of restoration, and a recent historian could conclude that Dawson was the logical successor to the mantle of authority worn by Wade Hampton in the desperate struggle to restore white rule.[3]

But while Dawson occupied center stage, especially in the decade of the eighties, his independence of thought and behavior and his own ambition to remain the Warwick of South Carolina politics frequently brought him

---

1. Quoted in James Welch Patton, "The Republican Party in South Carolina, 1876–1895," in *Essays in Southern History*, ed. Fletcher Melvin Green (Chapel Hill: University of North Carolina Press, 1949), p. 99.

2. Winthrop Jordan, *White Over Black: American Attitudes Toward the Negro, 1550–1812* (Chapel Hill: University of North Carolina Press, 1968), p. 429.

3. William Hepworth Dixon, *White Conquest* (London: Chatto and Windus, 1876), pp. 153–58; and Sir George Campbell, *White and Black: The Outcome of a Visit to the United States* (London: Chatto and Windus, 1879), p. 330. William James Cooper, Jr., *The Conservative Regime: South Carolina, 1877–1890*, Johns Hopkins University Studies in Historical and Political Science, ser. LXXXVI, no. 1 (Baltimore: Johns Hopkins Press, 1968), pp. 81–83.

into conflict with other elements in the Conservative-Democratic regime.[4] Through Dawson's eyes, the historian finds new understanding of the complex pattern which underlay the political economy of the Redeemer period. The Conservatives were not of one mind. There were, to be sure, those who looked with nostalgia to a romanticized past, but there were far more who wanted to build on the work of the 1850s in charting a course into the 1880s and beyond. In 1888 Congressman Samuel Dibble wrote Dawson saying, "I regard it absolutely necessary for Charleston to own and control, with her own capital, either Steamship communication from her own port Northward, or Railroad connection with the interior. To do both would be better."[5] These were not the words of men content to rest their accomplishments on an idealized view of a romantic past, nor were they the words of men mired in the despond of agrarian invective which Ben Tillman employed to wrest control of the state government from its Conservative occupants.

It could be that to view South Carolina's Conservative regime through Dawson's eyes would be misleading. He was after all an outsider. His English birth influenced him to speak with what C. Vann Woodward called "the voice of Manchester to the New South."[6] *Harper's Weekly* found it a "decided advantage for the State of South Carolina . . . that the editor of its chief journal was not American born, because he was unswayed by the traditions which cannot but unhappily affect in some degree the native Carolinians." Shortly after Dawson's death, the *News and Courier* commented that "born and bred elsewhere, he sometimes failed in the instinct which would have made him better able to understand the people he had so served." But the paper also remembered that "stranger as he came to us, he might sometimes on that very account have been better able to see us as others did, and by reason of it be the better able to advise."[7] But if Dawson's sensibilities were not precisely those of native South Carolinians, he nonetheless had a large following in the state and his paper completely dominated the forum of public debate. Whatever Dawson's view, it was a matter of great consequence to the policy and the thinking of South Carolina's ruling elite.

---

4. In South Carolina, Democrats preferred the label *Conservative* to avoid the odor of treason which still surrounded the name *Democratic* and to distinguish themselves from the *Radical Republicans.*

5. Samuel Dibble to Dawson, March 10, 1888, Francis Warrington Dawson Papers, Duke University Library, cited hereafter as Duke.

6. C. Vann Woodward, *Origins of the New South, 1877–1913,* vol. IX, A History of the South (Baton Rouge: Louisiana State University Press, 1951), p. 146.

7. *Harper's Weekly,* March 23, 1889; and Charleston *News and Courier,* March 14, 1889, clippings, Dawson Papers, Duke.

An examination of Dawson's role in the era of Redemption makes it readily apparent that certain terms, applied to South Carolina's Redeemers, are inappropriate. Chief among them is the term *Bourbon*. As William Watts Ball once said of that word, "Demagogy invents an epithet and parrots it until ignorance adopts it."[8] Dawson and his friends were no Bourbons, if that expression implies an inability to forget the past and a concomitant failure to learn from it. Indeed, they frequently used the term themselves to criticize opponents both within and outside their party. Moreover, the label *conservative* cannot be taken in the traditional context of resistance to change. As one historian noted, "In the political vocabulary of the 1870s, . . . the terms 'conservative' and 'liberal,' innocent of the meanings which the twentieth century would invest them, functioned more often as synonyms than as antonyms."[9] This study, then, will make reference to the expressions *Conservative, conservative Democracy,* and *Conservative regime* without intending any implication of Bourbonism.

Another term which has been improperly used is *restoration*. If properly conceived the concept of restoration does not necessarily imply social or political regression and has the additional benefit, in the case of South Carolina, of linking the Redeemers to their antebellum past in a way that throws light on both periods in the state's history. In fact, the year of Francis Warrington Dawson's death, 1889, might be considered the end of a long and productive era in the life of the Palmetto State. It marked the one-hundreth year of South Carolina's statehood under the Constitution, less the four-and-a-half years of rebellion. For the brilliant and conservative William Watts Ball, it was a *fin de siècle* of another sort, marking the end of a century in which "the old notions and standards" held sway. For Ball, the election of Benjamin Ryan Tillman as governor in 1890 represented the ascendance of democracy over an aristocracy of wisdom which distinguished South Carolina from its beginning.[10]

Ball clearly felt that what the Redeemers of South Carolina attempted in 1876 was no less than a restoration of the antebellum way of life, at least in terms of how power should be exercised and by whom. But in choosing the right leaders, the Redeemers still overlooked the one critical element that crept into the body politic during the interregnum of Reconstruction: "the democracy imported in the constitution of 1868, it was their undoing, the poison still works."[11] Just as the Stuart monarchs could never turn back the

---

8. William Watts Ball, *The State that Forgot: South Carolina's Surrender to Democracy* (Indianapolis: Bobbs-Merrill, 1932), p. 182.

9. Jack Pendleton Maddex, Jr., *The Virginia Conservatives, 1867–1879: A Study in Reconstruction Politics* (Chapel Hill: University of North Carolina Press, 1970), p. xiii.

10. Ball, *State that Forgot,* pp. 181–82.

11. Ibid., p. 184.

parliamentary ascendancy latent in Cromwellian strife, so the leaders of South Carolina's restoration could not or did not completely rid it of the democratic residue of Reconstruction, imported as it were from the town meetings of Massachusetts, or perhaps more accurately from the factories along the Merrimac. The restoration was forced to blend the new with the old, with time and circumstance on the side of the democratic impulse. Strange as it may seem, "Pitchfork Ben" Tillman may have completed the work of Reconstruction—at least for the white man.

Few historians have agreed with Ball's notion that South Carolina's experience in the Redeemer era amounted to an attempt at restoring the progressive virtues of an earlier time. They either doubt the fact of restoration, because the term denotes reaction, or (what amounts to the same thing) they view whatever restoration occurred as reactionary. C. Vann Woodward found the term inapplicable for South Carolina. He argued that "Senators Wade Hampton and Matthew C. Butler, whose family connections, manners, and patrician outlook identified them with the Old Order, gave superficial color to the picture of Redemption as a 'restoration.'" Woodward believed that South Carolina's Redeemers were much more like their counterparts in other southern states, allying themselves with "the business interests—with the factory owners, railroad men, and merchants of Charleston, Columbia, and other cities." While their names and patrician bearing were of "authentic planter origin, their votes and deeds were of the middle class, and to that class the Redeemers lent all the prestige of aristocratic lineage and glorious war record."[12]

The most recent study of South Carolina's Redeemers took issue with Woodward's interpretation. William James Cooper, Jr., rejected Woodward's idea that the term *Bourbon* was essentially a misnomer. Cooper hoped to establish that "the theme of the Confederacy and of times past pervaded the Conservative mind." South Carolina's Bourbons, he maintained, "looked forward not to a better world but to a re-created one. For them, the best of all possible worlds had existed in ante-bellum South Carolina." From this vantage, Cooper also rejected Woodward's thesis that the Redeemers, as representatives of the merchant and professional class, were swept from power by an agrarian movement grounded in class antagonism. Believing that the Conservative "program had unity only in its loyalty to an idealized past," Cooper felt that time's inexorable dimming effect on memory did more than anything else to undo the Conservative regime. "Tillman swept them from power, not because he had a new and different program for meeting the state's difficulties. He won because he spoke a new rhetoric that appealed to a new generation."[13]

12. Woodward, *Origins,* p. 19.

13. Cooper, *Conservative Regime,* p. 20.

Neither Woodward nor Cooper fully develop the possibilities of restoration as a period of vital, creative energy. Despite Woodward's efforts to give the New South a Whig ancestry, his *Origins of the New South* adopted a Beardian chronology. Denying that "Redemption was in any real sense a restoration," he suggested that "it was rather a new phase of the revolutionary process begun in 1865."[14] On the other hand, Cooper's thesis of a Conservative regime wrapped in a shroud of Confederate gray was based on the assumption that looking back was inherently nonprogressive.

This study rejects, at least in part, both of these views. As chapter seven will indicate, a survey of South Carolina's Redeemers may be better served by ignoring the more dramatic break points of 1860 or 1865 and by addressing instead South Carolina's economic activity, particularly in transportation, during the period stretching from 1850 to 1880. Viewed in this manner, the efforts to restore the conservative Democratic rule which characterized South Carolina in the decade before the war seem less static, more economically progressive.

In further developing restoration as a dynamic concept, the historian might focus on the bolder, more daring aspects of the effort to take South Carolina out of the Union.[15] South Carolinians of the 1850s were not men of little faith. They were opting for a revolution no less potentially consequential than the American strike for independence some four score and five years before. As in the revolution of 1776, the rebels who met in 1860 were intent on preserving the existing political order from a growing imperial menace. Had success crowned their efforts, the values which underlay their particular political philosophy would no doubt have been canonized and laid as foundation for a new governmental approach to the problems of liberty and the dilemma of white over black. While the eventualities of such a turn of events seem philosophically and morally repugnant to generations inheriting the legacy of northern success, it cannot be gainsaid that the effort to maintain southern institutions contained the seeds of a dynamic new departure. In this context, the civilization to be restored was not necessarily in the throes of death; it could quite conceivably have been in the pains of rebirth.

As a corollary to this argument, and to take the theme of restoration one final step, the historian should give more attention to the type of society the Conservatives wished to restore. My own research indicates that they were seeking a society in which men of "sterling worth" made all the important decisions. With ex-Governor Benjamin Franklin Perry, they wanted to restore the integrity which they believed to have marked the

---

14. Woodward, *Origins,* pp. 21–22.

15. For a recent study treating the dynamic quality of the southern strike for independence, see Emory M. Thomas, *The Confederate Nation: 1861–1865,* New American Nation Series (New York: Harper & Row, 1979).

"American cluster of republics" at their beginning. They wanted a government which blended "the strength of monarchy with the wisdom of an
aristocracy and the virtue of democracy. Instead of the people assembling
en masse to make laws, . . . they [were to] choose representatives for their
wisdom and virtue to legislate for them."[16] To these Conservatives the
convention system of government, as opposed to the primary system, was
"an eclectic, a culling system."[17] Beginning at the ward level, the various
conventions were designed to sift through the available candidates until by
a natural process of selection only men of character and ability assembled
to discuss issues affecting the common weal. Conservatives believed that
under the primary system men had little opportunity to talk with each
other, being compelled instead to make demagogic appeals to the lowest
common denominator. In this respect South Carolina's Conservatives were
not unlike liberal reformers in the North, always seeking those qualities of
individual character and personal integrity which guaranteed a society
governed by the "best men." It was class loyalty, but no different from any
other class loyalty, except in numbers.

My investigation leads me to take issue with one final point in Cooper's
thesis. By divorcing rhetoric from reality, Cooper attempts to refute
Woodward's emphasis on class antagonisms between Redeemers and
agrarians. He draws attention to the fact that Tillmanism brought in its
wake no meaningful agrarian reforms and that the movement encompassed
nonfarmers, landowners, and tenants without making distinction. William
Watts Ball, whose conclusions supported Cooper in this evaluation of
Tillman's accomplishments, took the argument a step further, however,
and noted that "it would have been quite impossible to convince the tenant
farmers, the real 'wool hats,' that Captain Tillman was not a 'Moses' to
deliver them from bondage." Ball further observed that the "starched
shirts," particularly in Charleston, who made their way into the farmers'
movement, became "Tillmanites primarily because they resented domination of the local political powers." The editor concluded his evaluation of
Tillmanism with the following note:

> It stood for no natural lines of social cleavage; it awakened, it crystalized
> the class consciousness of the land-owner, fusing and confusing the class
> consciousness of the tenant with it, so that the last remained, from the point
> of view of results, in the identical condition of political torpor and strangula-
> tion that he has ever been in South Carolina. Consequently, the triumph of
> Tillmanism brought only a superficial change and there was no compensation

16. Benjamin Franklin Perry, *Biographical Sketches of Eminent American Statesmen with
Speeches, Addresses and Letters by Ex-Governor B. F. Perry,* intro. Wade Hampton
(Philadelphia: Ferree Press, 1887), p. 240.

17. William Watts Ball, *An Episode in South Carolina Politics* (n.p., 1915), .p. 36.

for the evils attending it; there were the accompaniments of revolution, the clamor, the angry divisions—but when all is said, the revolution was of a wheel without a hub.[18]

This study supports Ball's judgment that the rhetoric of change had its impact even if the reality failed to measure up. It sustains the judgment of Francis Butler Simkins that the manner of political debate inaugurated by Tillman "filled a real need in the life of rural South Carolinians."[19] Dawson and his Conservative friends certainly believed the Tillman movement to be fraught with class antagonism. And even if the farmers' movement in South Carolina did not dream the dreams of the genuine Populist or advance the programs that offered some hope of redress, it cannot be denied that their movement was fueled by the same needs and aspirations as those of farmers in other states. "It was clear that these people were convinced that somebody had done them great wrong, and that they meant to get even with their foes." It was also clear that if "one wore a starched shirt [it] was enough to place him under suspicion."[20]

In review, it is my conclusion that the South Carolina Conservatives showed a greater diversity of opinion over the nature and future of Redemption than Cooper finds, and that the dominant element among South Carolina's Redeemers more closely approximated Woodward's description. I also believe that the theme of restoration, if properly explored, offers an interpretive key for better understanding Conservatism in South Carolina as a dynamic, constructive force in the state's life, in contrast to the regressive tendencies emphasized in Cooper's thesis. Finally, I have sought to highlight the idea of class antagonism between Conservatives and the farmers' movement by focusing on rhetoric as an important component of reality.

Having established that basic overview, it remains to be said that Cooper's survey of South Carolina's Conservative regime is both careful and thorough. My quarrel with his work is clearly a matter of interpretation. I can appreciate the evidence which lends itself to the inferences he has drawn. I can also appreciate his effort to downplay the Beardian theme which runs throughout Woodward's orchestration of the class antagonisms of the period. My own view is a selective borrowing from both Cooper and Woodward, finding much more on which to agree than disagree, but it is also governed by a belief that reform in America has more often than not found its inspiration in efforts to restore and conserve past virtues. Historians may second-guess the South Carolina Conservative, who be-

---

18. Ibid., p. 6.

19. Francis Butler Simkins, *The Tillman Movement in South Carolina* (Durham: Duke University Press, 1926), pp. 88–89.

20. Ball, *Episode*, p. 3.

lieved himself to be a reformer, by finding deeper structures of economic motivation for his behavior, but in so doing they must inevitably discount the fact that what men think they are doing is quite as important as what they in fact do. And in South Carolina the keepers of the past must also work with a class of men who, while seeking economic security, remained for the most part "plain men of simple tastes and without exception poor."[21]

---

21. Ball, *State that Forgot,* p. 183.

Chapter I
Francis Warrington Dawson:
Nom de Guerre

Long before Caesar warned Antony about men with "lean and hungry" looks, people pondered the question of just what qualities enabled the ambitious to get ahead. Children in particular have searched the books for some key to success, or to discover some similarity between their present state and the lives of their heroes. Few eras indulged this penchant for hero worship with more enthusiasm than did the last three decades of the nineteenth century. In addition to the rugged individuals popularized by Horatio Alger, the presses were kept busy with a stream of "life and letters" publications which chronicled the virtuous lives of senators, governors, businessmen, statesmen, and even vice presidents. Conspicuous among the heroes of those decades were editors, particularly in the South, where men relied on the metropolitan dailies to tell them of their place in a union they had only a few years before fought to put asunder. Thus when two of the South's leading editors, Francis Warrington Dawson and Henry Woodfin Grady, came to their untimely deaths in 1889, they provided occasion for great public mourning.

In Charleston the news of Captain Dawson's death was greeted with that mix of horror and disbelief that attends the assassination of men whose personalities have become the individual property of each citizen. This communal transformation of Francis Dawson from private citizen to public man was testament to the lordly dominance he exercised over South Carolina in the 1880s. Through the *News and Courier* he controlled the flow of information, the character of public discussion, and the notoriety of public officials. For fifteen years he spoke with the voice of South Carolina's leading Conservatives, but because it was his newspaper and his editorial column, the voice carried with the unmistakable inflection and accent of his English heritage. When South Carolinians debated the best way to overthrow Reconstruction, Dawson commanded a powerful group of Conservatives who favored a policy of cooperating with kindred spirits in the Republican party, but when his counsel was rejected on that issue, he and his paper quickly became General Wade Hampton's "right bower."[1] With Reconstruction ended, he championed the wise and moderate coterie, which surrounded Governor Hampton, against the aspirations of the intemperate white supremacist Martin Gary. Always with an eye to the future and South Carolina's place in the restored union, Dawson asked

---

1. The origin of this sobriquet is likely the Camden *Journal,* quoted in the Charleston *News and Courier,* January 11, 1879.

his readers to build a society imbued with the attributes of Manchesterian liberalism; a society which tempered white supremacy with a guarantee of the law's equal protection to the Negro; and a New South infused with the virtues of the old. During the eighties, Dawson gave South Carolina a powerful voice in national party councils, and when farmer unrest began to threaten Conservative hegemony at the end of that decade, he carried the Conservative guidon into battle against "Pitchfork Ben" Tillman.

A year after his death those who knew him best sought to take the measure of his mark upon the state. On March 12, 1890, James Calvin Hemphill, who succeeded Dawson in the editor's chair, allowed the *News and Courier* to indulge in a moment's reflection:

> Looking back now, as South Carolinians, over the year that has passed— and we think the impression will grow more definite and distinct as the increasing distance of time brings us nearer to the proper focus—we cannot but realize that this Englishman, who came among us in his impetuous youth as a fighter of our battles, strove earnestly to make himself one of us; and while imbibing all that was best in the old South Carolina character, sought to combine with it the modifying influence of the spirit of the age. Indeed, our statute books and social customs show the impress of his vigorous thought and forceful action, and few will be found to deny that South Carolina is better for having as a citizen for twenty years, never out of politics and never in office, Captain F. W. Dawson.

But the impression grew dim with time. Those friends who at first wanted to erect a monument or name a street in his honor gradually returned to the routine of carrying on and forgot the debt they felt at first news of Captain Dawson's death. When it was all done, the only marker to commemorate the man, who Ben Tillman said bestrode South Carolina "like a colossus,"[2] was a small stained window in the Catholic parish church of Isleworth, England, where Dawson once served as an alter boy.[3]

Francis Warrington Dawson was a *nom de guerre*. He was born in London, England, on May 17, 1840, and was baptized Austin John Reeks. He was the oldest son of Mary Perkins and Joseph Austin Reeks, who were married in London, October 14, 1837. The Reeks family (pronounced Riks) traced its line back to the Wars of the Roses. "It was a proud family without nobiliary connections," wrote Dawson's son, "but proud of its name as one of the oldest Catholic families in England, no member of which had ever recanted under the persecutions of Henry VIII and Elizabeth, and several having been burned at the stake." Joseph Austin, like his father before him, had been educated and graduated with honors in

---

2. *News and Courier,* August 29, 1888.

3. From an article by Dawson's son, Warrington, written for the *News and Courier,* December 7, 1930.

the college of Saint-Omer in France, and it was assumed that young Austin John would follow in those steps; then misfortune struck the Reeks family. In the forties Joseph Austin made some disastrous speculations in the English wheat market and spent the remainder of his life dabbling in one commercial venture after another in a vain attempt to recover a lost fortune. In the meantime the family struggled to maintain the dignity which befitted their former station.[4]

Fortunately, a sister of Mrs. Reeks was able to step in and to make provision for Austin John's education. This aunt inherited a considerable estate when her husband, Captain William A. Dawson, was killed in the Sepoy Mutiny, and she intended that her nephew, Austin John, should be the beneficiary of her wealth. Her plans were to send the young man to Saint-Omer, after which she would purchase for him a charge as solicitor. So, with the aid of a tutor, Austin John began his preparations to enter the college and was on a "gentleman's tour" of the continent when he received word that his Aunt Dawson had suffered a stroke. Family lore has it that before he could reach her side some distant cousins laid claim to the estate and in classic fashion cheated him of his inheritance.

Thus, at the age of eighteen Austin John Reeks found himself without a vocation and without means for attaining one. Despite his excellent preparatory education, he did not have the money to purchase an office and had to bear the additional handicap of being a Roman Catholic in a time when many avenues were still closed to practitioners of that faith. Bewildered by his meager prospects, Austin John considered employing his excellent tenor voice in pursuit of a musical career and devoted other hours to writing plays, with one production appearing as a curtain-raiser in London.

One manuscript, which Austin John finished in June, 1859, revealed much about the makeup of the soon-to-be Francis Warrington Dawson. Titled "Never Judge by Appearances,"[5] the play was highly moralistic, involving a simple plot with no loose ends. The heroine, Emily Danton, is torn between "duty" to her husband, who is engaged in the mundane world of commerce, and her inner desire for a man more romantic and artistic. Enter Algernon Fitzclarence, a blackguard spoiled by the effete world of aristocratic privilege. After surveying the situation, Fitzclarence

---

4. The information on Dawson's life in England comes from a number of sources, the most useful being the excellent M.A. thesis by S. Frank Logan, "Francis W. Dawson, 1840–1889: South Carolina Editor" (Duke University, 1947). Logan did an outstanding job of getting information from Dawson's son, F. Warrington Dawson, Jr., through the use of written interrogatories. Copies of Warrington's answers will be referred to hereafter as Warrington Dawson Notes and may be found in the F. W. Dawson Papers, Duke University Library, cited hereafter as Duke. Quoted material comes from Warrington's article in the *News and Courier,* December 7, 1930.

5. A MS copy of this play can be found in the Dawson Papers, Duke.

makes a wager that he can steal Emily's affections and lure her from her husband. Emily, suffering those qualities of indecision allegedly attributable to her sex, finally succumbs to Fitzclarence's blandishments and particularly to his perfidious promise to stand for her husband's heavy debts.

With her conscience salved by the promise of aid to her beleaguered husband, Emily takes flight, all the while under the unseen but ever watchful eye of her kind old guardian, John Brown. During her brief flight she comes to realize what a scoundrel Fitzclarence is and how important Duty is. At this juncture Brown intervenes by having Fitzclarence arrested for an old debt, and the debauched aristocrat, seeing the consequences of his evil ways, conveniently exits by means of suicide. Emily, now much wiser for having learned that one should "never judge by appearances," makes the decent and proper decision to tell the whole story to her husband even though there were no witnesses save for the kind old Mr. Brown who leaves the choice to Emily. So Emily tells the truth, Brown explains it, and all is forgiven. And lest the audience fear for the husband's debts, the author wraps up that detail by having Mr. Brown stand good for the judgment.

The play was simple and direct, with a puritanical emphasis on duty and religion. Just before taking his life, Fitzclarence is forced to concede, "Virtues I have none, my vices are those of my class, and with no staff of religion to support me, little by little I became the thing I now am." Moments later, when Fitzclarence lies dead and no witness remains to reveal Emily's betrayal, dear Mr. Brown consoles the distraught heroine, saying, "Do not forget that a stronger arm than ours seems to be guiding our vessel into port. Never does it harm to trust in Providence if at the same time your own shoulder be put to the wheel." Duty and religion would remain the staff and rod in Dawson's approach to day-to-day living. He served his church quietly and devoutly, studiously avoiding any public display of his or any other religion. He once advised a writer for the *News and Courier* that she should avoid "too much scriptural quotation and too much of Christianity by name. . . . You know it is our object to inculcate the loftiest Christian morality, but we can't call it Christian, nor dare we . . . indulge in any appearance of dogmatism."[6] Those who later doubted his professed "religious" scruples against duelling did not know the man.

"Never Judge by Appearances" said as much about the Reeks family as it revealed about a young man's world view. Austin John's father was a combination of Fitzclarence and Emily's husband, Henry Danton. After failing in grain speculation, Joseph Reeks, ill-equipped for other work, became something of a *bon vivant* and was frequently absent from the

---

6. Dawson to Sarah Morgan, ca. April 22, 1873, ibid.

family. But Austin John respected his father and wished to become his apologist. At one point the young playwright has Henry Danton, a man of commerce who is on the verge of losing his fortune, cry out, "Stop! I forgot the doctrine of the world. Be a rogue if you like, but make a fortune, and you may have all London for your shoe-blacks. Be honest, and lose a fortune and New Gate [sic] is a thousand times too good for you." At another point Emily may well have described the gulf that Austin John felt separating him from his father. "My father was never prodigal of his love to me," she lamented, "[but] always enwrapped in the cold mantle of his pride he scarce deigned to notice my existence."

The estrangement of the father, coupled with hard times, could not have made growing up in the Reeks family an altogether happy experience. Another mouth was added to the household when a younger brother, Joseph William, was born in 1849.[7] Making ends meet became extremely difficult. Years later Captain Dawson recalled having collected old wine bottles, relics of better times, and having sold them in order to purchase medicine for his mother. The medicine was very much needed, for not long after, his sister, Teresa Mary, was born.[8] To the problems of privation were added some of the concomitant difficulties of marital stress in the Reeks household. It seemed to the young playwright as if married people made up their minds "to be as uncomfortable as they can, and [took] the greatest possible pleasure in placing thorns for themselves to sit upon."

While the family situation was difficult, it was not usually turbulent, with each member of the household having great respect for the others and with the mid-Victorian rules of family discipline generally prevailing. On at least one occasion, however, there was a great commotion at the Reeks's dinner table. The stormy blast was occasioned by Austin John's declaration that he wished to go and fight for the Confederate States of America. Joseph Reeks, fearing that his son might be captured in passage and denied the rights of a belligerent, argued that under such conditions he would be hanged as a pirate. To risk death was one matter, but to risk bringing dishonor to the family name seemed to be more than Austin John's father could take. The quarrel ended with young Austin John swearing that he would leave home "and be hanged under a name of my own."[9]

---

7. Joseph William Reeks was subsequently private chaplain to the Duke of Norfolk, Honorary Canon of St. George's Cathedral, Southwark, and at the time of his death in 1900 Dean of St. Peter's Woolwich, the Catholic Army Church. It was his mission to minister to the poor, and as a result he never acquired financial security. It became necessary in the eighties for Dawson to offer financial assistance. See Dawson's personal financial statement, 1887–89, in the box marked accounts, Dawson Papers, Duke.

8. Teresa Mary Reeks, born in 1854, married a distant cousin, Bernard Richard White, in the late seventies. She died on May 14, 1881, only months before the death of their father, Joseph Austin, August 31, 1881.

9. *News and Courier,* December 7, 1930.

So it was that Austin John Reeks, at the ripe age of twenty and without immediate prospects, made known his intention to assume a *nom de guerre* and to join the cause of the southern armies. For some time he had been following the course of the secessionist states in the London papers, and as he later put it, "I had a sincere sympathy with the Southern people in their struggle for independence and felt that it would be a pleasant thing to help them secure their freedom."[10] By the autumn of 1861 he was determined in his resolve and merely awaited opportunity's nod. The motivation was, no doubt, much more than an English liberal's desire to defend home rule wherever it might be threatened, or as Dawson later remarked, the "ruling idea" being "that the South was fighting, as the Barons fought at Runnymede, for liberty and self government and that it was my duty, as an English-speaking man, to take a hand in the fight."[11] Yet more to the mark may have been Ella Lonn's suggestion that "Dawson left out of the reckoning the love of adventure which was undoubtedly thrilling his heart."[12] Like Samuel Taylor Coleridge or Edgar Allan Poe before him, Austin John Reeks would go to war under an assumed name. "It was the spirit of the age, and most delightfully romantic!"[13]

The surname selected was not surprisingly that of his soldier uncle, Captain William A. Dawson, since it was to the Dawson's generosity that he would have owed his formal education. For his Christian name he took that of his patron saint, Francis of Assisi, and as a middle name he slightly modified the name of the Warren family who were near-relations. Having assumed his *nom de guerre,* there remained but one problem—just how to get into the fight. This difficulty was soon solved when the Confederate steamer, *Nashville,* docked at Southampton. On hearing of the ship's arrival, Dawson hurried the short distance from London to Southampton and implored the ship's commander, Robert Baker Pegram, to allow him to enlist in the Confederate States Navy. Dawson got nowhere at first because of his youthful appearance, but persistence finally paid off when the commander relented on condition that Dawson would ship "before the mast." Pegram no doubt believed that life as a common sailor would be so distasteful as to deter the ardent young man. Undaunted and elated, Dawson rushed out and bought a sea-chest "which, according to Marryatt's

---

10. F. W. Dawson, *Reminiscences of Confederate Service, 1861–1865* (Charleston: *The News and Courier* Book Presses, 1882), p. 3.

11. Dawson to Robert Reid Hemphill, June 28, 1876, Hemphill Family Papers, Duke.

12. Ella Lonn, *Foreigners in the Confederacy* (Chapel Hill: University of North Carolina Press, 1940), p. 56.

13. *News and Courier,* December 7, 1930. See also MS note by Warrington in Morgan Family Genealogy Box, Dawson Papers, Duke.

novels, was indispensible to a sea-faring man."[14] Dawson then settled down to wait and to watch the newspapers for a notice of the *Nashville's* departure date.

Soon tiring of the wait, the impetuous adventurer bid goodbye to his family and set out for Southampton. On the way he stopped off to pick up the bowie knife he had ordered made, a friend from Arkansas having assured him that such a formidable weapon was essential in America. Before boarding ship he also purchased a sailor's outfit which he described at some length:

> I wore a blue woolen shirt open at the neck; a black silk handkerchief, with ample flowing ends, tied loosely around the neck; blue trousers, made very tight at the knee and twenty-two inches in circumference at the bottom, and on my head a flat cloth cap ornamented with long black ribbons. I had besides, in the famous sea-chest, a pea jacket, sea-boots, and the necessary underclothing. As a reminder of my former estate, I retained a suit of dress clothes, and black Inverness cape.[15]

Dawson reported to the *Nashville* on New Year's day, 1862, and informed the somewhat incredulous officer of the deck that he had been ordered aboard by Lieutenant Commander Pegram. It took some talking, but Dawson finally assured the officer that he was indeed a sailor. In fact, his previous experience "in nautical affairs had been confined to sailing miniature yachts on the Serpentine in Hyde Park" and to the "knowledge obtained from the romances of Marryatt and Chamier, and Dana's excellent book: 'Two Years Before the Mast.'" For the next few weeks Dawson's routine was confined to scrubbing decks during the day and joining the crew at the "Rainbow" or the "Wheat Sheaf" at night. Visits to the taverns were a delight, especially one trip that ended in a row with sailors of the Northern persuasion.[16]

Then at 3:30 P.M., February 2, 1862, the *Nashville* weighed anchor and departed Southampton under a full head of steam. There was no time to look back, for the United States warship *Tuscarora* chafed under a restraining order from the British government which forbade her sailing for another twenty-four hours. To foil the chase which would surely ensue, Pegram steered a northerly course, and the next morning the crew was mustered into the service of the Confederate States of America. Dawson's eagerly awaited martial career had begun at last, albeit as a "landsman" or "boy."[17]

---

14. Dawson, *Reminiscences*, p. 8.

15. Ibid. See also Dawson to his mother, January (?), 1862, Dawson Papers, Duke.

16. Dawson, *Reminiscences*, pp. 10–14.

17. For accounts of the *Nashville's* voyage see Dawson, *Reminiscences*, pp. 13–29, and Lieutenant Commander Pegram's report in the *Official Records of the Union and Confederate Navies in the War of the Rebellion*, ser. I, vol.I, pp. 745–49.

Life with the crew was unpleasant. There were eight seamen, a mixed bag consisting of an Irishman, a Belgian, a North Carolinian, a Swede, a Cockney, a Frenchman, a Scot, and a Spaniard. Dawson found them to be "mean, treacherous, and obscene." Two days out and they had stolen the treasures of his carefully prepared sea-chest. Eighteen days later, Dawson was writing, "Time does not in the least reconcile me to the men in the forecastle! More and more do I detest and loathe them!"[18] Fortunately, the young landsman's excellent preparatory education came in handy, and he soon found himself more and more in the company of the officers, teaching one to read French. On the seventh or eighth day out, Dawson was rewarded by being moved from the forecastle to one of the extra state-rooms on the hurricane deck. After coaling in Bermuda, the *Nashville* made its run for the Confederate States, slipping through the blockade at Morehead City, North Carolina, on the morning of February 28.

In his report on the cruise, Lieutenant Commander Pegram could not have been more flattering in commending the services of Landsman Dawson:

> I also wish to call specially your attention to the sacrifices made by Mr. Frank Dawson, a young Englishman of high refinement and education, who left family, friends, and every tie to espouse our cause, and who, not to be put off by any difficulty thrown in his way, insisted upon serving under our flag, performing throughout the passage from England the most menial duties . . . in a manner that gained for him the admiration of every officer on board. I am now most desirous of retaining the services of Mr. Frank Dawson as my clerk, unless the Department can find some more appropriate position in which to place him.[19]

Pegram's request was granted, and Dawson was appointed a Master's Mate. Nor would it be the last time Frank Dawson was recognized and promoted for ability or gallantry.

With his newly acquired commission, the young Englishman accompanied Pegram on what turned out to be a whirlwind tour of the South, going first to Norfolk, then to the outskirts of New Orleans where federal forces made it impossible to go farther, and finally back to Richmond.[20] But life in the Confederate States Navy proved too dull for a man who had crossed an

18. Dawson, *Reminiscences,* p. 11, and Dawson to his parents, February 20, 1862, Dawson Papers, Duke.

19. *Official Records,* ser. I, vol. I, p. 748. See also J. Thomas Scharf, *History of the Confederate States Navy from Its Organization to the Surrender of Its Last Vessel* (New York: Rogers & Sherwood, 1887), p. 712. Shortly after Dawson's death, R. B. Pegram wrote another account of his experience with Dawson which appeared in the *Daily Norfolk Virginian,* July 21, 1889, scrapbook, Dawson Papers, Duke.

20. Dawson to his mother, May 16, 1862, Dawson Papers, Duke.

ocean to get into a fight, and securing the approval of Commander Pegram, he resigned his commission in June, 1862. Dawson was now free to do what he had wanted for some time: to join the Purcell Battery, commanded by his patron's nephew, William Pegram. The battery was attached to Field's Brigade, A. P. Hill's Division, and on the afternoon of June 26, 1862, Private Dawson moved with General Hill's column across the Chickahominy, towards Mechanicsville. It was the spectacle he had come for, and one he would never forget. There before him were "the gleaming bayonets, and waving flags, the rumbling of artillery, and the steady tramp of the men." As the columns of gray moved out to engage the enemy, he found the sight "both exhilarating and imposing." Later in the day, the young spectator became a participant, and stepping into the breach left by fallen comrades, he shed his first blood for the cause as an exploding shell threw him to the ground and sent a piece of shrapnel tearing through his leg.[21]

For his courage under fire and with the highest commendations, Dawson was commissioned a first lieutenant of artillery in August, 1862, and by April, 1864, had attained the rank of captain. From August, 1862, to October, 1864, he served as an assistant ordnance officer, I Corps, the Army of Northern Virginia—a position which placed him on Longstreet's staff. From October, 1864, to April, 1865, he was placed in charge of ordnance for Fitzhugh Lee's cavalry division. When the war was over, he proudly claimed to have been present for the following engagements: Mechanicsville, Second Manassas, Fredericksburg, Gettysburg, Chattanooga, Knoxville, the Wilderness, Spottsylvania, North Side James River, the Valley of Virginia, and Five Forks. He was taken prisoner near Williamsport, Maryland, September 14, 1862, and after a brief incarceration at Fort Delaware was released in October of the same year. He was wounded at Mechanicsville, 1862; at Harrisonburg, 1864; and at Five Forks, 1865.[22]

Dawson loved his life as a soldier. He was full of dash and dare, and despite certain antagonisms expressed toward foreigners,[23] he won the admiration and respect of those under whom he served. One observer remarked that among the Englishmen in the Confederacy "the fighting

---

21. Dawson, *Reminiscences,* pp. 47–50. Dawson to his mother, July 1, 1862, Dawson Papers, Duke.

22. MS record submitted to the Confederate Survivors' Association of the Charleston District, n.d., prepared by F. W. Dawson, Dawson Papers, Duke.

23. Ella Lonn, *Foreigners,* p. 419. For manifestations of this hostility toward Dawson see Fitzgerald Ross, *Cities and Camps of the Confederate States,* ed. Richard Barksdale Harwell (Urbana: University of Illinois Press, 1958), pp. 128–31, and W. Stanley Hoole, *Vizitelly Covers the Confederacy,* Confederate Centennial Studies (Tuscaloosa, Alabama: Confederate Publishing, 1957), p. 104. Dawson's own testimony is found in letters to his mother, June 26, 1864, and November 25, 1864, Dawson Papers, Duke.

exceptions were rare," but that "a notable one" was Captain F. W. Dawson.[24] His letters home were full of the war and his role in it. After being commissioned a first lieutenant he wrote to tell his mother the news, and with the drollery which makes deeper feelings easier to express, exclaimed, "What a happy moment it will be when, the war concluded, I may visit England, and with my 'blushing honors thick upon me' tell you the tale of my perils in 'the eminent and deadly breach,' describing to you all the 'pomp, pride and circumstance' of glorious war."[25] Of Fredericksburg he later wrote, "Never in my life do I expect to see such a magnificent sight again. From the crest of a hill . . . the whole scene of conflict was before our eyes, and at our feet, the glorious sun shining out as if the bloodshed and slaughter were unknown to the beautiful earth—the screaming of shells and the singing of rifle bullets adding a fearful accompaniment to the continued booming of the heavy guns." It was at the sight of this same desperate field that General Robert E. Lee is said to have turned away and said, "It is well that war is so terrible, else we should grow too fond of it." But to a young adventurer writing his mother it was "the 7th pitched battle in which I have been engaged, and I hope before the war closes to extend my role of honor."[26]

Adding to his pleasures in the South, Dawson achieved a ready acceptance by Virginia society. Soon after his arrival Captain Pegram introduced young Dawson to Mr. Nathaniel Raines, a wealthy planter from Sussex County. Raines was so impressed with the young English soldier that he virtually adopted him, and thereafter "Oakland," the Raines's plantation, became Dawson's second home. But it was in Richmond that Dawson spent his gayest hours. Mrs. Burton Harrison recalled that this "clever, handsome, venturesome English lad" was accustomed to being met at our parties and to being received in our drawing rooms.[27] These private parties became a Richmond institution. The people who gathered were "known as the 'Quiet Set' to the giddier ones," but it was "possibly the best and most compensating portion of Richmond society." These gatherings, which Dawson frequented, were the origin and home of the famous "Mosaic Club."[28] It was here that Dawson reacquainted himself with Clarence

---

24. Thomas Cooper De Leon, *Belles, Beaux and Brains of the 60's* (New York: G. W. Dillingham, 1909), p. 333.

25. Dawson to his mother, August 3, 1862, Dawson Papers, Duke.

26. Ibid., April 23, 1863. The Lee quotation comes from Donald Bridgman Sanger and Thomas Robson Hay, *James Longstreet* (Baton Rouge: Louisiana State University Press, 1952), p. 114.

27. Mrs. Burton Harrison, *Recollections Grave and Gay* (New York: Charles Scribner's Sons, 1911), pp. 178–79.

28. De Leon, *Belles,* pp. 201–12. Dawson also speaks of being a founder of the Richmond Club in his *Reminiscences,* p. 164.

Cary, the officer he taught French while on board the *Nashville*. Cary, later to become a prosperous New York attorney, in turn introduced Dawson to the handsome James Morris Morgan of Louisiana, a man who later would figure prominently in Dawson's life. The beautiful Haxall sisters, one of whom Dawson engaged to marry, were also to be found among the guests. The Raineses, the Pegrams, the Carys, the Haxalls, and many others formed a web of friendship that led Dawson to exclaim, "It seems so strange that I should have had so few friends in England, when I have such hosts of them here."[29] The Richmond *Examiner* even took some time to punctuate this feeling of acceptance when in 1863 the paper acknowledged Dawson's gallant service and expressed the hope that after the war he would find some southern girl and settle among them.[30]

It was the web of friendship, the acclaim, and the quick advancement through the ranks that led Dawson to make both his adopted name and his adopted land permanent. In June, 1864, he explained to his mother that he had "won everything that is honorable in my life under my present name & to that I must forever adhere."[31] When the war was over, he momentarily vacillated between staying and returning to England but finally announced:

> Here I have a high position and a high reputation; in England I should be less than nobody; here I have a thousand friends where in England I have none; here the whole people are linked together by sufferings and hardships borne together, by perils shared in common, and by a hope for the future that will last while a solitary Virginian exists.

In bidding farewell to his family, he apologized for "the old wandering instinct in my blood" and prayed that "Joe may be able to give you . . . that personal care which cannot come from me."[32]

But even as he was staking his future with the state of Virginia, his prospects did not look good. No job offered any real security. He served variously as a bookkeeper, an editorial assistant for the Richmond *Examiner* and later the *Dispatch* and finally as an assistant superintendent for an express company. In between jobs he thought of being a farmer, but more frequently dreamed of being a soldier once again. At war's end he confided that "the profession of a soldier would be my choice above, far above, any other occupation with which I am acquainted." In moments of despair he

---

29. Dawson to his mother, March 25, 1866, Dawson Papers, Duke. Dawson was engaged to Miss Mary Haxall until he introduced her to Alexander Cameron of tobacco fame, whereupon Mary "unceremoniously jilted" her English suitor, *Reminiscences*, p. 165. Dawson was previously engaged to a Miss Botting in England.

30. Richmond *Examiner*, (?), 1863, scrapbook, Dawson Papers, Duke.

31. Dawson to his mother, June 1, 1864, ibid.

32. Ibid., July 28, 1866.

took heart from the thought that "this Country is still on the brink of a volcano, or may have another War, who knows, and then Hurrah! for the old cause; it may be years, what matter? I could wait a century patiently to have one more blow at them before I die."[33]

In less passionate moments, Dawson knew there would be no more war and no more soldiering for an ex-rebel, and he turned his attention to a future in business with such enthusiasm that a Yankee would pale by comparison. In a letter home he noted that the "habit here" was for every man to go into business for himself, "and the majority of the community, except the very *crème de la crème,* is made up of self-made men. There is room for it here! The country is always expanding, and every man has a chance." It was in this same hopeful spirit that he wrote his last letter from Virginia.

> There must be some strange influence in the atmosphere in this Country. Think of my having been an officer in the Navy, an officer in the Army, a book-keeper, the Editor of two newspapers, and Ass't Supt of an Express Co. in five years and succeeding in all of them. Jack of all trades, my dear Madam, and now waiting for something new to turn up. When in a jump I may find myself a doctor, pedlar or travelling preacher.[34]

Not long after this cheerful letter, the express company, which Dawson later bitterly compared to an "almshouse for Confederate officers of high rank,"[35] was in financial ruin and his next job was a "jump" indeed, taking him away from the state he had grown to love.

On leaving Virginia, Dawson was turning his back to the last group of people who would remember him as a private citizen. They would call back the memory of a lean, muscular young man who was almost tall at five feet and ten inches. They would remember his clear, steady, light blue eyes, rather deep set in a face that had been bronzed by the Virginia sun but was at war's end still frustratingly without manly beard. They would remember a light baritone voice, quick to laughter, shaped by the accent of the cultured Englishman—a voice which could rise to the heroic tenor when called on to sing in the parlors of Richmond. He was good-looking, and his dark brown hair, when allowed to grow, gave his prominent features the countenance of a poet. An absorbing conversationalist with an intense, forceful personality, he was the kind of young man who had no trouble securing endorsements and letters of recommendation. Dawson's son later "got the impression that his [father's] Virginia friends . . . had deeper penetration into his true character and personality, knowing him more as his own family knew him, than was the case of a majority of his Carolina

---

33. Ibid., June 5 and November 13, 1865.

34. Ibid., July 28 and October 2, 1866.

35. *News and Courier,* December 30, 1880.

friends." But, as his son conceded, the Carolinians knew him as a public man, "in a setting of politico-economic complexes," not as a private man.[36]

The call to leave his beloved Virginia came from Bartholomew Rochefort Riordan. Dawson first met Riordan when the two worked together on Henry Rives Pollard's Richmond *Examiner*. They shared a room and took their meals at Zetelle's restaurant, all the while braving the dangers of working for the fiery Pollard. Dawson in particular occupied the "unpleasant position" of being "adviser and best man for Pollard in his principal rencontres." One of the more spectacular fracases involved a shoot-out in the rotunda of the House of Representatives in which the tassel of the cane on Houdon's statue of George Washington was shot away. The job got so dangerous that on another occasion Dawson could be found hastily scribbling out a will while reporting actions from the floor of the House of Burgesses.[37] While Dawson dodged bullets, Riordan applied his fifteen years' experience in journalism back at the *Examiner* office and dreamed big dreams. His previous service on the New Orleans *Delta* and the Charleston *Mercury* convinced him that Dawson was just the kind of man needed to launch a successful newspaper venture, and so he proposed that the two of them start a cheap and popular newspaper in Charleston. In making the proposal, the more experienced Riordan commented, "Of course you know Dawson you could not do the editorial writing, but we could engage a man to do that for us."[38] Given the later course of events, it was to prove an amusing observation.

The time was not yet right, however, and Riordan soon left for Washington, while Dawson moved over to the *Dispatch* and subsequently to the National Express Company. Nothing more transpired on the subject until October, 1866, at which time Dawson received a letter from no less a figure than Colonel Robert Barnwell Rhett, asking Dawson to come to Charleston and to serve as the *Mercury*'s assistant editor. Rhett had been informed that a bright young man in Richmond was just the person needed to get the old newspaper going again, and the informant was none other than Riordan, who had just returned to Charleston as assistant editor of the *Courier*. So with no other prospects and anxious to join his friend, Dawson packed his belongings, taking special care to include a set of "shirt studs and sleeve buttons of gold, with the Confederate flag exquisitely enamelled on each." He had been presented these tokens in appreciation for services rendered to the Hollywood Memorial Association of Richmond, and they

---

36. Warrington Dawson Notes, Dawson Papers, Duke.

37. MS copy of will in Dawson Papers, Duke. See also Dawson to his mother, March 25, 1866, Dawson Papers, Duke; and Dawson, *Reminiscences*, pp. 153–58. For a vivid description of Pollard see George W. Bagby, *The Old Virginia Gentleman and Other Sketches*, ed. with intro. Thomas Nelson Page (New York: Charles Scribner's Sons, 1911), p. 217.

38. Quoted in Dawson, *Reminiscences*, p. 158.

were his most valued possession next "to the love of my dear parents."
With the war only a year and a half behind him, Francis Warrington
Dawson arrived in Charleston on November 10, 1866, and immediately
concluded, "I think I shall like the place, and, indeed, shall not have time
to dislike it."[39]

Another year would pass before Riordan and Dawson could consum-
mate their Richmond scheme of establishing a popular newspaper, a
scheme concocted, one would suspect, over dinner at Zetelle's. In the
meantime Dawson was establishing new friends among the French Catho-
lics of Charleston, and it was in that circle that he met Virginia Fourgeaud.
In less than three months they were engaged. A letter to his mother
described Virginia as "22 years of age, a fervent Catholic, very handsome
and accomplished, a charming singer, a polished woman, and a devoted
and affectionate child."[40] After their nuptial mass, May 1, 1867, Dawson
and his bride moved in with the Fourgeaud family at 8 Rutledge Avenue.
What the marriage lacked in fervor, it compensated in general satisfaction.
Virginia's health was never good, but she and her family supported and
sustained the upstart journalist in some very difficult and trying times. The
fortunes of the *Mercury* were sagging, and so were their payments to
Dawson. The Fourgeauds would have done even more, but for the failure
of a large mercantile firm which spelled financial disaster for two of
Virginia's uncles.[41]

Still, Dawson was never long without connections and financial backers,
and by the fall of 1867 he and Riordan were ready to seize the main chance.
With help from the president of the South Carolina Railroad, they moved
in on the ailing Charleston *News* and bought a third interest for $6,000.
The *News* had been started with New York capital in 1865 and had
flourished for a brief time before mismanagement brought the paper to its
knees. With Benjamin Woods of New York City agreeing to hold the other
two-thirds interest and to remain a "silent partner," Riordan and Dawson
set out to survey what they had bought. They found a dilapidated newspaper establishment, a daily circulation of about 2,500, and a debt of over
$20,000. "But we were very cheerful about it," Dawson reminisced, "and
our confident expectation was that, in about five years, we should be able
to retire from newspaper work, in part, and live at our ease on the property
we had accumulated."[42] To make good the promise, the two men worked
feverishly, boosting circulation, getting solid commitments from adver-

39. Dawson to his mother, November 15, 1866, Dawson Papers, Duke.

40. Ibid., February 1, 1867.

41. Ibid., July 12, 1867.

42. Dawson, *Reminiscences,* pp. 172–74. See also Dawson to his mother, October 24,
1867, and Dawson to W. J. Magrath, October 19 and 26, 1867, Dawson Papers, Duke.

tisers, and above all getting the news on front page. It was aggressive, hard-hitting journalism, the likes of which Charleston had never seen. The Charleston *Mercury,* unable to sell its warmed-over passions of an earlier era, succumbed to the inevitable in October, 1868, leaving only the *Courier* to rival the *News.*

The *Courier* limped on for another five years, and just at that moment when Dawson had expected to be living a life of ease, he and Riordan prepared to risk their hard-earned gains on a desperate gamble. The *Courier* was going on the block, and the question was whether Riordan and Dawson could acquire the South's oldest newspaper or whether a "ring" would form to buy up the property and engage in costly competition. To add to their difficulties, the owners of the *Courier,* representing "the old people in Charleston," were resolved that the *News* should not be the victors in this struggle. As before, Dawson worked assiduously to line up financial backing, and to conceal his activity, he secured the services of a local realtor to do his bidding at auction. The friends of the *Courier* were apparently not well organized and thought the bid made by Dawson's agent to be friendly. The result was that on April 3, 1873, Riordan, Dawson & Co. secured the *Courier* at the incredibly low price of $7,100, some $3,000 less than Dawson was willing to pay.[43] The Edgefield *Advertiser,* awestruck by this coup, correctly observed that the oldest paper in the Palmetto State had been auctioned for a song.[44]

Though previous owners of the *Courier* did all in their power to block the sale, the contract was binding, and on April 7, 1873, the first edition of the Charleston *News and Courier* hit the streets. The marriage of the *News* and the *Courier* was to be followed in nine months by another wedding. On December 6, 1872, Virginia Fourgeaud died of the consumption she had fought so valiantly for years. In that same month, while still grieving the death of Virginia, Dawson was called to Columbia where an old friend from the war, James Morris Morgan, lay incapacitated by a gunshot wound. During the visit, Morgan introduced the young editor to his sister, Sarah Ida Fowler Morgan. Dawson was immediately struck by her delicate beauty and extraordinary intelligence and in what smacked of unseemly

---

43. A number of letters from Dawson to Sarah Morgan in March and April, 1873, relate the details of the sale. Warrington Dawson later edited these letters and offered comments about the purchase of the *Courier.* Both the letters and a MS copy of Warrington's notes are in the Dawson Papers, Duke. The Francis Warrington Dawson Papers in the South Caroliniana Library, University of South Carolina, contain a number of the original documents involved in the transaction. See also Joseph Walker Barnwell, "Reminiscences of the *Courier* and Its Editors," *The News and Courier,* 125th Anniversary Edition, May 1, 1928; the recollections of William E. Simmons in *The Sunday News,* May 20, 1923; and Herbert Ravenel Sass, *Outspoken: 150 Years of The News and Courier* (Columbia: University of South Carolina Press, 1953), pp. 34–37, 110–12.

44. Edgefield *Advertiser,* April 10, 1873.

haste determined to marry her. In fact, the winter months of 1873 found Captain Dawson pursuing his lady-love with such ardor that readers of their correspondence are left to marvel at the suitor's ability to summon sufficient time and attention to establish the *News and Courier*.

Up to the time Dawson met Sarah, her life had been a perfect southern tragedy. She had been born into a wealthy Louisiana family, the youngest daughter of Thomas Gibbes Morgan and his wife Sarah. At the time of her birth, February 28, 1842, Morgan was Collector of the Port of New Orleans, but shortly thereafter the family moved to Baton Rouge, where Morgan had been appointed Judge of the District Court. Baton Rouge was a natural setting for the flowering of a southern girl. Blue-eyed and golden-haired, possessed of a remarkably good complexion, she was, according to her son Warrington, only four feet and eight inches tall, petite even by the standards of her time. Physical beauty was only the beginning of her attractions. She could write as she thought, with grace, wit, strength, and style. She enjoyed music, singing a bit and playing the guitar, at least until Frank occasioned to mention one day in their courtship that he could not bear the thought of a woman going "tingy-tang-tang on a guitar."[45] She was also thought by some to have special psychic talents, having been the seventh child of a seventh child (her mother), and she often searched the meaning of dreams and supernatural phenomena. Her education was excellent, though not finished by the time war broke out. Much of her study was undertaken in Europe, where she acquired an appreciation for the French language and culture.[46]

The war brought with it the rude destruction of this garden of a child's delight. The most serious blow came in November, 1861, when her father died. He occupied a very special place in her life and was the only person other than Frank Dawson who ever called her Sarah, the other members of the family calling her Zay or Sadie. By May, 1862, Baton Rouge was in federal hands, and in August the Morgan mansion was sacked by federal soldiers. Of the nine Morgan children, one, Henry, was killed in a senseless duel shortly before the war; the eldest son, Philip Hickey, sided with the Union, though he refused to bear arms against the Confederacy;

45. *News and Courier*, December 7, 1930.

46. Some of the more useful sources on Sarah's life are: Sarah Morgan Dawson, *A Confederate Girl's Diary*, intro. Warrington Dawson, ed. James Irving Robertson, Jr., Civil War Centennial Series (Bloomington: Indiana University Press, 1960); Edmund Wilson, *Patriotic Gore: Studies in the Literature of the American Civil War* (New York: Oxford University Press, 1962), pp. 263–77; Katherine M. Jones, *Heroines of Dixie* (New York: Bobbs-Merrill, 1955), pp. 121–23, 128–38, 168–71; *The National Cyclopedia of American Biography*, 23 (New York, 1933), p. 301; and Dale Bertrand Jonas Randall, *Joseph Conrad and Warrington Dawson: The Record of a Friendship* (Durham: Duke University Press, 1968). Chapter two of the Randall work contains an excellent biographical summary of the Dawson family. See also the Morgan Family Genealogy Box in the Dawson Papers, Duke.

the oldest daughter, Lavinia, also wound up on the federal side, being married to Colonel Richard Coulter Drum, later Adjutant General of the Army. The three remaining sons joined arms with the Confederacy, with Thomas Gibbes, Jr., and George Mather both being killed in action, while the youngest, James Morris, survived the trials of a rebel reefer. Only women and children were left to carry on the day-to-day routine of home. There were Judge Morgan's widow; a married daughter, Eliza or "Lilly," with her five children; and the unmarried daughters, Miriam and Sarah.

In the next to last entry in the diary Sarah began as a Confederate girl and ended as a southern woman, she wrote:

> Last Saturday, the 29th of April, seven hundred and fifty paroled Louisianans from Lee's army were brought here—the sole survivors of ten regiments who left four years ago so full of hope and determination. On the 29th of April, 1861, George left New Orleans with his regiment. On the fourth anniversary of that day, they came back; but George and Gibbes have long been lying in their graves.

Thus ended the nightmare of constantly dreading the "pain it would bring to see their comrades return without them—to see families reunited, and know that ours could never be again."[47]

Being forced from the Eden of her childhood, Sarah eventually came with her mother to South Carolina where her brother Jimmie had arranged the purchase of the former Wade Hampton plantation some four miles below Columbia.[48] It was there that Dawson pursued his love of Sarah Morgan with a devotion and ardor that could only have been learned from a Walter Scott romance and applied in the mid-Victorian South. Of the Hampton plantation where he spent every available moment, Dawson wrote:

> It is a hallowed place to me; the rough granite blocks by the whirling creek; the sylvan throne among the pines; the 'long walk,' all too short, to the boundary fence; the fallen tree on the hill-side; the quiet little room, with its closed shutters; & the memory of the hours & days of sweet communion with you. Every spot has its sacredness to me.[49]

The ardent suitor needed such an idyllic spot to help overcome the obstacles set between him and his future bride, not the least of which was his previous marriage. Sarah was concerned lest Frank's affections be

---

47. S. M. Dawson, *A Confederate Girl's Diary,* intro. Warrington Dawson (Boston: Houghton Mifflin, 1913), pp. 439–40.

48. James Morris Morgan, *Recollections of a Rebel Reefer* (Boston: Houghton Mifflin, 1917), pp. 316, 342, 346–47.

49. Dawson to Sarah Morgan, June 11, 1873, Dawson Papers, Duke.

divided. His religion also gave pause, not that Sarah felt a deep prejudice on the subject so much as she saw it as a barrier to a complete and unencumbered relationship. Before their marriage Dawson told Bishop Patrick Nieson Lynch that he could never in good conscience require Sarah to abide the Church's proviso concerning the rearing of children in a mixed marriage, but he also promised in good faith that his children would receive a Catholic education. In later years, the children would go with their father to Catholic services in the morning and with their mother to Episcopal worship in the evening. To accomodate the educational pledge, they spent the better part of 1886 and 1887 in Europe because the parochial school in Charleston was considered inferior. As it turned out, neither of the two children adopted the Catholic faith.

Perhaps the most difficult of all the obstacles was the irresponsibility of Jimmie Morgan when it came to providing for his mother and Sarah. Shortly after bringing them to South Carolina, Jimmie decided to marry for a second time, which forced Sarah and her mother to seek other accomodations. Into this breach stepped Captain Dawson, who managed the impossible task of finding a home for Sarah and her mother in Charleston, making basic provision for their financial security, while at the same time courting his coy mistress. It was a testimony to his tact, kindness, and sensitivity that he could at once honor the canons of courtship and act in the capacity of a near-relation, and that he could combine those two roles in an era which took a dim view of such intimacy, practical though it may have been.

Proving that persistence has its rewards, Frank finally overcame all objections, and he and Sarah were married on January 27, 1874, in the Gadsden House on Meeting Street—the home Dawson had secured for Sarah and her mother. The ceremony which united this Catholic and Episcopalian was performed by Bishop Lynch, the same man who had won fame by gathering Charlestonians in his cathedral to celebrate the breakup of Union in 1861. Sarah's mother died shortly thereafter and the young couple moved from the Gadsden House, but not before their first child, Ethel Morgan, was born on November 17, 1874. They next took the historic Lightwood House, which according to legend was frequented by the unhappy sister of Colonel Isaac Hayne, who had been hanged by the British in 1781. This house was located at the southeast corner of Meeting Street and Lightwood Alley, and it was here that Francis Warrington Dawson, Jr., was born on September 27, 1878. Two years later, while out riding, Sarah finally saw the house that she declared would make her happiest. She jotted down the number, 25 Bull Street,[50] and rushed home to prevail upon her husband to buy it. It was in this house that Ethel and

---

50. The number was changed to 43 shortly after the Dawsons moved there and is presently listed as 99.

Warrington grew up and that the Dawsons' third child, Philip Hickey, was born February 9, 1881. Philip died six months later on one of the hottest days of the year—a tragic beginning for a residence which would experience another tragedy before the decade was out.

One observer thought the Dawson home on Bull Street to be as representative of the new order in the South as was its owner.[51] The house was built before the war on plans secured from abroad and was patterned on the English country-house which found great favor in parts of the South from 1830 to 1850. The Bull Street residence consisted of three floors. The four large rooms at the ground level were used for storage, Sarah considering the floor too damp to be healthy. An imposing flight of white marble stairs led to a broad piazza—Sarah, following the New Orleans practice, called it a gallery—on the second level, the roof of which was supported by massive pillars. On entering the central hallway at this level, a visitor would have been invited into the drawing room which ran the full length of the house on the right side. It was the most spectacular room in the house, being actually two large rooms, with great wall mirrors at each end, carved marble mantlepieces, and a small semicircular room opening out to the side for the house had bays on each side. The large drawing room could be made more intimate by means of huge sliding doors which rolled together at its center. Across the hall was a smaller library and a dining room, separated by a graceful curving stairway which led to the third floor bedrooms.

The children slept in the rooms above the library and dining room. Frank and Sarah shared adjoining rooms on the other side. Frank would work long hours into the night at the desk in his room, while Sarah would sit with a book, often drowsing, but ever ready to answer questions Frank might have concerning a quotation or proper phrasing. Outside, the steady whir of crickets would echo off the high back and side walls of the family compound and make its way out into Bull Street through the trellised wirework which surmounted the low front wall. In the back, along the left side wall, the servants slept above the stables and waited for the ring of Captain Dawson's bell which would signal the beginning of another day at 43 Bull Street.

Dawson started the day with a cold bath in a tin hat tub, using a large sponge. He preferred this shivering abuse to the hot water bath that was available. He followed this invigorating ceremony by attiring himself in a perfectly tailored black cutaway coat with waistcoat to match, gray-striped trousers, an ascot of gray or finely striped white-and-black silk, a straight collar, immaculately shined shoes, and gloves which always appeared to be brand-new. All this would be crowned by a derby hat, except in summer

---

51. From a sketch by Josiah Carter in *The Union*, February 5, 1886, scrapbook, Dawson Papers, Duke.

when he wore straw. The family would then gather for breakfast, usually about 9:00 or 9:30. Breakfast was heavy, consisting of meat or fish, eggs, hominy, and two or three hot breads. After breakfast the children assembled in their father's room for prayers "which were pleasantly short." Captain Dawson returned for dinner at the unholy hour of four o'clock, the usual hour in Charleston being three, but Dawson's work schedule made the later time preferable. After dinner, Frank retired to his room for a nap, the inviolability of which Sarah guarded against visitors and children. For the children it was "a time of penance." Early in the evening Ethel and Warrington would have a light supper, then stories and bed. Frank usually did not return until eleven or midnight, at which time Sarah would rise and dress—"no negligee or teagowns, but a careful toilet, with all the bulky and unnecessary garments belonging to that day, and generally in her favorite pale blue, every shining golden hair in place."[52] The two then sat down to a cold supper and afterwards talked and read until two o'clock in the morning.

It was a pleasant life. The Dawsons were important people, and they entertained frequently. In such a family the father was invariably the dominant figure in everything from table conversation to household manners, yet Dawson was a benevolent autocrat. Each child was made to feel that his was an important contribution to the family discussion. Each felt that life had a special focus on his goings and comings. Ethel later recalled that as an "offset" to the uneasiness she felt over her father's safety, she had the "satisfying feeling that we were very important people." Under such conditions "'my people' were always interested in what I said or did." She remembered "singing 'I'm Called Little Buttercup' into one of the early phonographs, for the delectation of a select gathering," and she could also recall the feeling of self-assurance which she acquired because her "likes and dislikes were of great importance."[53]

Despite the demands of his public life, Dawson was a devoted husband and father. An associate remarked that "every one with whom he was thrown, soon felt and realized that what he lived for principally was for his wife, and his children at home."[54] Sarah reciprocated this devotion as both a wife and a confidant, but she suffered from a frustrating lack of self-confidence and from ill-health which plagued her most of her married life. The ill-health was the combined result of a painful back injury she sustained in a carriage accident during the war, the tortuous undergarments of the

52. Description of the Bull Street residence and the family routine is drawn principally from Warrington Dawson Notes, Dawson Papers, Duke, and from a fifty-five page typescript reminiscence by Ethel Dawson Barry, given the author by Dr. Herbert Barry, Jr., of Boston, cited hereafter as Ethel Barry, "Reminiscences."

53. Ethel Barry, "Reminiscences," p. 8.

54. Augustine T. Smythe to Sarah Dawson, March 16, 1889, Dawson Papers, Duke.

period, and frequent miscarriages. Sarah also dwelt on parapsychic phenomena, particularly seeing and conversing with ghosts. It was the one thing about her that Frank "really and openly minded."[55] All the above, coupled with the subordinate role women were expected to assume, made Sarah an indecisive woman as long as Frank was alive. Her preoccupation with death, suffering, and dreams, along with her general indecision, were indulged by Frank, not so much because it was expected behavior in that day, but because he loved and admired her. Rare were the expressions of exasperation as in the letter where he fretted, "Do try to fight against such timidity, or you will break me down as completely as yourself. . . . You make me very miserable with your sufferings, & if you put your mind to it you could end them." On another occasion he wrote, "You are so constituted that things pain you that no one else would waste a thought on. You take life too hard, and I have no idea that you can change."[56]

Frank enjoyed his children immensely. Romping, practical joking, story-telling, and table conversation with his children were a constant source of pleasure. He was strict without being a stern disciplinarian, always preferring to pose alternatives which made the proper conduct or behavior obvious. It might be said that while Sarah was an excellent mother, Frank was better suited, emotionally and temperamentally, for the job of rearing children. On a few occasions he intervened with advice to Sarah on how the children should be treated. These letters revealed much about Frank as a father and about the family as a unit. In one letter he advised:

> Ethel has my temper. . . . The best way is always to let her alone, and be ready to welcome the first sign of softening. You will do her real injury . . . if you treat her outburst as anything important. Do not, I beg you, make her feel like a criminal. It is a thing to laugh at, not grieve about, and I have more confidence in her fiery temper than in my poor boy's womanly softness.[57]

In another letter he wrote:

> Yes, I think that you are too ambitious about Warrington, not because I doubt his probable capacity, but because it is so much better not to court disappointment. If he grows up what we wish and is successful it is all very well, but if he has an uneventful and quiet life, he will probably be happier. I confess that I care for nothing myself, except that he should be a good man. . . . When you and I have done what seems best, and we believe to be best, there is an end of our responsibility.[58]

---

55. Ethel Barry, "Reminiscences," p. 37.

56. Dawson to his wife, July 25 and August 19, 1882, Dawson Papers, Duke.

57. Ibid., August 12, 1882.

58. Ibid., November 23, 1886. After Sarah's death her sister, Lavinia, wrote Warrington and said, "Her great tender heart overflowed with love for us all—but her *Son* came first and above all else in the world" (June 23, 1909, ibid.).

As the letters indicated, the family tended to divide, not sharply but definitely, with Frank and his daughter and Sarah and her son forming alliances of mutual temperament.

Such was life on Bull Street, but when the iron gate swung shut and Dawson headed for 19 Broad Street, there was a perceptible change in the man. He was headed for the editor's chair which made him a powerful and influential figure in South Carolina. The children first learned of their father's dual role when the Dawsons became one of the first families in Charleston to have a telephone. Shortly thereafter Ethel chanced to hear a burst of oaths emanating from the gadget, and though her mother assured her that it was another voice cutting in, Ethel knew very well that it was her father calling from the office. In the *News and Courier* offices Dawson was without peer, and his dominant and forceful personality shaped a newspaper of remarkable quality. "Denouncing, arguing, demanding reform, in season and out," wrote Robert Hilliard Woody, "Dawson's pen was persuasive and eloquent, often . . . being a determining factor in the course of events." As if to underscore that point, Woody concluded, "Dawson was a power in the state and he knew it. One may hesitate to assert it dogmatically, but the writer thinks that never in South Carolina's turbulent history has a single paper so dominated the thought of the state."[59]

In achieving this preeminent position, Dawson was ably served by the men who surrounded him. Chief among them was B. R. Riordan, the man who introduced Dawson to South Carolina journalism. Despite Riordan's initial expectation that Dawson would be most valued for his managerial ability, Riordan soon realized that Frank Dawson was, first and last, an editor and that it was he who would have to shoulder the managerial burden. All who knew them recognized that a better combination could not have been made, with Dawson doing the thinking and writing and Riordan running the business end. Riordan had a number of handicaps which precluded his being as effective as Dawson in the editor's chair. The first was a physical infirmity, a clubfoot, which caused him severe discomfort. The second was a notoriously bad marriage, which interfered with his work and made him a vulnerable target for the *News and Courier*'s enemies.[60] These liabilities, coupled with an accountant's inherent cautiousness even when the moment called for action, did not prevent Riordan from making the *News and Courier* a solid enterprise and a respectable investment. Riordan left Charleston in 1884 to enter business in New York, and his place was ably filled by General Rudolph Siegling, a

---

59. Robert Hilliard Woody, *Republican Newspapers of South Carolina*, Southern Sketches, ser. I, no. 10 (Charlottesville: Historical Publishing, 1936), p. 52.

60. For correspondence bearing on Riordan's unfortunate marriage see Dawson to his wife, August 1, 1873; August 20, 1874; February 6 and 15, 1879.

prominent Charleston banker and president of the News and Courier Co. "To the men who worked with them and under them," wrote the paper's historian, "Dawson, Riordan, and Siegling were 'the great triumvirate.'"[61]

Dawson was also ably assisted in his editorial wars by a reportorial staff of unsurpassed quality. William Watts Ball said that *The News and Courier's* writing staff was as large then as it is now [1932] and in ability was superior to any staff that any newspaper in South Carolina has had at any time."[62] The illustrious group included at one time or another: Alfred Brockenbrough Williams, later to become editor of the Greenville *News* ; Carlyle McKinley, a poet "who nearly crossed the border-line of genius";[63] Robert Means Davis, subsequently a prominent member of the faculty of the University of South Carolina; Yates Snowden, historian; and James Calvin Hemphill, "the quite conventional Associate Reformed Presbyterian 'Seceder' from the up-country" who succeeded Dawson as editor.[64]

The search for talent was aggressive. Perhaps the *News and Courier's* stormiest acquisition was Narciso Gener Gonzales, who was brought to the "Old Lady of Broad Street" after scooping her on an important story. And while the tale smacked of printer's ink, it was typical of the fashion in which Dawson operated. In many respects Gonzales was the brightest jewel in the *News and Courier's* crown of reporters. Though his years on the paper were turbulent and spent in frequent quarrels with Dawson, his reports from Washington and Columbia were vivid and were read avidly. To Dawson's face Gonzales complained of low pay and on occasions of being muzzled, and to Dawson's back he referred to the boss as "Dumbiedikes," the "Grand Mogul," or the "Tycoon." On one occasion the Carolinian with a Cuban name complained of having been "Dawson's darkey" long enough and declared himself eager to "escape from Dawson's continual ordering and hectoring."[65] But despite the clash of these two personalities, Gonzales stood to learn much from Dawson, and Dawson was certainly well served by Gonzales. Conceding that "the irrepressible correspondent would have been a trial to any employer," Gonzales's biographer concluded that the correspondent's respect for his employer never diminished.[66] It might be added that Dawson would have

---

61. Sass, *Outspoken*, p. 45.

62. William Watts Ball, *The State That Forgot: South Carolina's Surrender to Democracy* (Indianapolis: Bobbs-Merrill, 1932), p. 171.

63. Ibid., p. 172.

64. Lewis Pinckney Jones, *Stormy Petrel: N. G. Gonzales and His State* (Columbia: University of South Carolina Press, 1973), p. 87.

65. N. G. Gonzales to his sister, December 1, 1882, Elliott-Gonzales Papers, Southern Historical Collection, University of North Carolina, cited hereafter as SHC.

66. Jones, *Stormy Petrel*, p. 123.

admired the future accomplishments of his fiery reporter: Gonzales went on to found and edit the Columbia *State*.

Captain Dawson was an indefatigable journalist who insisted on supervising all aspects of the paper's composition, down to the most minute detail. At noon each day he assembled the reportorial staff and assigned the day's work, a great portion of which he reserved for himself. Working fourteen and sixteen hours a day, he was a man who did not know how to rest without "cutting loose absolutely and going to Europe."[67] Even then he wrote editorials in advance of his leaving and left behind specific instructions as to how the paper would approach various issues. A memo to J. C. Hemphill before the Dawsons departed for Europe in 1883 gave the following instructions:

> Editorial advice: avoid all sore subjects with regards local affairs; Support R.R. bill; Reduction tariff—looking always to free trade; no reduction whiskey & tobacco; Demo's take what can get in present Congress; Civil Service Reform; To win, natl election, must deserve to win; Let alone all liquor questions as State and County issue; Run as much as possible on matters of national concern . . . New York Times pretty safe guide on tariff questions; keep all pamphlets; . . . Railroad law—to stand for two years.[68]

Before leaving for Europe in 1886, Dawson cautioned that it was "imperative that you avoid all rows and wrangling with any person or persons in the State and I desire that the paper shall not in any way . . . be taken out of or beyond its present lines of policy."[69] Dawson even required that copies of the paper follow him on his travels, and he took time to send back comments and more advice on the paper's editorial policy.[70]

Such caution, however, was not what made the *News and Courier* one of the exemplary papers of the South, and readers of Dawson's paper could tell when he was away. During the 1883 trip abroad, Gonzales remarked, "Matt Tighe, our latest man and Dawson's stenographer, writes me that 'the editorial side of the paper has lately been worse than the sophomoric slop of a college journal' and I think he is about right. Riordan only cares to write about 'wishy-washy' things and doesn't do that with vim."[71] Dawson's style was vigorous, aggressive, and courageous. He believed a newspaper had to take a position and make it known. As he put it, an editor had "to write for or against something; for or against an idea; for or

---

67. *The Union*, February 5, 1886, scrapbook, Dawson Papers, Duke.

68. Dawson memo to J. C. Hemphill, ca. February, 1883, ibid.

69. Dawson to J. C. Hemphill, July 25, 1885, ibid.

70. Dawson to J. C. Hemphill, March 15 and April 2, 1887, Hemphill Family Papers, Duke.

71. Gonzales to his aunt, March 13, 1883, Elliott-Gonzales Papers, SHC.

against a party."[72] Dawson embodied the concept of "personal journalism." Jonathan Daniels, who thought Dawson was one of those editors who was bound to be heard, once observed that "the crusading editor in 'personal journalism' has always been a man about to disappear," but the Tarheel editor could also take heart in an observation made by Charles Dana:

> Whenever in the newspaper profession . . . a man rises up who is original, strong, and bold enough to make his opinions a matter of consequence to the public, there will be personal journalism; and whenever newspapers are conducted only by commonplace individuals whose views are of no consequence to anybody, there will be nothing but impersonal journalism.[73]

The attributes which made Captain Dawson such an exemplar of personal journalism were there from the beginning. In the face of overwhelming odds, he matched his courage, ambition, and wit against men who like himself were the flotsam a war had set adrift to find their fortune. He could have settled for far less. His ability and personality would have given him a ready acceptance in any enterprise, but he kept gambling for better. Even in the selection of a wife, he chose a woman whose uncommon mind could challenge and sharpen his own. He was what a later generation would call a rugged individual, and he had that lean and hungry look. When Lee surrendered at Appomattox, Dawson had only a Confederate five-dollar bill, a pen-knife, and a three-cent stamp, along with a right arm still useless from a bullet wound received at Five Forks. When his life ended on March 12, 1889, he so dominated South Carolina's public life that a man like Ben Tillman would seek power, not by attacking an elected official, but by attacking the editor of the Charleston *News and Courier*.

Dawson began his career as a journalist, as he had begun his life as a sailor and a soldier, knowing next to nothing about the trade, but he did know that to make a mark a man must stand for something. Following that instinct, he made the *News and Courier* indispensable reading for South Carolinians and sure copy for big-city journals in the North. He was not always on the side of popular opinion, as will be seen in the campaign which ended Reconstruction in South Carolina, but even those he antagonized conceded his genius and read his paper. Perhaps it was this quality that made Captain Dawson a respected if not always a well-liked man. Dawson's son later attributed what he believed to be his father's lack of acceptance in the Palmetto State to an "extraordinarily bitter quality about political strife in South Carolina."[74] Whatever the case, it may have been well, and it was certainly fitting, that young Austin John Reeks traded in a baptismal legacy for a *nom de guerre*.

---

72. Sass, *Outspoken*, p. 44.

73. Jonathan Daniels, *They Will Be Heard: America's Crusading Newspaper Editors* (New York: McGraw-Hill, 1965), pp. 309–10.

74. Warrington Dawson Notes.

Chapter II
Puritan and Cavalier:
Striking the Golden Mean

No state underwent a more thorough reconstruction than did South Carolina. Its black majority was by all democratic counts an inexhaustible reservoir of political power. No state could boast a more talented or more influential cadre of black leadership. Whites of whatever political persuasion or personal inclination were compelled to recognize this fact of political life, and they spent at least as much time in coming to terms with the black majority as in devising ways to reestablish white supremacy. To that degree, the inexorable drive among white South Carolinians to acquire political supremacy was checked, at least for a time, and the white community was forced to accept not-so-traditional alternatives in race relations.

The more lasting result of this assertion of humanity on the part of blacks was that racism, as a root cause of inhumanity, would never assume the status of accepted political theory. Not that the South and the nation were without advocates of racism as political doggerel, but that the more important debate, the actual speaking of the public mind, would center on euphemisms for, or assumed consequences of, visceral notions of racial inferiority. Advocates of white supremacy would have to argue such points as corruption, ignorance, and incompetence, reflecting as they did questions of taste and manners, or more basically, questions of class as opposed to race. Thus the success of the black majority, and perhaps of Reconstruction in general, was to deny the option of a nationally acceptable political regime grounded in an articulated theory of racial supremacy. Despite the later career of Jim Crow and the pervasive racism which underlay it, the debate would be forced to issues that were more suggestive of remediation than grounds for permanent enslavement.

Ironically, the ability to give the lie to stereotypes of racial inferiority and to force the discussion to questions of class played into the hands of those who sought to convince the nation that Reconstruction had been a dismal failure. Under the banner of reform these men talked about qualifications for membership in a ruling class. Even blacks splintered over the question of what sort of person should rule, making not-so-subtle distinctions among themselves as to color and status before emancipation, with the result that they jeopardized the racial solidarity so essential to the success of Reconstruction in South Carolina.[1] By the time they recognized

---

1. An excellent discussion of the politics of color and status is found in Thomas Holt, *Black over White: Negro Political Leadership in South Carolina during Reconstruction,* Blacks in the New World (Urbana: University of Illinois Press, 1977).

their peril and tried to regroup, those intent on reestablishing white rule had seized the initiative on the equation between class and government. The critical period for this transition from Reconstruction to Redemption in South Carolina stretched from the summer of 1874 to Christmas, 1875. Simultaneously this year and a half marked the fruition of a friendship between Daniel Henry Chamberlain and Francis Warrington Dawson. So interwoven were the stories of political transition and personal friendship that one cannot be told without telling the other.

The transition began when South Carolina took steps to elect its last Reconstruction governor. From the time of his election in the fall of 1874, Daniel Henry Chamberlain moved with the majority of his party to reform the abuses, both real and imagined, of the preceding years of Radical rule, but to the mortification of his fellow Republicans, he also moved in the direction of the conservative white minority. Such a move should not have been surprising, for Chamberlain was born and educated to associate with better men than the mass of freedmen who formed his constituency. He was five years Dawson's senior, having been born in the town of West Brookfield, Massachusetts, June 23, 1835, the ninth of ten in a farm family of modest financial circumstances. All the children were urged to a good education, and after some years as both student and teacher in the academies near his home, Chamberlain entered Yale College at the age of twenty-four. Excelling in oratory and English composition, he graduated fourth in the class of 1862. At the insistence of friends he entered Harvard Law School where he stayed for little more than a year before leaving in the fall of 1863 to fight for a cause that had long enlisted his sympathies.[2]

Despite protests from patrons who helped raise the money for his education, Chamberlain obtained a loan of $250 with which he insured his life for enough to repay his benefactors. He acknowledged the validity of his friends' assertion that a man of his education and ability should not throw his life away in a war that lesser men could fight, but he wrote, "Years hence I shall be ashamed to have it known that for *any* reason I did not bear a hand in this life-or-death struggle for Union and for Freedom."[3] With a lieutenant's commission in the Fifth Massachusetts Cavalry, Chamberlain came to Virginia in the spring of 1864, and on April 3, 1865, with his commander, Charles Francis Adams, Jr., he rode into Dawson's adopted capital a conqueror.

Like Dawson, he was a man without immediate prospect when mustered out of service, and again like the young Englishman, he made his way to South Carolina by chance. When a Yale classmate, James Pierpont Blake,

---

2. The biographical information on Chamberlain comes from Walter Allen, *Governor Chamberlain's Administration in South Carolina: A Chapter of Reconstruction in the Southern States* (New York: G. P. Putnam's Sons, 1888), pp. 524–26.

3. Ibid., p. 525.

drowned off Edisto Island, Chamberlain was called on to administer the estate, arriving in January, 1866. While in the Sea Islands, Chamberlain acquired a plantation and attempted the planting of cotton, but was not especially successful. Thus, the future governor entered South Carolina Republicanism by the back door, having at first no idea of helping the freedmen, but only later coming to it, after the Radicals in Congress had set the course of Reconstruction and offered a measure of protection for those interested in developing a political career. Selected in 1867 to attend the Constitutional Convention, he served on its Judiciary Committee with distinction and consented to become the Republican candidate for attorney general, which office he held for the next four years. Declining to seek office in 1872, Chamberlain sat out the next two years before becoming his party's nominee for governor in 1874.

Chamberlain was at best a reluctant Radical and more often than not found himself identifying with the conservative, or bolting, faction of his party. In 1872 he gave strong consideration to the prospect of becoming the bolters' candidate for governor against the regular party nominee, Franklin J. Moses, Jr. He even served as vice president of the Taxpayers Convention of 1871, a gathering which amounted to little more than a Democratic caucus on Republican excesses. With such a background there was little surprise when, in the summer of 1874, Chamberlain began to feel out the prospects of an alliance with Dawson. Dawson had only a short time before attained virtual dominance of the Charleston press and was now in a position to speak for South Carolina's Conservatives. Chamberlain's first feeler came in July when he wrote the editors of the *News and Courier* asking why his subscription had been terminated. With a touch of disarming humor characteristic of the ex–attorney general, he acknowledged being out of favor with the editors but could not imagine they "would go to the extent of refusing to *sell*" him a paper. Promising to pay up if he were in arrears, Chamberlain concluded, "The News & C is like surgery to me—painful but necessary! I wish I could add healthful."[4]

As yet Dawson saw little profit in making friends with Chamberlain and in fact was on the eve of making Chamberlain's last remark prophetic. Dawson was preparing some radical surgery for the prospective gubernatorial candidate. Two days after receiving Chamberlain's inquiry about the paper, Frank wrote Sarah, who, expecting their first child, was spending the summer in the Catskills: "Tomorrow I open on Chamberlain, who at this moment stands a better chance than [Governor] Moses of obtaining the Radical nomination." Dawson conceded that it would be hard work but thought he could prove the carpetbagger to be a "whited sepulchre"

---

4. Chamberlain to Dawson, July 31, 1874, Francis Warrington Dawson Papers, Duke University Library, cited hereafter as Duke.

and the difference between Chamberlain and Moses to be "the difference between a footpad and a forger."[5] True to his word, Dawson launched the attack on August 4, declaring that the *News and Courier* had "proper warrant for saying of Mr. Chamberlain that, while he has not the vulgar audacity of Moses, he is more culpable as well as more adroit than that profligate debauchee, and is even less worthy than he is to fill the executive chair." The *News and Courier*'s harangue continued for a week. Like a relentless prosecutor, Dawson unfolded a list of indictments accusing Chamberlain of complicity in the major portion of Radical malfeasance. In the midst of the exposés Dawson wrote Sarah complaining that his head was "almost dazed with groping after light in this Chamberlain crusade."[6]

The series of articles was attributed to almost everyone but Dawson. The papers supporting Chamberlain, particularly the Orangeburg *News*, noted that Franklin Moses, Sr., had been closeted with the Charleston editors for two hours the day before the first exposé appeared. These papers accused the editors of selling out, for an alleged price of $20,000. Though the charge was false, the Moses people were in fact negotiating with the *News and Courier* for columns and supplements to broadcast a Moses speech. The price was a much more modest $250 on which the *News and Courier* cleared $150, but the circumstances were sufficient to arch a few eyebrows.[7] At first Dawson was amused by the various allegations, but the humor soon wore thin, leading the young editor to confide, "The hard part of it is that after having made the name of Moses nauseous in the mouth of any American citizen we should be charged (by the radicals) with having sold out to him, merely because we are exposing the character of a man who is as bad as Moses."[8]

Frank obviously found great relief in confiding to Sarah his increasing role in the events of August and September, 1874. At one point he explained that he could not come to her side "because (although Riordan does not see it) the interest of these poor unfortunate people which I have

---

5. Dawson to his wife, August 2, 1874, ibid. No South Carolinian better fit the stereotype of the scalawag than did Franklin J. Moses, Jr. Son of a prominent Sumter family, Moses turned renegade after the war and was elected governor in 1872. While his father, Franklin Moses, Sr., won the respect of the state as Chief Justice from 1868 to 1877, the younger Moses gained an odious reputation as South Carolina's most corrupt Reconstruction governor.

6. Dawson to his wife, August 5, 1874, ibid. The exposés appeared in the *News and Courier,* August 4–10, 1874.

7. Among those alleged to have authored the articles were General James Conner and a well-known political maverick in Charleston, James Baxter Campbell, Dawson to his wife, August 13, 1874, Dawson Papers, Duke. The charge made by the Orangeburg *News* was published and denied in the *News and Courier,* August 17, 1874. The facts surrounding Dawson's negotiations with the Moses people are found in two letters from Dawson to his wife, August 10 and 11, 1874, Dawson Papers, Duke.

8. Dawson to his wife, August 20, 1874, Dawson Papers, Duke.

in keeping wd unquestionably suffer."[9] Even then his campaign against
Chamberlain was entering a more serious stage, for Dawson was joining a
conspiracy the purpose of which was to oust both Chamberlain and Moses
through the agency of President Grant. The plot was not unrealistic.
Evidence indicates that two years before, Grant had at least entertained
the idea of commissioning former Governor James Lawrence Orr to clean
up South Carolina.[10] Despite the failure of this earlier effort, the conspira-
tors had reason to believe that this time they had the ear of the president.

With the aid of ex-Governor Andrew Gordon Magrath, William Lee
Trenholm, and General James Conner, Dawson worked feverishly to
secure Grant's support for the candidacy of General Joseph Brevard
Kershaw, a resident of Camden and symbol of aristocratic integrity. On
August 17 he wrote Sarah that he had received a pledge of support from
the Grant administration, but that as yet the conditions could not be
fulfilled. By the twenty-ninth he could report more encouraging news. His
"friend in Washington" had wired saying that the substance of Dawson's
plan had been accepted by the president and the principal members of his
cabinet. On the thirty-first Dawson met Kershaw at the depot in Charleston and conferred for several hours. The result was a telegram to the White
Sulphur in Virginia telling General Conner to go at once to Washington to
protect their interests. With understandable relief Dawson sent the following message to his wife on the evening of September third. "Tonight comes
the first indication that the pledges from Wash'n will be kept. Grant's own
organ speaks briefly and pointedly agt Chamberlain. God grant it may
stick."[11]

The euphoria was short lived. The very next day Dawson wrote, "Dear:
my politics go wrong." Grant had forsaken them, and the foiled conspira-
tor blamed the failure on a combination of circumstances, chief among
them being the inability of "our own people" to work together. With some
exasperation he concluded, "I am tempted to abandon the fight, which

---

9. Dawson to his wife, letter fragment, ca. August, 1874, ibid.

10. Joel Williamson, *After Slavery: The Negro in South Carolina During Reconstruction,
1861–1877* (Chapel Hill: University of North Carolina Press, 1965), p. 399. Williamson
indicates that this deal was "by no means clear," but the fact that Dawson and his compatriots
renewed the approach to Grant in 1874 suggests a strong feeling on their part that the
channels to the administration were open. Whether Dawson was a party to the 1872
bargaining is not known, but he was a strong supporter of Orr. When Orr withdrew from
consideration in favor of the bolting reformer Reuben Tomlinson, Dawson decided to remain
neutral in the contest.

11. The story of the conspiracy is found in Dawson's letters to his wife, August 17, 18, 25,
27, 29, and September 1, 3, 4, and 8, 1874, Dawson Papers, Duke. The purpose of the
Kershaw candidacy was to solidify the white minority for future action. Dawson's letter of the
twenty-fifth stated, "He [Kershaw] will make a strong run, & be beaten, if the rads hold
together. But we must keep on fighting till we win."

harrasses me, tires me, interferes with my business & costs me time & money; but if I do, who will try as I have tried?" Reflecting the new mood, the *News and Courier*, which had been predicting the imminent overthrow of Chamberlain, warned on September 8 that there was no hope of the Republican State Convention's casting off both Chamberlain and Moses. On the same day Dawson wrote Sarah saying "the jig is up in Washington." Grant was thoroughly committed to Chamberlain, but "a rebuff should not . . . prevent us from persevering to the last in advocating Peace, Justice, Good-will."[12]

Sarah must have smiled at these rather self-promoting letters, but she also knew that Frank was not about to abandon the fight. In fact Dawson still had a few ideas on how to go about securing peace, justice, and good will. In a hastily scribbled letter from the floor of the Republican Convention, he wrote, "I take this moment to say only that I am waiting here for the completion or failure of my bargain to beat Chamberlain. The convention has been in session since 10 & no nomination yet. I am anxious, tired & suspicious of everything." Dawson's bargain was a last-ditch effort to bribe the Republican Convention into rejecting the Massachusetts carpetbagger. "They beat me out by using more money than I had," he wrote on his return to Charleston. "Chamberlain was nominated & I had those anxious days & nights for nothing."[13] On the same night Josephus Woodruff, a former reporter for the Charleston *News* turned scalawag, made a more practical assessment of the consequences. If the Republicans were intent on endorsing that "lovely set of Christians," he would simply have to "try and make peace with Chamberlain. When a man is king the subjects must obey."[14]

Dawson would ultimately reach the same conclusion but by a different route, and for the moment he was in no mood for a coronation. In the weeks ahead he turned his editorial page to the support of Judge John T. Green, the bolting reformer, in an election that would flex the muscle of the awakening white minority. But Chamberlain would go on to victory that autumn in an election that saw Republicans attack corruptionists at the local level as vigorously as reform was advocated by both factions in the gubernatorial campaign. In truth the advocates of honest government in South Carolina never broke cleanly along party or color lines. Those who eventually thought reform a matter of party were only indulging the rhetoric of the victor. In the sense of having no party or factional identity, reform was no different from corruption. It would have been strange indeed had Confederate brigadiers, scalawags, conservative businessmen,

---

12. Dawson to his wife, September 4 and 8, 1874, ibid.

13. Dawson to his wife, September 12 and 13, 1874, ibid.

14. Josephus Woodruff Diary, September 10 and 13, 1874, photostatic copy, Duke.

carpetbaggers, blacks, whites—all men caught in an unstable society—not sought at one time or another the rewards that only the intercession of government could provide. In the scramble for position there was never more than a thin line between influence and bribery, favoritism and theft, or good intentions and abuse of power. Only a few of the more unscrupulous stripped away all sense of propriety and fattened themselves on the flesh of a society struggling for a new order. Out of this milieu arose a cacophony of voices seeking a more stable and certain exercise of government. Perhaps the strangest irony of all was that the beguiling call for reform brought the weak (those needing the social protection of Reconstruction) and the strong (those desiring the economic protection promised by Redemption) to the same banner—with disastrous results, as it turned out, for the weak.[15]

So when Chamberlain's inaugural address detailed a plan for decency, he was expressing more than a personal conviction; he was summing up a case that had been building since before 1870 and which intensified through most of 1874. With virtual unanimity the Conservative press announced its guarded support for this articulate gentleman from Massachusetts who promised a puritanical housecleaning in Columbia. Dawson expressed the general approval when he wrote, "Mr. Chamberlain has placed his foot on the rock of a living principle, with the eye of a great nation upon him, and the light of a great future breaking all around him. He holds in his hands the heart of an heroic State, and upon his nerve depends the hope of a splendid national organization."[16] These were fine words from the pen of a man who had only months before attempted to destroy Mr. Chamberlain through conspiracy, bribery, and editorial vitriol.

There were more pleasant days ahead in the developing friendship between Dawson and Chamberlain. Friendly editorials from the *News and Courier* during Chamberlain's first session with the legislature seemed to warm the governor to the possibility of final acceptance by the very class of South Carolinians to which he belonged by education and taste. Leading Conservatives sensed that their new governor would be susceptible to this kind of class pressure. "I think that Mr. Chamberlain will be compelled to do what is in his power for the cause of reform and economy," wrote one Conservative. "He knows that he is now on trial before the whole country: his reputation as a public man as well as an individual is at stake."[17] For his

---

15. Since Francis Butler Simkins and Robert Hilliard Woody's pioneering revisionist study, *South Carolina During Reconstruction* (Chapel Hill: University of North Carolina Press, 1932), historians have not been reluctant to concede South Carolina's Republicans a major role in the reform movement. By far the stoutest defense of their efforts in that direction is found in Williamson, *After Slavery*, pp. 397–405.

16. *News and Courier*, December 11, 1874.

17. James Hemphill to William Ramsey Hemphill, November 13, 1874, Hemphill Family Papers, Duke.

part Chamberlain was only too willing to abandon his followers of the previous autumn and to embrace those who had conspired to defeat him. Accusing the vast majority of his party of insincerity on the issue of reform, he told Dawson, "My inaugural chilled them, my special message enraged them, and nothing keeps them from attacking me . . . except the power of my office and the support which the Conservatives and the country at large give to me in all my efforts at reform."[18]

Chamberlain was soon able to reciprocate Dawson's support. In late winter and early spring of 1875 Dawson found himself trapped in litigation that would mean life or death for the *News and Courier*. Charges for criminal libel had been brought against Riordan and Dawson by Christopher Columbus Bowen, a notorious scalawag who had been variously a member of the 1868 Convention, a congressman, and a member of the General Assembly, and was at that time sheriff of Charleston County. Bowen held power on the fringe of the Radical hierarchy, thrown there when, as congressman from the Charleston district, he persisted in his opposition to the powerful machine created by Governor Robert Kingston Scott. Such political independence had cost Bowen his congressional seat in 1870.[19]

Despite this difficulty, Bowen maintained his reputation as a genuine Radical and could always count on a solid following among blacks and the working poor in his bailiwick of Charleston County. Partial control of the influential Customs House patronage for the Port of Charleston helped explain his independence,[20] but equally important in this respect was the work of his wife. She was the independent, strong-willed Susan Petigru King, who broke her previous, respectable marriage in order to go to Washington to work in the Republican administration. Many attributed her maverick inclinations to her lineage, her father having been Charleston's most famous Unionist, James Louis Petigru. Susan and Bowen met in Washington and were soon married, only to discover that Bowen had overlooked the matter of divorcing his first wife, a detail which led to his conviction on a charge of bigamy. Susan remained steadfast, and Sarah Dawson later wrote that Bowen's marriage to Susan had much to do with his success among blacks in aristocratic Charleston. "The intimation to the negro," Sarah observed, "that he [Bowen] was one of them, married to a scion of ancient white supremacy who was ready to level all class distinctions, more than sufficed to influence them."[21]

The particulars of Bowen's case against Riordan and Dawson were as follows. On October 23, 1874, Dawson reopened charges that Bowen,

18. Chamberlain to Dawson, February 18, 1875, Dawson Papers, Duke.

19. Williamson, *After Slavery,* p. 396.

20. Holt, *Black over White,* pp. 116–19.

21. Sarah Morgan Dawson note on Susan Pettigrew (*sic*) for Warrington Dawson, November 12, 1908, Dawson Papers, Duke.

while a captain in the Confederate army stationed near Charleston, instigated the murder of Colonel William Parker White. The allegation urged that Bowen was enraged when Colonel White preferred certain charges that led to Bowen's court-martial. To get revenge, Bowen enlisted the aid of Eli Grimes, a young soldier from Lee County, Georgia (Bowen's home before the war). Grimes was at first unable to summon sufficient nerve to get the job done, but under threat of death, Grimes finally gave way to Bowen's demands and ambushed Colonel White in April, 1864.

White lived long enough to implicate Bowen, who was quickly thrown into a Charleston jail. When federal troops entered Charleston the following year, Bowen was released and began his career as a scalawag. An attempt to bring the case to trial in February, 1871, failed when Eli Grimes jumped from a train just outside Charleston and fled on foot. It was generally believed that Grimes died in the swamps, and the case was accordingly dropped for lack of evidence. Dawson was now, in the fall of 1874, reopening the case in an attempt to discredit Bowen.[22] Josephus Woodruff, who heartily disliked Dawson, branded the attacks on Bowen as "vulgar and scurrilous," but concluded that "people like this sort of journalism and Bowen's enemies and rivals admire it."[23]

Believing himself safe from prosecution, Sheriff Bowen decided to enter libel proceedings against the proprietors of the *News and Courier*, and it was generally believed that he chose criminal libel to avoid direct personal involvement—it would now be *South Carolina* v. *Riordan and Dawson*. On February 3, 1875, the Grand Jury filed a true bill, and Dawson found himself in the uncomfortable position of having to prove his case against Bowen or be convicted. An air of gloom hung about the *News and Courier* offices until Bowen's former wife, hearing of the case, wrote Dawson from Kentucky saying she had reliable information that Eli Grimes was still alive and residing in Lee County, Georgia. The weeks that followed found Dawson in feverish, often clandestine, activity to locate Grimes and bring him to Charleston. He wrote Sarah apologizing for his long absences and warning her that "there is nothing before me for months save trouble & risk."[24]

Besides Riordan and his wife, Dawson took only two others into his confidence during this period of desperate and delicate proceedings. The first was his brother-in-law, Jimmie Morgan, who would actually bring Grimes to trial, and the second was Governor Chamberlain, the only man who could make the extradition of the Georgian possible. None of these

---

22. For a full statement of Bowen's charges see *News and Courier*, April 21, 1875.

23. Josephus Woodruff Diary, October 10, 1874, photostatic copy, Duke.

24. The manner in which Dawson learned of Grimes's whereabouts is described in James Morris Morgan, *Recollections of a Rebel Reefer* (Boston: Houghton Mifflin, 1917), p. 355. The letter to Sarah is dated March 12, 1875, Dawson Papers, Duke.

accomplices, however, knew the full scope of Dawson's plan. He first learned of Grimes's whereabouts on Tuesday, March 24, and on the following Friday night he left for Columbia, reaching the capital early the next morning. Dawson went straight to the governor's office where, after a conference of several hours, the editor emerged with the two things he wanted—the necessary papers to extradite Grimes and a promise of executive clemency for Grimes should he testify under oath. Chamberlain was only too happy to oblige Captain Dawson. With one stroke of a pen he could do much to knit his new alliance with the editor of South Carolina's leading Conservative newspaper and at the same time strike at a long-time foe in the Radical camp. Before leaving for the Kimball House in Atlanta that same afternoon, Dawson hastily scribbled a note to Sarah, *"All goes well, Very well!"*[25]

On the very next day, Sunday, March 29, Dawson secured a conference with Georgia's Democratic governor, who was only too delighted to honor the request for extradition. Dawson left the governor's mansion in Atlanta with a paper directing the sheriff of Lee County to hold Grimes for twenty days, at the expiration of which time, if South Carolina had not made claims, Grimes was to be set free. Two short days after conferring with Chamberlain, an exhausted Captain Dawson was in Lee County, 150 miles south of Atlanta, confronting Eli Grimes with his proposition. The discussions with Grimes could not have been easy. The poor "cracker" was exceedingly reluctant even to talk about going back to Charleston, and he belonged to a large, menacing clan of poor whites—the kind of family that would later people Faulkner's novels. Nonetheless, with the aid of the sheriff, Dawson was able to get Grimes into custody and telegraphed success on Tuesday, the thirty-first of March.[26]

On the third of April, having left Grimes lodged in the Lee County jail, a relieved Dawson was back in Atlanta, where he telegraphed Riordan to set the machinery of their plan in motion. Dawson had already seen to it that his brother-in-law would serve as Chamberlain's deputy in the extradition of Grimes, but as he was never too sure of the dependability of Sarah's brother, he urged Riordan to be certain that Jimmie boarded the train as scheduled. When Morgan arrived in Lee County, he learned to his dismay that Grimes, with the aid of his clan, had flown the coop. Despite warnings from the sheriff of the dangers involved, the headstrong Morgan proceeded to Grimes's shack, where, after a scuffle which involved Grimes's semi-nude wife, Jimmie arrested Eli and ushered him back to jail. Mor-

---

25. Dawson to his wife, March 26, 28, and 30, 1875, Dawson Papers, Duke. Quoted material in letter of March 28.

26. The papers ordering Grimes's extradition are undated but may be found among Dawson's personal correspondence of March and April, 1875, ibid. The telegram of March 31 was from Dawson to his wife, ibid.

gan's troubles were only beginning. The next morning they found Grimes's body crumpled on the floor of his cell, unconscious. The poor devil, determined not to go back to South Carolina, had tried to incapacitate himself by smashing his head against the bars of his cell. Thereafter, under strict orders from Dawson, Morgan never let Eli out of sight. Dawson's telegraph attempted to instill in Jimmie the gravity of the situation: "All my trust is in you," he wired, "much of my fortune & reputation is in your hands." As an afterthought Dawson warned, "Make G understand that if he backs out he will swing for it."[27]

The trial began on Monday, April 19, even as Grimes was being smuggled secretly into the city. The newspapers of the state, particularly those belonging to the State Press Association, which Dawson had been instrumental in forming the year before, transformed the trial into a *cause célèbre* for freedom of the press. The state was ably represented by Solicitor Charles Wilson Buttz and by David Timothy Corbin, a perennial favorite for the state senate from Charleston County and a man who remained active in Republican party affairs long after Reconstruction was over. Counsel for the defense was equally capable, represented by leading members of the Charleston bar, including General James Conner. The presiding judge was Jacob Pinckney Reed, a white Republican with leanings as conservative as his middle name. As expected, the dramatic moment came when the defense called Eli Grimes. Bowen laughed in disbelief then blanched when he saw his old accomplice appear as from the grave. Grimes did his job on the stand well enough, but the impact of his testimony was somewhat diminished by a blistering cross-examination administered by the prosecution.[28]

After seven exhausting days of testimony and argument, the case finally went to the jury. Judge Reed's charge was interesting. After standing on the cutting edge of new judicial precedent with the declaration that either truth or the absence of malicious intent would serve as a defense, he proceeded to lecture the prosecution for prejudicing their client by arguing that acquittal of Dawson was tantamount to the conviction of Bowen. Given the evidence, there was little mistaking the implication of Judge Reed's remarks, that the *News and Courier*'s allegations against Bowen were grounded in truth. The judge went one step further and cautioned the jury against a mistrial—there having been rumors that such would be the case.[29] The jury went into seclusion at seven o'clock on the evening of the twenty-sixth and failed to reach a decision that night. Reports indicated that there was a lone holdout for conviction and that he was a diehard

27. Dawson to B. R. Riordan, April 3, 1875; Dawson to J. M. Morgan, April 7, 1875, ibid. For a description of the difficulties involved in arresting Grimes and bringing him to trial, see Morgan, *Recollections*, pp. 355–59.

28. For a complete report of the trial see *News and Courier*, April 20–27, 1875.

29. Ibid., April 27, 1875.

radical from the Bowen camp. On the following day the jury declared itself unable to reach a verdict when two blacks changed their votes to favor conviction. Though not acquitted, Dawson considered the verdict a victory, and Bowen never attempted to reinstitute proceedings.

Through it all, Susan Petigru Bowen remained one of the most interesting characters in staid old Charleston. Her defiance of all that Charleston society held most dear was brought off at great personal sacrifice, but her determination gained the grudging admiration of the community she scandalized. Writing of Susan many years later, Sarah Dawson remarked, "To her, Bowen owed all that he accomplished in South Carolina—a record to make angels weep. She knew the vulnerable point in every [armor] and she never hesitated to strike it venomously." Every Saturday, Susan published over her own signature, a tale of some well-known citizen in a "dirty little paper" devoted to Bowen's cause. No one bought the paper, it being a point of honor not to. But through Frank, Sarah got copies of the little sheet, and each week Sarah would be "surrounded by petitioners who secretly read and were ashamed."[30] After Susan's death in December, 1875, Bowen married the seventeen-year-old daughter of ex-Governor Franklin Moses, Jr., and to the end he remained an influential figure in Charleston politics. He died in New York City on June 23, 1880.

To all Conservatives the events following the Bowen episode clearly foreshadowed an impending crisis between Radical rule and the forces which looked to a restoration of the supremacy of white rule in South Carolina. The Radicals, disturbed by Chamberlain's apparent truckling before the white minority, seemed determined to unglue the alliance that had been forming between the governor and the Conservatives. Dawson, fortified by his recent assistance from Chamberlain in the Bowen case, was ready to parry the Radical attack. On May 14, 1875, he published an editorial in which he retracted his earlier judgment of the governor and announced "that, whenever all the facts shall be known, the record of Attorney-General Chamberlain will be found every whit as clean as the record of Governor Chamberlain." The governor signified his pleasure with the *News and Courier*'s latest course, writing, "It is doubly valuable to me *privately* because you and I know that it is the result of conviction and not of bargain. Let the tongue of the world 'wag as it will,' that is a precious fact to men who are trying to use their powers for the good of all their fellow citizens."[31] Forgotten was the exposé Dawson had so carefully developed to defeat Chamberlain the previous August.

---

30. Sarah M. Dawson note on Susan Pettigrew (*sic*) for Warrington Dawson, November 12, 1908, Dawson Papers, Duke.

31. *News and Courier*, May 14, 1875. Chamberlain to Dawson, May 15, 1875, Dawson Papers, Duke.

Chamberlain believed that the plot to crush the reform détente between his Independent Republicans and the Conservatives was being engineered by Senator John James Patterson, or "Honest John" as he was known because of his well-publicized efforts to bribe his election to the United States Senate. Chamberlain believed that Patterson was "now in Washn pouring his venom on me 'squat like a toad' at the ear of the President and spitting his venomous filth on me at every chance."[32] The Radical strategy was to discredit their maverick governor by convincing Washington and South Carolina that Chamberlain had been deeply involved in the scandals of the Scott Administration, 1868–1872, and under the guise of reform was even then plotting further perfidy. The campaign first manifested itself in May, 1875, with an effort to implicate the governor in the abuses for which ex-Treasurer Niles Gardiner Parker was then being tried. These charges, involving irregularities in the management of the Sinking Fund Commission, eventually led to Parker's conviction by a Republican judge and jury.[33] Chamberlain steadfastly refused to respond to these allegations of wrongdoing until his enemies came forward and made a formal charge. Such a statement of particulars was not forthcoming, and Chamberlain did not publicly deny involvement until August.[34]

Even while efforts were under way to associate Chamberlain with Parker's crimes, anonymous correspondents from Charleston and Columbia were filling the New York *Sun* with lurid details of every conceivable corrupt practice of the former attorney general. All the charges raised by the *Sun* had been thoroughly aired before with the exception of a letter from Chamberlain to Hiram H. Kimpton, former financial agent for the state. The letter, written in January, 1870, indicated that Chamberlain had taken advantage of his position as attorney general in a scheme to buy up the Greenville and Columbia Railroad along with other lines which would form a northwest passage from the Atlantic. The scheme was as old as railroading in South Carolina and into 1870 remained entirely legal. It even attracted such latter-day apostles of integrity as Martin Witherspoon Gary.[35]

---

32. Chamberlain to Dawson, May 11, 1875, Dawson Papers, Duke. It is alleged that Patterson was never brought to trial for bribing his election because Chamberlain, acting as a secret attorney for Patterson, moved to have the jury quashed on grounds that it had been improperly drawn. The judge, R. B. Carpenter, having just been elected by the same body, sustained the motion, Simkins and Woody, *Reconstruction*, pp. 136–37.

33. Allen, *Governor Chamberlain's Administration*, pp. 145–46. This was not the first time Parker tried to implicate Chamberlain in his own wrongdoing. In the spring of 1870 Chamberlain threatened to bring Parker to trial for land frauds. Parker countered with a threat to drag Chamberlain down with him. Whereupon, for no known reason, the charges were dropped. Williamson, *After Slavery*, p. 398.

34. Chamberlain to Dawson, May 11, 1875, Dawson Papers, Duke. *News and Courier*, August 10, 1875.

35. The alleged conspiracy of correspondents is described in Allen, *Governor Chamber-*

But the charge that Chamberlain had taken advantage of an office entrusted to him by the people of South Carolina was serious. As soon as the June 5 issue of the New York *Sun*, which contained a copy of the alleged correspondence, reached Dawson's desk, the editor rushed a clipping to the governor. Chamberlain replied immediately. He told Dawson that he was content to leave his defense entirely in the editor's hands. He did say that he could not confirm or deny the authenticity of the letter, but even if genuine, he did not think it suggested fraud. Chamberlain confessed, "That I hoped to make money—dreamed of thousands—there is no doubt, but I never knew of or consented to any transaction, even in that connection, which involved any injury to the State as I then understood it."[36]

The governor's confidence was not misplaced. Dawson was intent on cementing the new alliance between Chamberlain and South Carolina's Conservatives. He characterized the action of the *Sun* as an apparent attempt "to ruin Governor Chamberlain, and with him those citizens who see in him the mainstay of honesty and decency and ability in this State." Saying "this is no crime," Dawson went on to suggest that the ex–attorney general had acted no differently from a Vanderbilt, a Garrett, or a Scott. He accused the *Sun* of being the agency through which the Patterson-Whipper-Moses ring hoped to alienate the Conservatives from the governor, thereby insuring the success of the Radical ring. The ominous portent of this collusion between local Radicals and the northern press could be seen in the all-important judicial elections scheduled for winter. "The anti-Chamberlain Ring," warned Dawson, "propose to drop Judges Reed, Maher, Townsend, and Shaw. Charleston is to be honored with the judicial presence of a Whipper or a Worthington."[37]

---

lain's Administration, pp. 141–45. The letter to Kimpton is dated January 5, 1870, ibid., p. 143. For Gary's involvement see a MS contract, in Gary's hand and signed by J. J. Patterson, August 5, 1871, Martin Witherspoon Gary Papers, South Caroliniana Library, University of South Carolina, cited hereafter as SCL. The contract affirms an agreement between George S. Cameron, Thomas S. Sterns, and J. J. Patterson to purchase stock of the Blue Ridge Rail Road from the state and further acknowledges that Gary and Patterson were equal partners in the purchase. A letter from Sterns to Gary, February 28, 1874, ibid., further indicates that Thomas A. Scott was involved to the tune of $300,000.

36. Chamberlain to Dawson, June 9, 1875, Dawson Papers, Duke. It has been as difficult for historians as for contemporaries to resolve the enigma of Chamberlain's close contact with the corruptionists and his apparent good character. The best explanation is found in Robert Means Davis's notebook, "Campaign of 1876," R. M. Davis Papers, SCL. Davis, a contemporary, observed that as attorney general Chamberlain knew about some of the frauds but refused to reveal them, even though he did not profit personally. "This is not a very high position to take; but Chamberlain was young, he had a future before him, and in 1868–70 it seemed as if nothing could stay the flood."

37. *News and Courier* editorials, ca. June, 1875, reprinted in Allen, *Governor Chamberlain's Administration,* pp. 142–45.

By June, 1875, the Radical attack on Chamberlain had found most of the Conservatives rallying behind their reform governor. It was generally believed that the test of the new alliance would indeed come in the winter judicial elections. Judge Alfred Proctor Aldrich of Barnwell, former champion of secession and one of the eight holdouts against emancipation in the 1865 convention, best summed up the new position of the Conservatives. In a letter to William Dunlap Simpson, later lieutenant governor under Wade Hampton, Aldrich acknowledged that Chamberlain would have "a harder fight next winter than he has yet had with the Radical Ring." One Radical told Aldrich that "Chamberlain was going too fast and that we 'Celestials' [Conservatives] . . . would kill him off with his own party and prevent him from carrying out his policy of reform." The old judge felt it imperative that all good Conservatives should stand fast behind the governor. With hard work and organization the Conservatives could hope to outmaneuver the Radicals in the legislature that winter and "beat them in the elections next year."[38]

Though the Conservatives were apprehensive about their impending battle with the Radicals, the summer and fall of 1875 must have seemed in retrospect the halcyon days of their alliance with the Independent Republicans. The months following Chamberlain's first legislative session found the governor toasting and being toasted in the camps of his former enemies. He made the rounds of all the social, literary, and patriotic festivals, or, if unable to attend, he sent ingratiating messages of regrets. The governor even commended the existence and work of the Conservative rifle clubs that would be used in another year to bring about his defeat.[39] By their invitations and their plaudits the Conservatives were driving ever deeper the wedge that would separate the governor from the Republican constituency that had elected him. It was in this heady atmosphere of acceptance that Chamberlain decided to honor an invitation from Dr. William H. Whitsitt of Greenville to present prizes for excellence in Greek. On the evening of December 16, 1875, while Chamberlain was extolling the virtues of classical learning, the South Carolina legislature rose in rebellion against the Conservative-Independent Republican detente. Black Thursday had come.

---

38. A. P. Aldrich to W. D. Simpson, June 30, 1875, W. D. Simpson Papers, Duke. A foreign observer, William Hepworth Dixon, commented on this Conservative strategy and Chamberlain's receptiveness to it. Noting that Chamberlain was "listening more and more to the White minority," Dixon remarked, "Like other strangers, Chamberlain is open to the softer influences of society. He likes to sit at good men's feasts and bask in the smiles of well-born women. A podesta in Verona or Ferrari, seldom, if ever, stood beyond the reach of social courtesies; and the podesta of South Carolina shows a disposition to respond, so far as he can meet these White advances without fear of estranging his coloured friends, *White Conquest* (London: Chatto and Windus, 1876), pp. 150–51.

39. Allen, *Governor Chamberlain's Administration,* pp. 115–39.

The election of circuit judges provided the occasion for the rebellion. Taking advantage of the governor's temporary absence, the legislature elected ex-Governor Franklin Moses, Jr., and a popular Negro legislator, William James Whipper, to the Sumter and Charleston circuits respectively. Choices more acceptable to the Conservative-Democratic minority might have been made. Indeed, the leaders of Reconstruction had traditionally assigned these sensitive judgeships to conservative whites, but the Republicans, sickened by Chamberlain's obvious apostasy, were bent on making the affair a test of loyalty by choosing from among their more notorious partisans.[40] To no one's surprise, the election threw South Carolina's Conservatives into paroxysms of indignation and provided the catalyst for the resurgence of white rule in the Palmetto State. Joining in the chorus of outrage, Chamberlain cried out, "if there ever was an hour when the spirit of the Puritans, the spirit of undying, unconquerable enmity and defiance to wrong ought to animate their sons, it is this hour, here, in South Carolina. The civilization of the Puritan and the Cavalier, of the Roundhead and the Huguenot, is in peril."[41] In keeping with such crisis rhetoric, December 16, 1875, would forever be remembered by the sobriquet Black Thursday.

The Sunday following that episode was not a day that stood apart in the saga of South Carolina's deliverance from Reconstruction. Yet it was a day that brought together two principals in the story, men who, in seeking the middle course of reform, helped break the back of Republican dominance and pave the way for a minority rule in South Carolina as complete as the Negro majority ever dared dream. As Dawson and Chamberlain greeted each other, they had every reason to congratulate themselves on their merging courses of action in the year just ending. Their growing alliance and friendship had been born of mutual concern with rooting out the corruption of the preceding eight years, and their efforts were praised by South Carolina's most honored citizens. Both men welcomed the praise, for they had now passed the better part of a decade in a state distinguished by an overweening pride in its lineage and a natural distrust of the interlopers that a lost war had thrust in its midst. Little could either man realize at the time of their meeting on December 19, 1875, that the lasting acceptance of one would come at the expense of the other and that both reputations would suffer in an effort to prolong their now admired alliance.

Arrangements for the meeting were made by Dawson. On hearing of the legislature's action Dawson immediately sent a telegram to the governor requesting an audience. Chamberlain was relieved to see his new friend. Not only was it a chance to get his side of the story published, it was also an opportunity for Chamberlain to discuss the course of action he would take.

---

40. Holt, *Black over White*, pp. 185–86.
41. Allen, *Governor Chamberlain's Administration*, pp. 200–201.

The governor had been accepting Dawson's counsel on the matter of the judicial elections for some time, and in October he had written the editor saying "I agree with you entirely in regard to your position [on the impending elections]. I see no escape from it, and it solves one of our greatest difficulties." Dawson had been arguing from various precedents that Chamberlain could refuse to honor objectionable elections to the ermine on the ground that the incumbent judges in the Charleston and Sumter circuits were entitled to full terms because they had been elected to fill places vacated in the middle of a term.[42] Chamberlain had already decided to act on the basis of this advice when he and Dawson sat down to their interview that Sunday.

Before getting down to business, Chamberlain may well have laughingly reminded Dawson that it was little more than a year ago that Dawson was publicly urging the Republicans to reject Chamberlain in favor of men like William James Whipper—such were the politics of Reconstruction.[43] In any case, Dawson asked why Chamberlain decided to honor his speaking engagement in Greenville, when the Senate had already voted to consider the elections on the sixteenth. It was the question on the minds of most Conservatives, for it had been Chamberlain's presence that blocked Whipper's election the year before. The governor explained the events in terms of a conspiracy. He told Dawson of sending a note to Speaker Robert Brown Elliott requesting that the House delay the election so that he could honor the Greenville invitation. Elliott replied that, while he was personally committed to vote for the Thursday election, he felt safe in assuring the governor of a delay. With this promise, Chamberlain made arrangements to leave but took the precaution of scheduling an early return should events go awry. And, of course, no sooner had Chamberlain departed than the plot matured.[44]

Elliott himself seconded the nomination of Whipper, declaring the vote to be "a test of fidelity to the Republican party."[45] With this call for unity

---

42. Chamberlain to Dawson, October 11, 1875, Dawson Papers, Duke. The case of *Wright* v. *Charles,* Sup. Ct. S.C. (Richardson's Reports, vol. 4, p. 178) was argued as a solution for the impending election dilemma in the *News and Courier,* October 9, 1875. See also Chamberlain to Dawson, December 27, 1875, Dawson Papers, Duke, in which Chamberlain asks Dawson to explain the governor's position on the elections, saying, "I would have it done here, but our paper [Columbia *Union Herald*] don't *travel* much, you know!"

43. *News and Courier,* August 31, 1874. Before the judicial elections, Whipper, a carpetbag Negro from Beaufort, had a good reputation among Conservatives. See Williamson, *After Slavery,* p. 331. This was due in part to Whipper's opposition to Robert Smalls and close association with the bolting reformers in 1872, Willie Lee Rose, *Rehearsal for Reconstruction: The Port Royal Experiment,* intro. by C. Vann Woodward (Indianapolis: Bobbs-Merrill, 1964), p. 390.

44. The interview was published in the *News and Courier,* December 20, 1875.

45. Allen, *Governor Chamberlain's Administration,* p. 198. Allen described Elliott as "a colored carpet-bagger from Massachusetts, an ex-member of Congress, a person of consider-

and with vote-trading on the other judicial offices, both Whipper and
Moses were elected by substantial majorities. Governor Chamberlain's
biographer called it a "moral earthquake." Alfred Brockenbrough Williams, then a young newspaper reporter, still vibrated with the sense of
Conservative outrage when he wrote many years later, "The year 1875
closed with the most respectable Governor and the worst and most violent
legislature Reconstruction had given South Carolina or any Southern state.
The culminating crime of the legislature was the election . . . of Whipper,
black, bestial, dissolute Carpetbagger, and Moses, former governor, rejected for reelection by his own party, known through the country as 'the
robber governor,' lowest of the low."[46]

Chamberlain also explained in answer to Dawson's questions that his
presence would have made no difference for the consipracy had been too
carefully concocted. "The color line, the party line, and the line of
antagonism to my Administration, all were sharply drawn." The immediate effect, Chamberlain predicted, would be the reorganization of the
Democratic party, but with an eye cocked to the future he declared, "I do
not allow myself to think that the good and honest men of South Carolina
will find it impossible, because they are organized as Democrats, to give
their help to whomsoever shall be best able to undo the terrible wrongs of
last Thursday." Chamberlain was clearly ready to repudiate the majority of
the party through which he had once hoped to achieve "the solution of the
most difficult and one of the most interesting social and political problems . . . this century has presented."[47] He seemed almost too willing to
place the future of Reconstruction in South Carolina and his own ambitions in the hands of men who had a vested interest in destroying the
former, if not the latter.

When Dawson left Chamberlain, he was convinced as never before that
the carpetbag governor would be the instrument of South Carolina's
redemption. As the interview closed, Chamberlain gave assurances that he
would overturn the elections of Whipper and Moses, and on the next day
he made it official, concluding his proclamation with a most curious
suggestion that "in some cases, presenting similar legal questions, it might
not be required of the Governor to decline to issue commissions, the

---

able education, superior oratorical power, and unsurpassed influence as a politician among his
people." Elliott's biographer concurs in the conspiracy thesis. She contends that on December 15 Elliott deliberately engineered the vote to delay the elections as a "red herring to get
the governor out of town." Peggy Lamson, *The Glorious Failure: Black Congressman Robert
Brown Elliott and the Reconstruction in South Carolina* (New York: W. W. Norton, 1973),
p. 222.

46. Allen, *Governor Chamberlain's Administration*, p. 193. Alfred Brockenbrough Williams, *Hampton and His Red Shirts: South Carolina's Deliverance in 1876* (Charleston:
Walker, Evans & Cogswell, 1935), p. 27.

47. *News and Courier*, December 20, 1875.

circumstances of the present case compel me to this course."[48] While the
Grant administration along with most of the nation's press supported
Chamberlain's decision, the governor was not altogether happy with
suggestions in the New York *Times*, the *Nation*, and the Springfield
Republican that his ground was "purely technical." Asking Dawson to
correct this erroneous view, Chamberlain wrote, "The ground is not
technical, nor even *legal* in the common meaning; it is fundamental and
strictly constitutional."[49] When the South Carolina Supreme Court later
sustained Chamberlain's action, it was sustaining more than law. It was
giving judicial sanction to a Conservative view of what was fundamental
and constitutional—that the "best men" should rule.

Since the election of 1874, the Puritan governor and the Cavalier editor
had moved from open hostility to cautious regard and finally to mutual
admiration. They seemed to have struck what one newspaper called "that
golden political mean the people so much admire and the country in her
poverty and desolation so sadly needs."[50] There was magic in their work.
By their adroit management the extreme elements of the state appeared to
be held in check. But if they seemed to control the center, it was only an
illusion, for the center was in reality only the pinched waist of an hourglass,
incapable of preventing the sands from running their course from one
extreme to the other, creating only a fleeting sense of equipoise at time's
midpassage. The efforts of Dawson and Chamberlain to secure rule by the
"best men" only succeeded in dislodging Chamberlain from his Republican
constituency. The hourglass was turned on end. The thin rope of sand
began to flow inexorably in the direction of the extreme Democratic forces
which by fraud, intimidation, and violence would secure the state for its
white minority. The episode of the judges was in truth only a touchpoint in
the events leading to the overthrow of Reconstruction, but it exercised
such a spell over South Carolina's *viri boni* as to provide "the key to the
problem why so many good Conservatives desired a fusion with Chamberlain up to the nomination of Wade Hampton."[51]

48. Allen, *Governor Chamberlain's Administration*, p. 197.

49. Two letters from Chamberlain to Dawson under same date, December 27, 1875,
Dawson Papers, Duke.

50. Abbeville *Medium,* February 9, 1876, scrapbook, Dawson Papers, Duke.

51. R. M. Davis, notebook, "Campaign of 1876," R. M. Davis Papers, SCL.

Chapter III
"Aut Bourbon, aut Nihil":
The Spirit of '76

In 1876 South Carolina Conservatives launched the campaign that delivered the state from Reconstruction. As the year dawned, the Democrats were by no means certain about the course of action they should take. A majority favored some sort of fusion with the reform-minded Republicans led by Governor Chamberlain, the foremost champion of this policy being Dawson. Another group preferred to take the state "straight-out." These firebrands were much impressed with the "Mississippi plan," which delivered that state from its black majority by fraud and intimidation. The most outspoken advocate of a straight-out fight was the legendary Bald Eagle from Edgefield, Martin Witherspoon Gary.

As the months passed the Straight-outs became more and more earnest and the debate more and more heated. Robert Means Davis, then on special assignment from the *News and Courier* and later a professor of history and political economy in the University of South Carolina, wrote in his campaign notebook that "such a condition of affairs was unfavorable for compromise," and with feelings aroused to fever pitch, he predicted a greater probability of success for the "extremists."[1] Success for the extreme Democratic forces was guaranteed on a hot day in July when the little town of Hamburg erupted in racial violence. One day after the initial incident at Hamburg and three days before violence broke out, Dawson wrote an editorial declaring that the real issue of 1876 was Governor Chamberlain, for "if he could be eliminated altogether from political calculations, there would be absolutely no differences in the Democratic ranks."[2] At the time Dawson wrote the editorial he was right—Chamberlain was the issue—but even as the editor wrote, events at Hamburg were overturning all political calculations based on assessments of men and their worth. Hamburg was transforming the issue of 1876 into what Martin Gary had said it was from the very beginning: race.

But for the moment, fusion was the talk of the state. It had been tried with limited success in 1870, 1872, and 1874. Fusion, or Co-operation as it came to be called, was a strategy as old as minority politics itself and, as a political theory, seemed at home in the state that produced John Caldwell Calhoun. Its defining characteristic during the era of Reconstruction in South Carolina was the forging of the white minority into a bloc which

---

1. Robert Means Davis notebook, "Campaign of 1876," R. M. Davis Papers, South Caroliniana Library, University of South Carolina, cited hereafter as scl.

2. *News and Courier,* July 5, 1876.

could then be used to form a majority in alliance with dissident Republicans. It is interesting that fusion's only numerical success (and it was qualified) came in the 1874 opposition to Chamberlain—the very man who now made Co-operation appear a viable alternative. General James Conner, a leading Charleston fusionist, expressed the sanguine hopes of his conservative friends in the spring of 1875. "Both city and state are improving politically, financially & morally," he wrote William Porcher Miles. "Chamberlain has disappointed his party & pleased his enemies by his conduct." Noting that the governor's main strength now lay with the Conservatives, Conner looked forward to the fall municipal elections when Charleston's better elements could organize to "elect our own Mayor, if our people will go earnestly to work."[3]

The Charleston municipal elections, which Conner looked forward to with so much hope, were billed everywhere as a test case for fusion, and rightly so, for the politics of Co-operation cannot be understood if divorced from Charleston. It was in her business community that the policy was born and nurtured, and a twenty-eight-year-old editor could claim paternity. Writing in 1876, Dawson noted that as early as 1868 he attempted to form a combination with the colored people for the aldermanic elections and "that the first political meeting ever held in Charleston in which respectable democrats & colored men sat together was arranged & organized & the expenses paid by me." The meeting was held in a vacant store on Hayne Street, with Thomas Y. Simons of the *Courier* serving as coadjutor.[4]

. But even while the young editor was assiduously manipulating political fusion with one hand, he was revealing its fatal flaw with the other. A letter to his father in August, 1868, underscored the duplicity that could never be masked. "We shall have our City election here in a short time," Dawson wrote, "and that will decide whether this fair City is to be ruled by white men or negroes."[5] Such duplicity led one historian to declare, "Fundamentally, fusion did not succeed because it misrepresented not only the basic attitudes of the great mass of white voters, but the deep-seated feelings of the fusionist leadership itself."[6] Fusion was simply another route to white supremacy.

Despite fusion's lack of success in South Carolina, the results of the Charleston municipal elections of 1875 offered encouragement to those

---

3. Conner to Miles, May 12, 1875, William Porcher Miles Papers, Southern Historical Collection, University of North Carolina, cited hereafter as SHC.

4. Dawson to Robert Reid Hemphill, June 28, 1876, Hemphill Family Papers, Duke University Library, cited hereafter as Duke. See also the Abbeville *Medium,* February 9, 1876, scrapbook, Francis Warrington Dawson Papers, Duke.

5. Dawson to his father, August 26, 1868, Dawson Papers, Duke.

6. Joel Williamson, *After Slavery: The Negro in South Carolina During Reconstruction, 1861–1877* (Chapel Hill: University of North Carolina Press, 1965), p. 354.

Conservatives who were looking toward an eventual alliance with Governor Chamberlain, and the final count was seen as a personal triumph for Dawson. Victory, however, proved to be Pyrrhic, for it was achieved in spite of the visceral white supremacy which permeated fusion and at the price of deep divisions within the Charleston business community, divisions that would cast a long shadow over fusionist aspirations for 1876.

The election matched the Republican incumbent, George Irving Cunningham, against the candidate of the Citizens' Conservative Party, John Andreas Wagener. Cunningham was a man of good character who made an adequate living as a butcher, while Wagener, a man of considerable wealth and a former mayor, was considered to be the "most beloved of all the Germans."[7] At that time, the Charleston Germans comprised a substantial section of the business community, controlling altogether some six million out of an estimated thirty million dollars' worth of real property in Charleston.[8] The choice for Conservatives would have seemed obvious to any but those involved in the crazy-quilt pattern of Charleston politics in the 1870s. In what came to be one of the most bitterly fought contests of the period, Dawson was found supporting the Republican, Cunningham, while the editor's archenemy, the scalawag Christopher Columbus Bowen, was to be found in the camp of John A. Wagener.

Wagener had been elected mayor of Charleston in 1871 on a fusion ticket and, despite his bitter personal quarrel with Dawson in 1875, remained an advocate of Governor Chamberlain up to the nomination of Wade Hampton in August, 1876. Many of his friends, however, were loath to follow this subsequent course of loyalty to fusionist principles, for there ran a current of antagonism between the German community and native Charlestonians that Dawson's editorials only deepened. Wagener claimed to have won election in 1871 without support from "the Carolinians" (native Charlestonians) and to have lost in 1873 as a result of their opposition. One of his embittered political lieutenants declared in the 1875 campaign that "the Germans did not want the support of the Carolinians."[9] Wagener's decision to run in 1875 was made without benefit of counsel from the regular Conservative hierarchy, and his strategy was to call Conservative ward meetings without going through normal channels and thereby to gain recognition through a *fait accompli*. To compel recognition still further, his faction assumed the parallel label of Citizens' Conservative Party.

This division in ranks was too tempting for the opportunistic Bowen. He immediately began maneuvering to do in his rival in the Republican camp,

---

7. Davis, "Campaign of 1876."

8. *News and Courier,* October 9, 1875.

9. Ibid., August 25, October 1, 1875.

Mayor Cunningham, who had become increasingly friendly with the "Broad Street clique." By gradually insinuating his men into the ward meetings of the Citizens' Conservative Party, Bowen gave substance to the charge that the Wagener party was merely a psuedonym for the Bowen-Wagener faction. As the campaign heated up, more and more Conservatives dropped out of the Citizens' party, and Wagener's reliance on Bowen became too great to repudiate. Charge and countercharge both marked and marred the contest. Wagener asserted that only "Broad Street" supported Cunningham, and may have hit closer to the mark than he knew when Dawson answered rather lamely that working men were also included in the Conservative-Independent Republican effort. At the same time Dawson blamed the whole Wagener campaign on Bowen's scheming. "The [Bowen] plan," Dawson charged, "was to play upon the ambition and natural sympathies of the Germans, who have hitherto, as a rule voted with the Conservatives, and to lure them on to an acceptance of his aid in electing a so-called Conservative ticket for Mayor and Aldermen."[10]

Dawson's editorial attack demonstrated the awesome power of an unopposed political press. He argued that there were three parties in Charleston—Conservative, Independent Republican, and Radical. He told his readers that the election of 1874 established the principle of Co-operation between the first two and, as a result, guaranteed Conservative representation in the General Assembly equal to their numbers as a minority. Any faction which divorced itself from the regular Conservative organization Dawson branded as Radical. The election of Wagener, he warned, would destroy the Conservative-Independent Republican coalition for good government and "would bring in its train Bowenism on the bench next winter, rampant Bowenism in the County in 1876 . . . and Bowenism unchecked and uncontrollable in the City." By late September the *News and Courier* was no longer running any letters friendly to the Germans, and Dawson reached new heights of editorial vitriol, declaring Wagener a "so-called Conservative candidate" who relied for his election on such Negro votes as his allies could import or command and German dollars could buy.[11] Such blatant political propaganda, along with good organizational work, produced a 2,000-vote majority for Cunningham and cries of Co-operation vindicated.

But far from vindicating fusion, the election of 1875 more nearly foreshadowed its doom. The white minority was not welded into a solid bloc, though a sizable majority did follow Dawson's lead. Cunningham's election was more the product of factional alliances unique to Charleston than the result of a neat three-cornered structure of Conservative, Inde-

10. Ibid., October 4, September 22, 1875.

11. Ibid., September 20, October 1, 1875.

pendent Republican, and Radical that Dawson felt essential to fusion. This kind of division would not likely be duplicated in a statewide election where Reconstruction itself was at stake. Furthermore, Dawson's vigorous editorial attack betrayed the white supremacy latent in any fusionist rhetoric. His vicious charges against Bowen drew the inevitable Conservative equation between corruption and black rule. His insistence that Co-operation would work only if Independent Republicans and Conservative Democrats maintained party identity made it unmistakably clear that a majority could be fabricated only if sufficient numbers of blacks could be duped into voting Conservative under the guise of a Republican label; the Negro would never wittingly fuse with the party of his oppression. Finally, Dawson's editorial attitude toward Wagener underscored the point that no candidate, regardless of his status in the community, could be a proponent of good government if his candidacy depended on a constituency with a black majority. Fusion politics depended on enough defections to insure the election of whites; more than enough would threaten its raison d'être.[12]

Dawson likely indulged one of the more common delusions of white supremacy; that blacks could not understand the slurs against race when couched in the language of good government and class. If so, he had only to go to one of his own reporters for proof that black sensitivity to racial slights did affect the politics of fusion. Writing a year later, Means Davis noted with some alarm the action of Charleston delegates to the Episcopal Diocesan Convention in refusing to seat black delegates. "Thus, in Charleston," he wrote, "the stronghold of the fusion political policy, a firebrand was thrust in this religio-social question. Here was another disturbing element. If the whites would not admit blacks to Church Conventions, how long would Democrats allow blacks in political office? The Republican politicians were shrewd enough to ask these questions."[13]

Beyond revealing the philosophical bankruptcy of Co-operation, the election of 1875 raised a more practical consideration about the Conservative alliance with Chamberlain. The alliance was inordinately dependent on the cohesiveness of the Charleston business community,[14] and the political debate of 1875 did much to strain those bonds. The ever-observant Means Davis again offered commentary. In the spring of 1876, he saw Charleston's businessmen and leaders as united behind fusion and opposed to Straight-out Democracy, but he also noted "several disturbing influences in the County." Chief among them was the lingering effects of the *News and Courier*'s antagonism of the German community in the munici-

---

12. Ibid., September 20 through October 9, 1875.

13. Davis, "Campaign of 1876."

14. Williamson, *After Slavery*, p. 402.

pal elections.[15] Nor were Dawson's parting comments on the election likely to salve the wound he had done so much to irritate. In a manner more patronizing than conciliatory, he urged the new city council to go out of its way to protect the defeated Germans because of their extensive property holdings and because the German community did not get the two representatives they would certainly have received had they remained loyal to the regular Conservative establishment.[16]

The embittered Germans immediately set out to establish a rival newspaper, and on May 1, 1876, the doors of the *Journal of Commerce* were opened for business. A letter to William Porcher Miles in December, 1875, sounding out his possible interest in editing the new paper, expressed a widely shared sentiment. Noting that the "chief subscribers are Germans and different elements are at work," the writer concluded, "an independent high paper is greatly needed."[17] This reaction to Dawson's dictatorial control over campaign rhetoric severely weakened whatever chances the pro-Chamberlain forces might have had in 1876, for as one student of these events observed, Dawson was the "political cat's paw" of the "top echelon financiers and businessmen of Charleston," the very people who would be essential to Chamberlain's success.[18] Whatever served to diminish Dawson's influence could only hurt the chances of fusion, but Dawson was still new to the power of his own press and had a lot to learn.

With the municipal election behind him, Dawson spent the early part of 1876 attacking the legislature, defending Governor Chamberlain, and counseling against a straight-out fight in the fall. Despite his journalistic failings in the municipal elections, he proved a master strategist in skillfully sandbagging against a rising tide of sentiment against fusion. Chamberlain spent the same time nursing sick headaches, which were no doubt aggravated by mounting attacks both from within and outside his party. His action in the recent judicial elections led to charges by high-ranking Republicans in Washington that the governor was preparing to desert his party and become a Democrat. These charges prompted Chamberlain to write Senator Oliver Hazard Perry Throck Morton of Indiana defending his Republicanism and declaring that his refusal to commission Whipper and Moses was absolutely essential to the continued ascendency of southern Republicanism.[19] When the letter was made public, the governor

15. Davis, "Campaign of 1876."

16. *News and Courier,* October 9, 1875.

17. Louis D. DeSaussure to Miles, December 26, 1875, William Porcher Miles Papers, SHC.

18. Williamson, *After Slavery,* p. 401.

19. The letter to Morton from Chamberlain was written January 13, 1876, and subsequently published in the New York *Herald,* February 25, 1876. A copy appears in Walter Allen, *Governor Chamberlain's Administration in South Carolina: A Chapter of Reconstruction in the Southern States* (New York: G. P. Putnam's Sons, 1888), pp. 229–34.

quickly realized the damage it might do him in South Carolina and sought Dawson's aid. Indicating that the letter was *"hot,"* he suggested that Dawson use some "righteous indignation" against those who would use the letter to hurt the cause of fusion.[20]

Sensing the temper of his readers, Dawson subtly transformed Chamberlain's defense of Republicanism into another clarion call for thorough Democratic reorganization. He argued that before Black Thursday the Democrats would have been willing, as a minority, to co-operate with the better class of Radical. But now that this class was overridden and scorned in their own party, the Democrats would expect the minority of upright Republicans to co-operate with them. Saving his best prose for last, Dawson stirred his readers by announcing "the time of the white minority has come."[21] The beauty of the editorial was that it said nothing while appeasing Straight-out sentiment. The strategy of the fusionists was clear: Democratic hotheads were to be kept busy organizing for a straight-out fight save for one office, the governor's chair. The headless ticket would be completed by a fusion with pro-Chamberlain Republicans. All the talk about who would co-operate with whom was just so much double talk, but it created the sense of a vigorous anti-Radical posture. Chamberlain certainly saw no threat in this strong prose, for he wrote the following day saying, "I think your treatment of the Morton letter *fair & wise,* and I am glad to say so to you."[22]

Apart from making a mockery of the original concept of fusion politics, fusion at the top only depended on far too many contingencies to succeed. At the heart of each stood the unanswerable question, Could either party accept a hybrid candidate at its head? The very act of organizing would create in the Democrats a heightened awareness of the grievances they had been nursing since the beginning of Reconstruction. Could they accept a symbol of carpetbagging Republicanism? If by some strange alchemy they embraced this Puritan interloper, could Republicans nominate a man their newly aroused enemies encouraged to apostasy? In retrospect the dream of a Democratic legislature with a reform Republican governor seems just that, an idle fancy. It was a testament to the spell Chamberlain cast over his influential Conservative allies and to Dawson's singular devotion to the cause of fusion that Co-operation seemed a viable alternative up to August, 1876. To all the imponderable questions, Dawson offered only hope. "The conclusion we reach," he told his Straight-out critics, "is, that if Governor Chamberlain succeed in his endeavor he will give Democrats and Republicans a pure and capable government, and if he fail with the Republicans, he will abandon the rascally leaders, while remaining a

20. Chamberlain to Dawson, January 26, 1876, Dawson Papers, Duke.

21. *News and Courier,* January 29, 1876.

22. Chamberlain to Dawson, January 30, 1876, Dawson Papers, Duke.

Republican, and leave the field open to the Democrats." The answer was tenuous at best, but then Dawson was asking for an act of faith, not offering a guarantee. "Good has come out of Nazareth," he concluded. "Shall we who see and know refuse to believe?"[23]

Dawson's personal war with the proponents of Straight-out Democracy intensified with increasing fury as spring yielded to the summer months of 1876. As secretary for the State Democratic Executive Committee, he counseled against any precipitate action on the part of the state convention that had been called for May 4. While he acknowledged a "preponderance of feeling in favor of straight-out nominations," he argued that it would be foolish to make nominations before seeing what the enemy planned.[24] His editorials during this period amounted to a rearguard action to prevent the up-country press from steamrolling public sentiment by putting forward Democratic candidates with charismatic appeal. Yet at the same time he proved willing to drop names in behalf of his own cause. When the May convention decided to delay nominations, he congratulated the delegates for joining the *News and Courier* along with "the Kershaws, the Mannings, the Conners and the Cothrans, faithful sons of South Carolina."[25]

During the early months of 1876, Dawson was reasonably fair in reporting Straight-out strength, but as the campaign wore on, he became less cautious with his facts and opinions. Then, encouraged by the delaying action of the State Convention, Dawson fired off an injudicious editorial that revealed for all to see the touchstone of the Conservative alliance with Chamberlain. Titled "Radical Democracy and Conservative Democracy," he charged the up-country Democrats with advocating a rule or ruin policy, saying that their courage and energy, rooted in their white majorities, availed the lower counties nothing. More specifically, Radical Democracy was a direct menace to Charleston. "Straight-outism, with its threat and bluster, with its possible disturbances and certain turmoil, is the foe of mercantile security and commercial prosperity." As a result the Conservative Democracy of Charleston, "and there [were] none other worth counting," would oppose to the last the Radical policy of running a full slate at any cost. Charleston simply could not "countenance any policy which [would] drive capital away, and render her powerless to aid and sustain the agricultural interests of the State."[26]

Dawson could not have made the point clearer. Fusion was a policy by and for Charleston with incidental benefits for the remainder of the state. For one who had managed the debate so skillfully up to that time, Dawson opened a wound as old as the state's invisible boundary between low and

23. *News and Courier,* February 7, 1876.

24. Ibid., February 24, 1876.

25. Ibid, May 8, 1876. See also editorials of March 30, April 11, 19, and 24, 1876.

26. Ibid., May 9, 1876. See also editorials of July 19, August 3, 1876.

up-country. Perhaps it was this indiscretion that Dawson had in mind when, writing many years later, he remarked, "If I had been born in South Carolina I should not have had so much difficulty in making myself and my actions understood."[27]

By June sentiment seemed to be running strongly in favor of Straight-out nominations, but since the public was without means for assessing its own sentiment, Dawson was able to create the impression that the debate over fusion was at the very least undecided. However, on the centennial celebration of the nation's independence, an incident took place that was to overthrow whatever presumption the fusionists could claim and that would lead in a direct line to Wade Hampton's nomination. The setting was the practically abandoned little town of Hamburg, Edgefield County, "a place of vanished hopes and strangled ambitions."[28] Years before, it had been a pretender to the trade of King Cotton, but Augusta, sitting on the opposite bank of the Savannah river, had long since won the urban battle for cotton. Now Hamburg was a desolate community, with weed-infested streets, deserted buildings, and a population made up mostly of blacks whose only real satisfaction came in being away from whites.

Enjoying their separation, the blacks of Hamburg were not reluctant to play "tricks" on whites who might be passing through, and on the Fourth of July, 1876, a company of Negro militia detained two young white men on their way back from Augusta to Edgefield. The two men, Thomas Butler and Henry Getzen, sought redress by swearing out a warrant against the militia captain for obstructing a public highway. The case was continued until Saturday, the eighth, and General Matthew Calbraith Butler of Edgefield, head of the State Democratic Executive Committee, was called in as counsel. Not only did the general appear on Saturday, but several hundred whites from Edgefield, Aiken, and Augusta also decided their armed presence was called for. It was a chance to settle some scores with the "uppity niggers"—Mississippi style.

Meanwhile some thirty to forty of the black militia withdrew to an old brick warehouse, a relic of Hamburg's earlier pretensions. Whereupon Butler decided that the case could not proceed until the militia had been

27. Dawson to General John Bratton, June 1, 1888, Hemphill Family Papers, Duke. Bratton had written apologizing for having suspected Dawson's motives in 1876 and for having opposed the editor's nomination to the Democratic National Committee as a result. Dawson expressed dismay at the thought of his loyalty's ever being questioned and seemed somewhat piqued, even at that late hour, over Bratton's admission.

28. Alfred Brockenbrough Williams, *Hampton and His Red Shirts: South Carolina's Deliverance in 1876* (Charleston: Walker, Evans and Cogswell, 1935), p. 27. This book was written, "reporter-fashion, from personal observation and knowledge," fifty years after the events and was serialized for the Charleston *Evening Post* and the Columbia *State*. Williams should be read by any student of the period, especially for his evenhanded judgments on the racial politics of 1876.

disarmed, and not surprisingly they refused. By this time enough whites
under the influence of enough whiskey decided the wheels of justice were
turning too slowly and shooting broke out. The first casualty was McKie
Meriweather, a young white from Edgefield, who was struck in the head
and killed instantly. The enraged whites then drew up a cannon and the
blacks were forced to flee their temporary fortress. As they ran, roving
bands of whites chased them down on horseback. The following morning
revealed a casualty count of six Negroes dead and four wounded, one white
killed and two wounded. A. B. Williams, then a reporter for the Straight-
out *Journal of Commerce,* later declared, "It seems certain that some of
the slain were told to run and were shot as they ran."[29]

Dawson led the way in expressing shock and indignation at this barba-
rous occurrence, a feeling generally shared throughout the state. He found
nothing in the actions of the Negro militia that could excuse the "cowardly
killing of the seven negro prisoners who were shot down like rabbits long
after they had surrendered."[30] The young editor was motivated by genuine
revulsion at the barbarity of the massacre and by a realization that if South
Carolinians did not vigorously and immediately repudiate the atrocity, it
would offer Republicans more than enough grist to feed their bloody-shirt
propaganda mills at the North. What Dawson did not realize was that
South Carolina's whites could never accept collective or individual responsibility for the act; that, despite initial revulsion, Hamburg would force a
closing of the ranks in a racial struggle that one contemporary correctly
described as a "grim clash of fears."[31] The editorials that Dawson began on
July 5 lauding the record of Governor Chamberlain would fall on deaf ears.
The ultimate casualty of that bloody Saturday was the politics of fusion.

Nonetheless Dawson dispatched Carlyle McKinley to the scene of the
Hamburg massacre and calmly continued his attack on the opponents of
Co-operation. Ignoring the pleas of friends, he moved to implicate the
entire Straight-out movement in the Hamburg tragedy, up to and including
General Butler.[32] When the General retaliated through the pages of the
Columbia *Register,* the *News and Courier* truculently suggested that if
Butler could prove them wrong they would gladly retract, but "until then
we shall not unsay a word we have said, and we are mindful enough of
Gen. Butler's services during the war to be careful to do him no injustice,

---

29. Ibid., p. 30.

30. *News and Courier,* July 10, 1876. The initial *News and Courier* reports on Hamburg
were taken from the Augusta *Chronicle and Sentinel,* which became a convenient excuse
when Dawson later backtracked on his initial judgments about Hamburg.

31. Williams, *Hampton and His Red Shirts,* p. 171.

32. Joseph Walker Barnwell, "Joseph Barnwell Recollections," 125th Anniversary Edition, *News and Courier,* Dawson Papers, Duke.

whatever may be his intemperance of speech."[33] Dawson later backed away from his direct challenge to Butler, but not to the movement he and Martin Gary represented. He argued that when Democrats advised a Straight-out ticket and that the state be carried on the "Mississippi plan," the popular understanding was that the state should be carried by fraud and violence. "To the unthinking masses, in such a County as Edgefield," Dawson wrote, "the Mississippi plan is the Hamburg plan."[34]

For once the editor very likely fingered the truth when he spoke of the popular understanding, but even here being right did not work in his favor, for the leading architects of the Mississippi plan, the men Dawson would have to contend with in party councils, did not see it as Dawson saw it. No matter how the "unthinking masses" interpreted their ideas, these men actually sought to avoid the killing of blacks; killing "Mister Nigger," as they put it, only brought in federal troops. As true white supremacists, they argued instead that efforts be directed toward intimidating the white Radicals who supposedly led the Negroes and that this intimidation be carried out by "abusing the candidates to their faces when they put in an appearance."[35] In another month the plan of denying free speech to Republican candidates would go into action and would be known in South Carolina as "dividing time."

For the moment, however, there were more personal scores to settle with the editor of South Carolina's leading Conservative daily. Before the campaign of dividing the time of Republicans could get under way, Dawson had received two challenges to duel. The first came from Martin Gary, the exemplar of white supremacy and the Straight-out movement. On July 22, Gary charged from the pages of the *Journal of Commerce* that Dawson had run up the "Black Flag" against him because he, Gary, had exposed Dawson's attempt to convert the white people of the state to the Republican party. Gary further expressed the hope that when the contest waxed warm Dawson would not run up the "White Flag." Dawson wrote his reply the same day and had it published in the *Journal of Commerce* on the twenty-fourth. Noting his public stand against duelling, he concluded, "Meantime, if Mr. Gary, who sets himself up as the champion of the shotgun policy, feels any solicitude as to the likelihood of my raising the 'white-flag,' at his coming, he should lose no time in resolving the doubt, unless he is content to be known throughout the state in the double character of slanderer and braggart." Being an honorable man, Gary dispatched General Butler to deliver his formal note, saying Dawson's action "must suggest to every 'man of honor' my course of conduct."

---

33. *News and Courier*, July 12, 1876.

34. Ibid., July 13, 1876.

35. General S. W. Ferguson to Major T. G. Baxter, January 7, 1876, copy, Martin Witherspoon Gary Papers, scl. Ferguson was considered the leading Mississippi expert on the "Mississippi plan."

Apparently not impressed with such bravado, Dawson dismissed the whole affair suggesting, "A hostile message, which it was a foregone conclusion that I should decline, may satisfy you. It certainly is not, under any circumstances, the most direct way to resent my course and maintain the position you had taken."[36]

This first challenge under the code came to nothing, and though remaining bitter political foes, Dawson and Gary eventually reconciled their personal differences. The second challenge came from a gentleman whose very name personified the legendary intemperance and fire-eating behavior attributed to South Carolinians. Robert Barnwell Rhett, Jr., was the kind of southerner from whom, observed the splenetic Henry Adams, "one could learn nothing but bad temper, bad manners, poker, and treason." Rhett's *casus belli* this time was found in a seemingly innocuous editorial published in the *News and Courier* of August 9. In this editorial Dawson was attempting to explain why Governor Chamberlain asked Grant about the possible need for federal troops at Hamburg. He addressed himself to the accusation that the *News and Courier* was trying to make Democrats believe that Chamberlain had not called the troops. This charge, Dawson insisted, was "a malignant falsehood, unsupported by the slightest semblance of truth." Though Dawson named no accuser, Rhett seized the opportunity to claim responsibility and to give insult. In a vile and slanderous attack, Rhett accused Dawson of journalistic cowardice. Making obvious reference to Dawson's recent run-in with Gary, Rhett derided the editor's alleged religious scruples saying, "Mr. Dawson . . . prefers to play the part of an insolent coward, and once more uses the editorial column to wound, while he slinks in safety behind what is, with him, but the shield of a base hypocrite."[37]

Rhett's motive was curious and had more to do with the *Journal of Commerce* than any personal slight at Dawson's hand. The newspaper, it will be recalled, had been formed in opposition to the *News and Courier* and had begun operation in May, 1876. Its first editor was imported from Virginia and, while a graceful writer, was woefully ignorant of South Carolina and her condition. He was reported to have written "with a state map before him that he might know whether Orangeburg or Oconee was nearer to Charleston." The situation did not improve much with the return of Rhett, for he, too, had been out of touch with the state and had not "the intimate knowledge of recent political history and the sure knowledge of

36. Letters and clippings treating the episode, including Gary's note of July 25, 1876, can be found in Dawson's scrapbook, Dawson Papers, Duke.

37. *Journal of Commerce,* August 10, 1876. Interestingly, it was to another Rhett, Alfred, that Dawson first made his religious scruples known. A letter from Dawson to Alfred Rhett, June 5, 1868, concluded, "It is proper for me to say now that, being a member of the Catholic Church, I cannot, under any circumstances, engage in a duel." See Charleston *Mercury,* June 13, 1868.

just what strings to strike that Captain Dawson had." The *News and Courier* with its superior wire service and organized state network was constantly getting the scoop on news items and lording this fact over its rival. These difficulties were compounded by the absence of a "practical general newspaper man in the establishment." The net result was to drive the demoralized staff of the *Journal of Commerce* "wild with impotent fury." A. B. Williams, who shared this frustration, believed Rhett took his action against Dawson because the *News and Courier* had finally strained the Colonel's nerves to the breaking point.[38]

At high noon on the eleventh of August, Colonel Rhett stepped out of his office and strolled along the north side of Broad toward Meeting Street. In his retinue followed A. B. Williams and three other members of his staff, it being expected in those days that office personnel should "take personal interest and part in all the rows of their papers and editors." Williams carried with him a thirty-eight, though "the really well-dressed man wore a forty-four." All along Broad Street doors and windows were crowded with men anxious to see the fight. A hush fell over the street as Dawson approached along the south side of Broad. With him was his brother-in-law, the irrepressible Jimmie Morgan. True to his word, both Dawson and Morgan were unarmed, though Captain Dawson must have done a lot of coaxing to convince his tempestuous relative of the wisdom in such a course. The width of a street separating them, the two parties approached. Not a word was spoken, and to the great disappointment of the crowd, not a shot was fired. The same scene was repeated on the following day.[39]

Rhett was satisfied, for he had fulfilled his commitment under the code which provided that one insult could not be effectively resented by another insult. "If a man called you a liar," Williams noted, "you were expected to hit, shoot or challenge forthwith. Answering that he was also one, 'so's your old man,' or anything like that, was counted mere idle persiflage and meaningless gossip."[40] For his part Dawson felt no compunction about resenting an insult in kind, and on August 11, he published a scurrilous attack on Rhett. Among other things, he called Rhett a "fire-eating Bobadil" who was taken in by the *Journal of Commerce* because he was known to have "a gun for hire." And lest readers suspected Dawson of "mere idle persiflage," he lashed out at Rhett for talking secession but not enlisting and for talking a Confederacy but weakening its leaders by his attacks upon them. Moreover, Rhett was charged with having asked Dawson to assume responsibility under the code for Rhett's actions while Dawson was an associate editor of the *Mercury*. As a final insult, Dawson

38. Williams, *Hampton and His Red Shirts*, pp. 32–33, 63–64.

39. Ibid., pp. 63–65.

40. Ibid., p. 65.

snapped that Rhett's newspaper ability was a recognized failure every-where and that Rhett was notorious for his bad debts.[41]

To the last, Rhett probably thought Dawson had made a fool of himself under the code and simply replied, as any good aristocrat would, that there was no dishonor in being in debt, only in airing it publicly as the *News and Courier* did. Thereafter, Dawson maintained a smug silence, content to clip Rhett's response for his scrapbook and to pencil in the margin, "The dishonor was not in being in debt, but in borrowing money with solemn promises to return it at a certain time, without any intention of doing so."[42] Thus ended a second challenge to duel, with Dawson convinced he had won the affair when he exercised the right to choose weapons, proving, at least in his own mind, that in his hand the pen was indeed mightier than the sword.

The matter of the duels was but the ruffled surface of an ocean of discontent which sprang from Dawson's overbearing treatment of a move-ment that had swelled to majority proportions among South Carolina's whites. It was never very pleasant to be on the wrong side of the Captain's editorial pen. "The truth is," observed A. B. Williams, "that, aggressive and outspoken and intolerant of opposition as Dawson was, he would have had a duel on his hands every week of every election year if he had continued to abide by the code."[43] Charles Richardson Miles, later attor-ney general and a warm personal friend of Dawson's, wrote a letter to his brother expressing a widely shared reaction to the *News and Courier's* domination of the news. On a trip to Columbia Miles was surprised to find that, contrary to the claims of Dawson's paper, "the idea of refraining from opposition to Chamberlain was scarcely entertained out of Charleston." He noted that Dawson's defense of Chamberlain after the governor had turned the Hamburg affair to partisan advantage only "excited suspicion and disgust and alienated very many good men who would otherwise have supported him." Miles's final comment seemed an ultimate protest against the artful intellectual dodges Dawson used in an effort to prevent the inevitable demise of fusion. "In our present condition," he complained, "any policy however wanting in wisdom foresight and breadth of vision—but which commends itself to the instincts and feelings of our people—and which will unite them—and enlist their enthusiasm and earnest effort; is better for us than the wisest policy which statesmanship can suggest."[44]

---

41. *News and Courier,* August 11, 1876.

42. *Journal of Commerce,* August 14, 1876, in Dawson's scrapbook, Dawson Papers, Duke.

43. Williams, *Hampton and His Red Shirts,* p. 53.

44. C. R. Miles to W. P. Miles, August 2, 1876, W. P. Miles Papers, SHC. .

By late July Dawson recognized the inevitable and was doing his best to beat a strategic retreat. When General Kershaw went over to the Straight-outs because Hamburg and the call for a state convention had predetermined the party's course, Dawson reluctantly conceded the point. He was resolved to stand fast in opposition to the Straight-outs, but promised not to "make the discussion irritating."[45] He continued to advise delay in nominating until the Republicans acted, and he shrewdly sought to burst the bubble that had started for Hampton by suggesting the dangers involved in selecting a conspicuous military leader. Using an editorial mast of "Watch and Wait and Win," he tried desperately to indicate a trend for postponement, announcing that "Abbeville had joined Charleston, Clarendon, Georgetown and Orangeburg in this decision and that Barnwell, Beaufort, Chester, Kershaw, Colleton, Darlington, York, Marion, Marlboro, and Sumter could be expected to join."[46]

The retreat remained orderly on all fronts save one, and on that front Dawson broke and ran shamelessly. The state that had taken his barbs and rejected his counsel would demand fealty on the issue of Hamburg if no other, and the arrogant young editor bowed to this ultimate test of racial solidarity. The line held by the *News and Courier* on Hamburg showed signs of weakness as early as July 15, but it did not break until August 12. Two days later the feature editorial characterized the two whites who precipitated the incident, Butler and Getzen, as citizens of good character and high standing. "In any Court of Justice," Dawson conceded, "their words would outweigh the words of excited and alarmed negroes who, in many cases, are proved to have made extraordinary blunders, if they did not foully perjure themselves." The same editorial revealed what constituted proof of perjury. "The averment of the negroes that the two white men interfered with them and would not pass on, although they could have done so, is rebutted conclusively by the affidavits of the young men themselves. They are men of character and standing." Perjury had become procedural, not substantive; blacks lied if white men said so. Through the entire editorial only one brief phrase recalled that "no one in South Carolina justified the killing of the negro prisoners," but there was no mistaking the conclusion that the provocation made it at least understandable.[47] After all, honorable men said so.

Dawson, spurned in his aspiration to be a delegate to Columbia, maintained his allegiance to Chamberlain until the State Democratic Convention met on August 15 to decide what had already been decided. Having pledged its word to abide the decision of the convention, the *News and Courier* greeted the verdict with banner headlines of "Wade Hampton

45. *News and Courier*, July 28, 1876. Kershaw's letter appears in this issue.

46. Ibid., August 4, 9, 1876.

47. Ibid., August 14, 1876.

and Victory!" It was difficult to discern which was the more audible, the ill-concealed laughter of Dawson's recent enemies or his own sigh of relief at being relieved of his heavy burden. The circulation of his paper had been badly damaged as the stop notices piled up in late July and early August. His son later wrote that his father "always maintained the principle that a newspaper while assuming the leadership of public opinion could not and must not fight against the unanimous will of the community which it represented."[48] Dawson left this ordeal deeply scarred by a community he only months before thought he knew so well. He was determined never again to suffer such a defeat at the bar of public opinion.

Dawson and Chamberlain had traveled a long way together since the summer of 1874. The reform record, the municipal election of 1875, and their successful handling of Black Thursday gave them a false sense of security in their combination and the politics of fusion. But they were attempting to be moderate men in a revolutionary society. There would be no golden mean. The sands of the hour glass were falling inexorably from one extreme to the other, with time on the side of the white minority. When Democracy "waxed mad," as Sarah later put it, "and cried, '*aut Bourbon, aut Nihil*,'"[49] their alliance was doomed and their immediate political fortunes crushed.

More damaging may have been the impact these events had on a friendship, for seldom is greater bitterness excited than when former comrades are forced by a divided society to choose sides. Dawson and Chamberlain labored long to prevent such a division, but when it came, their friendship yielded to the higher call of the constituencies which gave them political life. On the day Dawson bowed to the demands of Hamburg, August 12, Chamberlain was being harrassed and abused by a bunch of Red Shirts who were bent on dividing the governor's time Mississippi style. Though Dawson had a reporter on the scene, the *News and Courier* remained as silent as the chilling effect that fell across all free speech in the state of South Carolina.

No record remains of what the two men may have felt on the eve of their separation. Because Dawson had to give his newspaper over to Hampton and the Democrats, his use of the angry political rhetoric which characterized journalistic discourse made him appear the greater offender of a former friendship. But neither man was wont to use the damaging knowledge each had of the other. When forced to embrace the extremists in their

---

48. Comments by Warrington Dawson on a MS biographical sketch of his father, written by Sarah Dawson for the *National Cyclopedia of Biography,* but not published, Dawson Papers, Duke.

49. MS biographical sketch of F. W. Dawson written in 1894 at the request of J. T. White for the *National Cyclopedia of Biography,* 12:411, revised by Warrington Dawson, 23:300, ibid.

respective parties, men they had only months before denounced, they accused each other of treacherous duplicity and moral paralysis. Dawson's language was typical, declaring Chamberlain to be a moral "chameleon, taking the hue of what he feeds on."[50] Perhaps it was the anguished sense of personal failure that made each so self-righteous in his denunciation of the other.

In another year the victorious Democrats would investigate Dawson's alleged involvement in the corruption of Reconstruction even while the *News and Courier* was calling for the blood of Chamberlain on other charges. The harsh feelings of betrayal lingered for the remainder of the decade. Despite all this, the two men resumed a periodic and cordial correspondence in the eighties, apparently forgiving, if they could not forget the bitterness of 1876.

---

50. *News and Courier,* December 5, 1876.

Chapter IV
A Revolution Must Move Backwards

Mary Frances Waite, unmarried daughter of the Chief Justice of the United States Supreme Court, was a young woman of even disposition who liked to immerse herself in church work. For this reason, her father was astonished to find her in a state of considerable agitation on a cheerful Sunday morning in May, 1877. On further inquiry he learned that she had just returned from a church service, where she witnessed "the people of Charleston give thanks for their 'great deliverance.'" Nany, as she was affectionately known, was accompanying her father on his tour of duty on the Fourth Circuit, a responsibility members of the court had to endure until 1891. The chief justice reflected his daughter's concern. "The truth is," he observed, ". . . the people here are really, at this moment, in heart further from reconstruction than they have been since the war. They have received the first fruits of success . . . and they have gone back to their original idols." Despairing of his party's future in the South, he felt that President Hayes's only alternative was to appoint men from the enemy camp who possessed genuine merit and ability, men who had "the interest of South Carolina at heart and who [knew] its people." Admittedly the president's only recourse then would be to sit back and to hope that events would take care of themselves, but the chief justice saw no other way out of the present troubles. "The truth is," he concluded, "I am thoroughly disgusted."[1]

Morrison Remick Waite was a strong supporter of the administration's southern policy, but what he heard on the bench in Charleston that spring sickened him. He sat through accounts of the brutal slaying of a deaf and dumb boy, and of the murder of a father before his wife and children even as the father begged for his life and promised to vote Democratic.[2] More disheartening were revelations about a society which appeared to condone such activity. To a man like Waite, Charleston in May, 1877, must have seemed like a world turned upside down, where summer was winter and ponies rode men. The dream of a reconstructed South faded as men of the cloth celebrated a new Moses who, robed in Confederate gray, led his people out of the bondage of Reconstruction. It was truly a revolution gone backwards.

---

1. Morrison Remick Waite to his wife, May 24, 1877, Morrison Remick Waite Papers, Library of Congress, cited hereafter as LC.

2. C. Peter Magrath, *Morrison R. Waite: The Triumph of Character* (New York: The Macmillan Co., 1963), pp. 158–59.

What Waite saw was in part only what South Carolina's Democracy wanted him to see. The men of '76 knew it was their united effort that presented Hayes with a *fait accompli* that nothing short of raw force could change, a force for which the nation no longer had any stomach. They also knew it was a display of solidarity that would guarantee white supremacy, something for which the nation was now showing some stomach. But behind this carefully constructed façade lay stresses within the ranks of the white minority—stresses that had built up during the course of Reconstruction and its subsequent overthrow. The men who seized control in 1876 were not strangers to power. Most of them had traveled at least the outer edges of the circle of Republican influence, and their often devious behavior during that time made them as suspicious of each other as of the enemy. Moreover, their divisive struggle over the politics of fusion still rankled in the spring of 1877, aggravating the typical victor's dilemma over who had done most and therefore deserved most. Finally, those who won office in 1876 and again in 1878 were embarrassed by the tactics used to elect them and saw in the violence of their minions the chaotic seeds of their own undoing. These internal stresses made South Carolina's Conservative regime vulnerable to outside pressures. The men who condoned the fruits of violence in the spring of 1877 gradually tempered their rhetoric until by 1879 these same voices had become the harbingers of moderation, stability, and order.

Dawson's career in the two and a half years following Hampton's nomination in August, 1876, clearly revealed the tensions that underlay the new regime. Fulfilling his pledge to the Straight-outs, the editor did much during the canvass of 1876 and the period of the dual government to create the image of white solidarity. On the eve of the election he graciously conceded that "for the splendor of the canvass the people are primarily indebted to the up-country."[3] He became a principal strategist in the scheme whereby the Chamberlain government was denied operating revenues while Hampton received his tithe. When a native South Carolinian, Belton O'Neall Townsend, exposed the tactics of the late campaign, it was Dawson who answered for South Carolina, saying "these assertions are made against the concordant voice of the whole people, the statement of the most eminent gentlemen in the State, and the correspondence of the independent press of the country."[4] Dawson was even willing to eat political crow for the sake of unity. He quickly rallied behind Hampton's negotiations with Hayes for the removal of federal troops, though igno-

---

3. *News and Courier,* November 8, 1876.

4. Ibid., February 7, 1877. Townsend published his views in "The Political Condition of South Carolina," *The Atlantic Monthly* (February, 1877), pp. 177–94. Townsend took an orthodox view of the evils of Reconstruction, but wrote candidly about the violence used to overthrow Republican rule.

rance of Hampton's strategy found Dawson initially opposed to such unnecessary truckling.[5] And when the troops marched out at high noon, April 10, 1877, Dawson led the cry for Republican blood.

It was this cry for vengeance which first betrayed signs of intraparty weakness among the victorious Democrats. What should have turned into a parade of Republican venality was marred by revelations that Democrats had come dangerously close to the Republican tar baby. Nor were Republicans the only ones to suggest the complicity of their accusers. Democrats, still nursing grievances from the heated debate of the previous summer, seemed eager to point fingers as well. At the center of this storm of counter-charges stood the editor of the new regime's most powerful organ. Not to put too fine a point on it, Captain Dawson was charged with influence-peddling and bribe-taking. These charges resulted in Dawson's coming under the investigations that were designed to incriminate Republicans and a counter-punching libel suit that threatened the much desired harmony of the victors.

None of the charges against Dawson were particularly new. They first gained currency when the editor chose to remain neutral in the election of 1872. Supporters of Reuben Tomlinson, the Republican bolter, accused the *News and Courier* of having sold out to the Moses people. "The plain truth," Dawson later explained, "is that this paper offered its unqualified support to the lamented James L. Orr, if he would consent to be the candidate of the Reform Republicans for Governor." When Orr refused, Dawson felt his only choice lay "between a devil and a witch, and *The News and Courier* took no part in the canvass, beyond striving to elect the better of two sets of Republican candidates in Charleston."[6] These general allegations of influence-peddling remained largely unsubstantiated until Benjamin Franklin Whittemore, a white carpetbagger, took the floor of the senate in the special session of 1877 to read into the record certain letters from Dawson to Josephus Woodruff. It was a chance to get even, for Whittemore, a Northern Methodist minister who lost his congressional seat for selling a cadetship to West Point and who despite that transgression had maintained a creditable reform record, had long endured the *News and Courier's* cry for his blood.

The most incriminating letters were dated November 24, 1868, and January 30, 1869. They were addressed to Woodruff, who was at that time the Columbia correspondent for the *News,* where he took orders from Dawson. Woodruff later became clerk of the senate, in which position he

5. The breakdown in communication between Hampton and Dawson was no doubt encouraged by Hampton's lieutenants, many of whom were up-country Democrats and much closer to the Straight-out faction. Hampton's invitation to visit Hayes came on March 23 and the *News and Courier* showed little real understanding of the situation until March 28, 1877.

6. *News and Courier,* February 27, 1878.

acquired a facility for managing the corrupt flow of money. When Woodruff subsequently came under the scrutiny of the Joint Investigating Committee on Public Frauds, he seemed to relish his extensive knowledge of corruption, even to the point of editing his infamous diary for better effect.[7] Woodruff's hatred for Dawson was never concealed. He once told a friend that when "Dawson and family" boarded a train on which he was riding, he feared "an explosion or breakdown with so much wickedness as Dawson on the train."[8]

At the time Dawson wrote the letters (which bear repeating) he believed Woodruff to be a man of "fair average character."[9]

My Dear Woodruff:
    The enclosed is a reply to yours received this evening. You may show it where necessary, but do not let it be copied or kept. We think it will do all you want. The fact is that we want to make all we can, and will go as far as we can to support Scott and the government if we are treated well. We cannot be blind advocates. That would be to ruin our influence, if we could permit ourselves to adopt such a course. We must be independent, but we will always be more than just to our friends, and never personally abusive, because it is contrary to our views of propriety. Send all Bills, &c., that are printed, and post us about any scheme that wants puffing or crushing.
    All this *confidential*.
            Yours,
                    F. W. Dawson

The second letter, dated January 30, 1869, read:

My Dear Woodruff:
    What you have done so far is highly approved. A memorandum of your account, as it then stood, was sent on yesterday. As you collect money due us, pay yourself in full *first*, and remit balance, if any.
    We count on you to push the State printing (acts.) The best we can do is this. If we can get ten cents a line, which would be about twenty-four dollars per column, we can allow the paymaster twenty per cent. and yourself ten per

---

7. An edited version of the diary appears in Robert Hilliard Woody, "Behind the Scenes in the Reconstruction Legislature of South Carolina: Diary of Josephus Woodruff," *The Journal of Southern History,* 2 (February, 1936), 78–102, and 2 (May, 1936), 233–59. Notes for this study were taken from a copy of the original diary held by the Duke University Library, cited hereafter as Duke. That Woodruff edited his diary for effect is indicated by Joel Williamson, *After Slavery: The Negro in South Carolina During Reconstruction, 1861–1877* (Chapel Hill: University of North Carolina Press, 1965), p. 388.

8. Woodruff Diary, September 17, 1875.

9. The two letters cited may be found among others from Dawson to Woodruff in *Reports and Resolutions of the General Assembly of the State of South Carolina* (1877–78), pp. 1292–97, and in the *News and Courier,* June 12, 1877. Dawson's assessment of Woodruff's character is from *Reports and Resolutions,* p. 1339.

cent., which would only leave us a very moderate profit; if we can get twelve and a half cents a line, which is thirty dollars a column, or more, we can allow you twenty per cent, instead of ten. Now, you have the whole programme, and may blaze away at will. We are willing to give a helping hand to any up-country project, railroad or otherwise, and *free*. Keep us informed.

Yours,

F. W. Dawson

Dawson's response to the publication of these letters was immediate and hot. He said that for ten years the proprietors of the *News and Courier* had been denounced by the Republicans they sought to expose and by "malignant Democrats who were jealous of the success of our efforts." When his enemies were called on to prove their charges, they merely repeated themselves. Now Whittemore purported to give proof, but the letters proved nothing. At most, Dawson declared, the proprietors of what was then the *News* were accused of addressing Woodruff familiarly, seeking to obtain state printing, paying Woodruff a commission of 20 percent on bills collected, and not saying as much against the credit of the Scott administration as might have been said. Dawson met each allegation with contempt. Woodruff at that time was a trusted employee of the *News*, thus there was no reason not to address him informally. "When such time came that he could not be spoken to familiarly, he was not spoken to at all." The *News* did seek printing contracts like everybody else but charged the state less than was charged to private parties for the same work. Had they not paid Woodruff a 20 percent commission, he would never have collected the bills due. Finally, the *News* could hardly be charged with going easy on the Radicals. Certainly Governor Scott would not have thought so.[10]

The editorial ended with a ringing cry for justice. "Before the Senate the charges were made. Upon the journals of that body the lying speech of the scoundrel Whittemore is recorded. Of the Senate we shall ask that our conduct, as journalists' be examined . . . and to the judgement of that body we submit ourselves. The opportunity for which we have yearned has come. They who have charges against *The News and Courier* shall prove them, or eat their words." With the aid of Senator S. S. Crittenden of Greenville, Dawson addressed his question of privilege to the senate, and after some substantive and dilatory motions from the divers likes of Whittemore and Martin Gary, Dawson's reply to the charges was read, but not recorded, on the third of May. His testimony was not privileged to be recorded because Gary, still nursing grievances from the past summer, objected unless other parties to the dispute were given the same right. Finally, Whittemore moved the investigation of the editor be extended to cover all his activities, especially his charges against certain Radicals, and

10. *News and Courier,* May 2, 1877.

by that means Dawson got the thorough examination for which he called.[11]

The investigation would turn out to be even more thorough than Dawson could have wished. The inquiry which commenced in the senate was ultimately subsumed under the aegis of the Joint Committee on Frauds in the regular session of 1877–78. Again the Woodruff correspondence was paraded out, and again Dawson's defense had not budged. He once more suggested that his political enemies were not confined to one party and carefully indicated that only a strained construction of the correspondence could suggest wrongdoing. His testimony that he had charged the state some 30 percent less than his private customers was corroborated, and additional evidence indicated that the *News* charged 50 percent less than the Charleston *Daily Republican.*[12] Dawson's most persuasive defense came in an editorial crediting Horace Walpole with the dictum that "every man has his price." "But," the *News and Courier* added, "Walpole was too worldly-wise to suppose, as the thoughtless public are expected to do, that any person, occupying powerful and lucrative positions, would sell themselves to infamy and disgrace for a sum equal to two per cent of their gross income!"[13] The Committee on Frauds agreed and completely exonerated the *News and Courier,* saying, "Comment is unnecessary, for the evidence is, in itself, a sufficient tribute to the integrity of the proprietors of the *News* and the correctness of their accounts."[14]

To be accused by Whittemore and Woodruff, or even Martin Gary, was one thing, but when the same charges were raised by respectable Democrats, Dawson completely lost equanimity. The rival *Journal of Commerce* was the principal villain, and after enduring their raking around in the same old muck during May, June, and July, Dawson instituted libel proceedings in August, 1877. Surprisingly, Dawson was not going after his

---

11. *Journal of the Senate of the General Assembly of South Carolina* (Special Session, 1877), pp. 61–62, 82–83.

12. *Reports and Resolutions* (1877–78), pp. 1256–60.

13. *News and Courier,* June 16, 1877. Amounts of the printing contracts received by the *News* and the *News and Courier* from 1869 through 1876, by consecutive year, were: $1,436.95; $1,835.80; $1,694.07; $5,656.23; $467.74; $826.75; and $1,022.50. The entire sum amounted to 2 percent of the paper's income for the period. The bulge for the year 1872 would seem to indicate that Dawson received favors for remaining neutral in the contest between Moses and Tomlinson. Moreover, a significant portion of the correspondence between October 11 and November 27, 1872, Dawson Papers, Duke, deals with allegations that Dawson was selling out to the Moses people in return for printing contracts. At the same time the state printing was taken away from the Charleston *Daily Republican* and given to the *News* under terms of the "Printing Authorization," October 28, 1872. The motive behind the "Printing Authorization," however, seems to have been an effort by former members of the Scott organization to punish the *Daily Republican* for supporting Scott's enemy, C. C. Bowen, Williamson, *After Slavery,* p. 360. The *News and Courier*'s windfall for 1872 seems, therefore, more the product of Republican infighting than bribe-taking.

14. *Reports and Resolutions* (1877–78), p. 1256.

archenemy, Rhett, but the impeccable Charles Henry Simonton, part owner of the rival newspaper and powerful member of the Charleston legislative delegation. Simonton was an elegant member of the bar, an influential legislator both before and after the war, eventually becoming Speaker of the House during Redemption, and ending his career in the federal judiciary.

By all counts Simonton was not a particularly appropriate target, but the issue had become a deeply personal one for Dawson and reflected his intraparty feuds of the past year. At one point he confessed to Sarah that he did not "know whether to laugh or cry," that he had "been on the border land of each." On another occasion he lamented, "I do not expect either the honor or the blessings you promise me. . . . I have no faith in vindication coming by and with time or I should not have tried a libel suit." He adamantly refused an out-of-court settlement and repeated that a verdict of a few cents would be quite as satisfactory as thousands of dollars.[15] Dawson's friends begged him to cease and desist. C. W. Dudley of the Marlboro *Planter* wrote the editor saying his reputation was beyond reproach and that to continue would only aggravate divisiveness. James Conner pleaded that he stop his attacks on Simonton. Conner argued that Simonton had exerted his influence to restrain Rhett and that to persist would only lessen Dawson's influence. "The time is coming and not far off," Conner concluded, "when you will be, or can be, a great influence. Save yourself for that."[16] Under the pressure of such advice, Dawson eventually dropped the libel proceedings, but not before the Committee on Frauds had formally cleared his name.

Of more interest to a study of Dawson and his times were the records and notes the editor took and maintained during this period of investigation. They told a story of Democratic complicity, if not actual involvement, with the men and in the crimes that formed the subject matter of the Joint Investigating Committee. The notes were no doubt taken for purposes of self-protection and reveal a side of Dawson that could be vindictive when cornered. While the evidence was little more than a collage of hearsay, innuendo, and fact, it would have been difficult for the Hampton regime to have survived their publication.[17]

Dawson's allegations began at the top. Simonton was said to have sought an alliance with the Bowen faction in Charleston, to have made a fortune as receiver for the Bank of the State, never to have reported the enormous sums of money he had collected and disbursed in the campaign of 1876,

---

15. A series of ten letters, most undated, from Dawson to his wife, late July to mid-September, 1877, Dawson Papers, Duke.

16. C. W. Dudley to Dawson, November 28, 1877, and James Conner to Dawson, August 25, 1877, ibid.

17. Record Book in box marked "Drama, Poetry, and Accounts," ibid.

and to be a bond speculator of the basest sort. The unimpeachable Attorney General James Conner was charged with being cognizant of efforts to bribe the Returning Board in 1876. The notes further revealed that United States Senator M. C. Butler was, in December, 1877, negotiating with the soon-to-be indicted Hiram H. Kimpton on matters concerning recognition of the state's bonded debt.[18] Former Governor Andrew Gordon Magrath was said to have made an offer of $50,000 to secure recognition of the state debt, a step that would have brought riches to the holders of government securities. Two Hampton lieutenants, Alexander Cheves Haskell and Colonel James H. Rion, along with Senator John Brown Gordon of Georgia, were charged with employing the infamous Hardy Solomon to offer the Canvassing Board $60,000 to cast South Carolina's vote for Tilden, and that to protect Gordon, Senator Butler bought Solomon's silence by inducing the Committee on Frauds to drop their indictment of Solomon.[19]

Other notes revealed that Senator Butler was opposing Hampton's policy on the state debt in order to bring the governor to some unspecified terms. At the same time Hampton was threatening to expose the 1871 Gary-Butler combination with northern financiers in an effort to bring South Carolina's junior senator to terms on the state debt. Dawson himself maintained papers proving that Gary and Butler had conspired with northern bankers to force the Taxpayers' Convention of 1871 to recognize the entire bonded debt of the state, including fraudulent issues made under Republican rule.[20] Nor could Dawson dig very far into his own records without pointing a finger at himself. In 1871, Charles P. Leslie, the carpetbagger who grossly mismanaged the state's Land Commission, accused Dawson of having accepted a $2,000 bribe from the state's financial agent, H. H. Kimpton, in return for the *News*'s support of the Sterling Funding Bill, another scheme to make money off the government's ability to borrow. In point of fact, Dawson did get that amount of money from

---

18. Kimpton served as financial agent for the state during the administrations of Scott and Moses. Butler may have been attempting to ascertain what portions of the existing debt were valid, but the chummy relationship with Kimpton could have proved embarrassing.

19. Solomon was principal banker for the Republicans until D. H. Chamberlain crushed the South Carolina Bank and Trust Company by denying it exclusive rights to government deposits. Walter Allen, *Governor Chamberlain's Administration in South Carolina: A Chapter of Reconstruction in the Southern States* (New York: G. P. Putnam's Sons, 1888), p. 145.

20. Both the Dawson Papers at Duke and the Gary Papers in the South Caroliniana leave no doubt that Butler and Gary were to receive 10 percent of the profits realized "by the advance due from an endorsement of the public meetings." MS copy of an agreement signed by W. E. Everett, L. D. Childs, J. B. Palmer, and L. P. Southern, and accepted by M. C. Butler and M. W. Gary, April 17, 1871, Gary Papers, South Caroliniana Library, University of South Carolina, cited hereafter as SCL. When Gary later became a repudiator the whole messy affair was published in the New York *Sun*, February 1, 1878, and answered by Gary in the Columbia *Register*, February 12, 1878.

Kimpton, and while he later got statements from Kimpton saying that the transaction was "based purely upon banking principles" and that Dawson repaid the loan, such dealings with the wizards of corruption would not have set well with the state's average Democrat.[21]

None of the records and notes Dawson maintained could have stood normal evidentiary tests in a court of law. Many of the items suggested impropriety as opposed to illegality. Those which purported to show a clear violation of the law lacked substantiation. Such evidence could never convict, but it could destroy. All of which suggested that beneath the surface cohesiveness of the victorious Democrats they were vulnerable; that despite cries for Republican blood, Democrats could not probe deeply without bleeding themselves. Dawson and his friends were men living in glass houses.

Under these circumstances it was fortunate that a spirit of amnesty prevailed on the part of federal and state authorities which prevented a wholesale bloodletting in the courts. The South Carolina legislature took the first step toward amnesty on May 11, 1877. Hampton was authorized to request that President Hayes quash the proceedings against Democrats accused of violating the election laws during the campaign of 1876. In return South Carolina would *nol pros* all indictments, save the major crimes, arising from their fraud investigations. Many Republicans, fearing the worst from a Democratic inquisition, urged Hayes to accept the offer. After studying the matter Hayes agreed that "a general amnesty should extend to all political offenses except those which are of the gravest character" and that the federal government would proceed with only three indictments in the upcoming election cases.[22] Thus it came to pass that the Conservative hierarchs, in protecting their subalterns from the criminal liability incurred to elect Hampton, and the Republicans, anxious to avoid the consequences of their corruption, worked to suppress indictments and trials that neither could afford.

The election cases which the South Carolina legislature wanted quashed revealed yet another disturbing element in the surface calm of the Conservative regime. Despite early protestations to the contrary, the tactics used by Hampton's red-shirted legions to win Democratic hegemony embarrassed the Conservative hierarchy before the nation and threatened their quest for stability and order. The particular election cases pursued by the Hayes administration proved a special embarrassment. They involved atrocities committed in and about Ellenton, near Hamburg, on the day

---

21. C. P. Leslie to Dawson and Dawson to Leslie, August 1, 1871; Dawson to Kimpton, August 10, 1871, and Kimpton to Dawson, February 10, 1872, Dawson Papers, Duke.

22. The Hampton and Hayes correspondence is found in Hampton McNeely Jarrell, *Wade Hampton and the Negro: The Road Not Taken* (Columbia: University of South Carolina Press, 1949), pp. 170–87. Quoted material in letter from Hayes to Hampton, May 12, 1877, p. 176.

after Chamberlain's nomination. Precipitated by events unrelated to the campaign itself, the collision between blacks and whites at Ellenton left at least fifteen blacks killed and two wounded, with two whites dead and eight wounded.[23] The ratio of dead to wounded in the casualty count spoke to the dimensions of the tragedy. Republicans were of course quick to see in this horror the workings of the Mississippi plan.

It was to try election violations arising from this event that Chief Justice Waite traveled to Charleston in May, 1877. Before departing, Waite was fully informed of the administration's position on relaxing prosecutions and received a letter from Governor Hampton hoping that the chief justice would "find it consistent with [his] sense of duty to take such action as will tend to promote a restoration of peace & good will among all classes and both races here."[24]

Hampton need not have feared. In Morrison Waite, South Carolina was not getting a vindictive Stalwart on the bench. Waite was a man of patrician bearing. His education at Yale had given him a proper appreciation for the rights and property of states. Of greater significance for the Ellenton cases, he was a man who believed that the acts of private persons did not fall under the purview of federal authority. Moreover, Waite was favorably disposed to Hayes's southern policy and shared the centennial spirit of a restored Union. When asked to block the invitation extended to a member of the Lee family to read the Declaration of Independence on July 4, 1876, the chief justice replied:

> The nation has been preserved in its entirety and I preside over a court which is common to all its parts. In fact, I must not permit myself to know that it has parts. Neither can I, in my position, know the antecedents of any one—All are equal before me. It is my duty, in my place, to cultivate that feeling so that I may at all times and in all places be prepared to act without prejudice.[25]

The chief justice was an instant social success wherever he went. Only the month before he had thoroughly charmed Richmond's social elite, and Charleston was not to be outdone in courting the chief justice. But the felicitous spirit paled as the veil of blind justice was lifted in a trial that left Waite increasingly shocked and horrified. "You can hardly imagine the horrid details of our trial," he confided to Mrs. Waite. "There have already been developed about twenty murders in cold blood. I never before conceived of such a state of society. The testimony this morning was . . . sickening." Moreover, he was stunned at the manner in which the Negro

---

23. Ibid., pp. 77–80.

24. Hampton to Waite, May 11, 1877, Waite Papers, LC. See also Magrath, *Morrison R. Waite,* pp. 155–66.

25. Magrath, *Morrison R. Waite,* p. 137.

witnesses were abused and misrepresented by the Charleston press even though the deponents seemed "unusually intelligent for their condition." Such gratuitous abuse left him again troubled by his inability "to comprehend such a state of society." Though lavishly entertained that evening in the home of Judge Magrath, he lamented, "Somehow, I feel that the two sections will never in our times come together."[26]

The chief justice was anxious to hear what possible excuse could be given for such atrocities, and he did not have long to wait, for the South Carolina bar had done its homework. Waite was forced to concede that the defense made a strong case against their liability under the particular indictment (violation of election laws), "but nothing to excuse the inhuman barbarity of the conduct of some of the persons implicated. More unprovoked murder was never proven than has been shown in some of the cases, but unfortunately the guilty parties are not on trial for that."[27] Waite's charge to the jury was legally proper, if it failed to reflect his shocked sense of humanity. It must have rankled for him to write, "The Charleston papers, that have done [all] they possibly could to embarrass this trial and misrepresent it, said they could not ask for a change of a single word." Having discharged his obligation, the chief justice departed for Columbia where he gave Hampton a complete account of the Ellenton trials and expressed his idea of the governor's duty. An incurable optimist, Waite could leave South Carolina on the happier impression that Wade Hampton was "a gentleman."[28]

The first Ellenton Cases resulted in a mistrial and provided the grounds for a new appeal for general amnesty in 1878. On receiving this new request from the South Carolina legislature, Hayes and his attorney general sought Waite's advice as to what should be done. The chief justice maintained some judicial distance, because the cases might come before him again, but he did indicate that "the counsel for the United States conducted the trial of the 'Ellenton Cases' . . . with ability and good judgement." Attorney General Devens could not have mistaken Waite's conclusion. "The cases were thoroughly prepared, and, so far as I could discover, the government lost nothing through any fault of those to whom its interests were committed."[29]

Despite this indication of futility, the Hayes administration continued its investigation into the viability of the Ellenton cases,[30] but in April, 1879, the president gave up and decided to come to terms. In the flurry of

26. Waite to his wife, May 22 and 20, 1877, Waite Papers, LC.

27. Ibid., May 27, 1877.

28. Ibid., June 5, 1877.

29. Charles R. Devens to Waite, March 11, 1878, and Waite to Devens, March 25, 1878, ibid.

30. William Evarts to Waite, July 29, 1878, and Hayes to Waite, November 14, 1878, ibid.

negotiations which ensued Dawson served as principal mediator. By that time Dawson's fortunes within the Democratic party were mending, and the Republicans believed him to be the logical contact point with the Conservative regime. On April 17, Dawson, accompanied by Edmund William McGregor Mackey and Robert Smalls of the opposition party, appeared in Columbia to signal Hampton through Governor Simpson that the state's Republicans were ready to reach agreement on amnesty. Mackey requested that Dawson hold all papers relating to pardons and continuances until the negotiations were completed. Bargaining between Mackey and the Conservative regime continued until terms were reached on April 21. Thereafter, Dawson was charged with working directly with the United States District Attorney to see that the details were executed.[31]

The agreement called for the federal authorities to continue (i.e., not bring to trial) all cases arising under the election laws. In return the state agreed to pardon Francis Louis Cardoza and Robert Smalls and to continue its case against D. H. Chamberlain by name and all other cases "involving malfeasance on the part of any public officer of the State, or bribery or corruption of the public officers of the State, prior to Jan. 1, 1877." The state further agreed to *nol pros* its cases at some future time when federal authorities took the same action. Finally, the state relinquished its right to bring any further cases to trial arising from its investigation of public frauds.[32] Thus died the victors' right to bring the vanquished to justice. It was difficult to decide who was the more relieved.

One of the interesting curiosities of the whole episode was the role played by Daniel Henry Chamberlain. During this period of publicly anticipated vengeance, Dawson had seemed to clamor loudest for Chamberlain's indictment and trial, especially when it was rumored that the editor was going soft on his old friend. Now Chamberlain was the only Republican under indictment whose case was continued by name, and there was good reason. The ex-governor had been advising South Carolina Democrats on how best to effect amnesty. General M. C. Butler wrote Dawson during the delicate negotiations saying Chamberlain personally cautioned "that an immediate *dis*continuance on our part would not be advisable, and I agree with him. It would look very badly."[33] The old adage of politics making strange bedfellows never seemed more appropriate.

The reaction of the state to mutual amnesty was not generally favorable. Apart from the *News and Courier* and the Columbia *Register,* both in a position to know the inside machinations, the country press and their

---

31. John Cheves Haskell to Hampton and W. D. Simpson to Hampton, April 17, 1879, Simpson Letterbook, South Carolina Archives, Columbia, South Carolina. Particulars of the settlement are set forth in correspondence and memoranda, April 17–26, 1879, Dawson Papers, Duke.

32. Four memoranda, April 20 and 21, 1879, Dawson Papers, Duke.

33. M. C. Butler to Dawson, April 20, 1879, ibid.

constituents felt cheated. "The state quid for this federal quo made a distasteful pill for South Carolinians to swallow," wrote one historian. "The idea of refraining from prosecuting the bribe givers and bribe takers, the forgers and embezzlers who had bankrupted the state, was a hard one to take, and many and loud were the complaints."[34] Robert Aldrich, a leading Conservative, asked Robert Reid Hemphill of the Abbeville *Medium* to go easy on Governor Simpson for pardoning Cardoza and Smalls. He told Hemphill that "there was *a reason* for the sudden breaking down of all those prosecutions." Guilty or not, hundreds of "our men" would have gone to jail. "But our men," he confided, "especially in the lower counties, were not innocent (in a legal sense I mean). They made up their minds to carry the elections (as they should have done) and they violated the law at every step." Aldrich felt that simple justice could be gained for the red shirts by "simply foregoing the pleasure of seeing two niggers locked up in jail."[35]

It should have come as no surprise that the rank-and-file Democracy, in whose name amnesty had been sought, saw little reason to deny themselves the pleasure of going after the big knaves of corruption. After all, the state's major newspaper did much to encourage the idea that little fraud and violence had been employed unless justified in retaliation for Republican abuses. It was not until after the election of 1878, which, if anything, was attended by greater excesses than 1876,[36] that Dawson openly acknowledged the crimes that had been committed in the name of Redemption. On the third anniversary of Black Thursday, Dawson surprised his readers with the editorial caption, "Not Guilty, but Don't do it Again!" He told his audience that "no public man who values the present and has an eye to the future can afford to figure before the country as the champion of 'bull-dozing' or 'ballot-box stuffing.'" He acknowledged that there were many in South Carolina who were not moved by such considerations. "The good or bad opinion of the outer world, with its effect on trade, commerce and manufacturers, matters little to them." But even these men, Dawson charged, must surely be aware of the necessity for avoiding dissension and discontent in South Carolina. Their own political preferment depended on it. "We tell them, in all frankness," warned the editor, "that South Carolina will not tolerate lawlessness at elections. This revolution must move backwards."[37]

---

34. Jarrell, *Wade Hampton,* p. 138.

35. Robert Aldrich to R. R. Hemphill, May 10, 1879, Hemphill Family Papers, Duke.

36. Jarrell, *Wade Hampton,* p. 149. Jarrell wrote, "Many tales of fraud that properly belong to 1878 and subsequent elections probably attached themselves to 1876, according to the normal tendency of legends to concentrate on a single point."

37. *News and Courier,* December 16, 1878.

As important as the editorial confession were the circumstances which prompted it. South Carolina's *viri boni* were peculiarly sensitive about their national reputation. They had portrayed themselves as the very embodiment of order and the principle that only men of intelligence should govern. The tactics they condoned to win election now embarrassed them and threatened the order they promised to preserve. Dawson knew that South Carolina could not continue to wink at the violence that shocked the sensibilities of a man like Morrison Waite. So, when the New York *Evening Post* and *The Nation* both published articles condemning the violence in South Carolina but conceding some extenuating circumstances, Dawson saw his chance to confess past sins and make new resolutions for the future. "The State and the country," he told his readers, "are ready to render a verdict of 'Not Guilty; but don't do it again!' This we shall not deserve or receive, unless we give earnest of an intention to behave ourselves hereafter."[38] The confession was made. The guilt was placed squarely on the backs of men like Martin Gary and his followers. Having walked in the mud of their overzealous supporters, Dawson and his compatriots were somewhat belatedly lifting their skirts.

But Martin Gary, the Bald Eagle from Edgefield, posed a threat to the Conservative regime that would not down. His conviction that race was the only issue in South Carolina politics, combined with his insatiable ambition for high office, made him a lightning rod through which nascent opposition to Hampton's policy of racial conciliation could strike at any time. Gary was no rube. He probably bears the distinction of being the only man ever kicked out of the South Carolina College who finished his education at Harvard. His slight build was offset by a rigidly erect bearing, sharply chiseled features making his deepset eyes appear almost demonic, and a full mustache with goatee to balance his thinning, closely cropped hair. He could have served as prototype for the mint julep–sipping, race-baiting politicians who have adorned fiction and fact in southern history.

Gary's thirst for office was never slaked. His friend and neighbor from Edgefield, General Butler, beat him out for the United States Senate in 1876, Hampton thwarted the same ambition in 1878, and the state convention turned its back on his desperation bid for the governor's chair in 1880. Yet through it all he may have remained South Carolina's second most popular figure. Revered for his role in the campaign of 1876 and admired for his straight talk, his sympathizers were nonetheless committed to Hampton and his regime. Opposition to the regime was not a permissible route to power. One had to rise through the organization, and the Conservative hierarchy had little use for such an intemperate spokesman. So Gary chafed in the wings while his closest allies proclaimed that his *"politics today will be the politics of South Carolina in five years from this*

---

38. Ibid.

date."[39] And though the aborted affair of honor between Gary and Dawson was formally reconciled in December, 1877,[40] Dawson remained an immovable object in the path of Gary's ambitions. As a matter of conscience and politics, the editor could never countenance Gary's vociferous antagonism of the race issue.

Gary was initially reluctant to challenge Hampton openly and in early 1878 remained content to lay the responsibility for the governor's mistakes on "the lawyers of his administration."[41] Gary decided on a strategy that called for replacing the men then serving under Hampton with a new slate of officers to be nominated in the August convention. He urged his political confidant, Hugh Farley of the *Carolina Spartan,* to develop the rival slate by catering "to the ambitions of men all over the State" and recommended that Alfred Rhett be placed on the ticket from Charleston. Rhett would "keep Dawson overawed and [would] control the influence of the *Journal of Commerce.*"[42] But the strategy never got off the ground. In August, 1878, General John Doby Kennedy of Camden gavelled the convention to order and presided over a resounding endorsement of the Hampton regime.

Not daunted by the convention, Gary took heart from correspondents like the one who wrote saying Hampton was no longer regarded as infallible and was now seen "as the exponent of extreme conservatism and niggerism."[43] Gary had already decided to renew his bid for the United States Senate but knew his plans would be for naught if Hampton became a candidate for the same office. To insure that Hampton remained governor, Gary proved willing to give the lie to his known feelings on the race question. Under the ruse of letters to newspapers, he launched a campaign to prove that Hampton was "the only man who [could] keep the blacks and whites harmonized for the next two years" and therefore should remain governor. In a letter to Farley he enclosed a clipping from the Greenville *News* in which A. G. Garlington argued that "Governor Hampton is the

39. Ellerbe Bogan Crawford Cash to Gary, October 27, 1878, Gary Papers, SCL. For similar expression see Joshua Hilary Hudson to Gary, September 7, 1878, ibid. Few historians have disagreed with this judgment, seeing an obvious connection between Gary's politics and those of Benjamin Ryan Tillman. The best explanation of this connection is found in Francis Butler Simkins, *The Tillman Movement in South Carolina* (Durham: Duke University Press, 1926). For a history of Reconstruction and Redemption from Gary's point of view, see William Arthur Sheppard, *Red Shirts Remembered: Southern Brigadiers of the Reconstruction Period* (Atlanta: Ruralist Press, 1940).

40. W. D. Clancy to Dawson, December 5 and 8, 1877, and Gary to Dawson, December 8, 1877, Dawson Papers, Duke.

41. Gary to Hugh L. Farley, April 8, 20, and May 3, 1878, Gary Papers, SCL. Quoted material from letter of April 20.

42. Gary to Farley, April 13, 1878, ibid.

43. Ellis G. Graydon to Gary, August 19, 1878, ibid.

only man in the State, who has the confidence of the white and colored people. He alone can keep the Democracy united and give the colored people satisfaction."[44]

But Dawson and Hampton had other plans for their errant colleague. The *News and Courier* denied Gary access to its columns, and Hampton refused to speak from the same platform. Gary became so frustrated that he was forced to send an emissary to Dawson requesting newspaper space and offering to buy the space at advertising rates if the *News and Courier* refused to publish a political communiqué. Dawson was out of the office at the time and the request was made to Riordan. After contacting Dawson, Riordan replied that the *News and Courier* would publish one communication on the subject but reserved the right to make editorial rebuttal. Well could Gary proclaim that he had been "practically denied freedom of the *press* and the freedom of *speech*, if this is not political proscription and persecution, what is it?"[45] Hampton went on to be elected governor that fall and was honored with election to the United States Senate in December by a grateful legislature.

By far the most sparks flew on the issue of race. Both factions agreed that white supremacy was essential. Their differences lay over how it was to be achieved and what role would be assigned the Negro. Hampton favored a policy that would invite the Negro's participation with a vague promise that at some future date an educated black citizenry could approach some measure of political equality. Gary favored their complete proscription and subordination. Dawson carried the Hampton standard warning Gary that "no State can be ruled by repression, and long retain a republican form of government."[46] To this warning the Greenville *News,* one of the few Gary papers, retorted that "if Mr. Dawson and his followers keep up his 'leading ideas of moderation, toleration and liberality,' we will lose the state." The *News* was charitable, however, suggesting that Dawson's errors could be explained by his English birth, which made him unable to "understand the unwritten political law, which is made up of the customs, habits of thought, modes of reasoning, of certain repugnances and attractions of the inhabitants of the Commonwealth."[47] Gary was not

44. Gary to Farley, August 25 and September 8, 1878, ibid.

45. W. T. Gary to Gary, September 21, 1878, and B. R. Riordan telegram to W. T. Gary, September 21, 1878, Gary Papers, SCL. For Hampton's proscription of Gary see Gary to R. R. Hemphill, October 4, 1878, Hemphill Family Papers, Duke, and Gary to Farley, October 4, 1878, Gary Papers, SCL. Quoted material in letter to Farley.

46. *News and Courier,* August 29, 1878.

47. Greenville *News,* September 8, 1878. The article was a reprint from the Columbia *Straightout,* edited by Henry Farley, Hugh's brother. There are no extant copies of the *Straightout.* For a discussion of the few Gary newspapers see William J. Cooper, Jr., *The Conservative Regime: South Carolina, 1877–1890,* The Johns Hopkins University Studies in Historical And Political Science, ser. LXXXVI, no. 1 (Baltimore: Johns Hopkins Press,

so charitable, arguing that "only *English* men . . . like [Dawson] are on the fusion, miscegenation & Mongrel government policy."[48]

Gary's program to advance himself and his race failed for many reasons, not the least of which was his intemperate, volatile, angry rhetoric when the times called for Hampton and peace. A man who counseled his friends to "never admit that you have been hit or wounded," that the only approach was "to ridicule the idea of Hampton or Dawson reading [him] out of the party,"[49]—such a man might express deep-seated popular feeling, but not conventional wisdom. Furthermore, traditional assumptions of the white community, what the Greenville *News* called "habits of thought," rendered incredible the charges that Hampton was leading his people "into this dark pit of African rule—this worse than 'black hole of Calcutta.'"[50] It was an article of faith that no self-respecting white man, least of all the state's greatest war hero, would ever countenance such a course whatever might be his conciliatory language from the political stump. Gary should have listened to one of his wiser friends who advised him not to "come down too heavy on the *race* issue," that many who were in full accord with his "orthodox" views felt it "better not to proclaim such sentiments from the house tops." Gary's only mistake, concluded the friendly counselor, was in being a little in advance of his times, for "theorists may twist and distort the matter at will, but the *real* issue in this and other Southern States involves white supremacy and civilization."[51]

The machinations and the changing, often contradictory rhetoric in the period between the election of 1876 and the proclaiming of general amnesty in 1879 may have perplexed the people of South Carolina, but it was perfectly intelligible to the Conservative leadership. They were men who had been close, sometimes too close, to the centers of power throughout Reconstruction. They had engineered a counterrevolution the consequences of which threatened their own existence. The violence and the cries for vengeance which attended their insurgency were dragons' teeth, and they dared not reap the harvest. If Morrison Waite and his friends were willing to acquiesce in the backward thrust of the revolution wrought by Reconstruction, Francis Dawson and his compatriots were equally certain that the counterrevolution called Redemption "must move backward." The chief justice and the editor had one thing in common—both placed a premium on order. Neither could allow the passions of Reconstruction or Redemption to challenge the maxim that the best society was

1968), p. 59. Gary tried to get the Abbeville *Medium* to publish the same article, Gary to R. R. Hemphill, September 25, 1878, Hemphill Family Papers, Duke.

48. Gary to R. R. Hemphill, September 25, 1878, Hemphill Family Papers, Duke.
49. Gary to Farley, October 10, 1878, Gary Papers, SCL.
50. Greenville *News,* October 6, 1878.
51. J. H. Hudson to Gary, September 7, 1878, Gary Papers, SCL.

one which entrusted its care to men of ability, worth, and intelligence. Dawson also had one thing in common with Martin Gary. Both believed that what was at stake was "white supremacy and civilization." But Dawson believed there was an orderly way of accomplishing the objective. He was convinced that Gary's way would guarantee white supremacy at the expense of republican institutions where only the best men ruled.

These countervailing tensions created the vital nexus linking the aspirations of South Carolina's Conservative regime with a national community. Dawson and his associates could never make perfect restoration of the status quo antebellum. South Carolina's institutions would hereafter be justified in terms acceptable to a national constituency. A later group of southerners, romanticizing an agrarian past, would call it cultural slavery. To the men of '76 it seemed more like peace. It may have been neither here nor there, but it was a way of carrying on.

With the declaration of general amnesty in 1879, Dawson left for Europe and a much-needed vacation. He departed with a sense of accomplishment. He had fought his way through a bitter internecine party struggle and had regained a commanding position in the councils of the new regime. Even when he was in the midst of investigation by the state legislature for alleged printing contract violations, his party honored him with unanimous election as its county chairman. The year before he had not even been selected as a delegate. Well could he exclaim to Sarah, "The whirligig of time!"[52] After the initial difficulty of launching his libel suit against the *Journal of Commerce* he wrote, "I have never felt stronger in the State than I now do, our God be praised! The night is near at an end."[53] Even those who accused him of not knowing South Carolina and its people were willing to concede "the magnetism of his genius," and when Dawson served as chief mediator in the final negotiations for amnesty, he was not only cementing South Carolina's restoration but his own restoration as the "political cat's paw" of the Conservative regime.

Dawson did not inherit his position in South Carolina. As his detractors frequently pointed out, the editor was not one of them. Dawson gained influence through ability, intelligence, genius, and energy—the very qualities so much admired by Morrison Waite. In hard times he built a newspaper that now required $75,000 a year to operate, and a journal that no politician could do without if he wanted his story told. Dawson's lecture to the people of South Carolina on the occasion of the death of the *Journal of Commerce* was instructive. He began by recounting that the *Journal* had been formed when the *News and Courier* had been assailed for having the courage of its convictions in the city elections of 1875. To the "unthinking" it seemed that the *News and Courier* was on the wane, "and a wish to

---

52. Dawson to his wife, July 20, 1877, Dawson Papers, Duke.

53. Dawson to his wife, September 6, 1877, ibid.

hasten the moment when it should sink below the horizon actuated . . . many persons from whom we had differed or . . . had been constrained, at times, to oppose." The *Journal of Commerce* had hundreds of stockholders who wanted to injure the *News and Courier*. They failed, and there was a moral. "Personal antagonism" was not enough to win a place for a new journal.[54] Proving, perhaps, that a cock will crow.

---

54. *News and Courier,* July 25, 1878.

Chapter V
Liberal Reform: The Search
for a Larger Synthesis

Liberal reformers of the nineteenth century have not fared well in comparison with their twentieth-century counterparts. Several maxims of political economy seemed to pave the way for a newer, less prejudiced, more worldly understanding of the nature of politics, business, and society. First, the modern observer discovered that inflation was not necessarily bad, that it was essential to maintain growth, and that a government by experts could regulate this growth for the benefit of all. Second, monopolies or oligopolies were not an unmitigated evil, the nation was better off because the New Nationalism of Herbert Croly triumphed over Wilson's New Freedom, and the new industrial state was entirely too sophisticated to indulge profit maximization at the consumer's expense. Finally, true liberation was achieved with the knowledge that corruption had its advantages, that the Plunkitts of Tammany Hall were essential to acculturation, and that political graft was often the means of promoting worthy social ends.

Compared with the affirmative action reformers of the twentieth century, who supposedly understood the new political economy, the naysayers of the Gilded Age seemed appropriately characterized as "man milliners." In any confrontation with the real world they could be counted on to react ostrich-like. Eric Goldman, seeing the history of American reform as a rendezvous with destiny, denounced liberals like Edwin Lawrence Godkin, Charles Eliot Norton, and George William Curtis for being patricians or American Tories who refused to soil their hands in the dirt of democratic politics. From such a vantage Ulysses Simpson Grant became, not an unwitting tool of corruptionists, but a man who "knew his America."[1] Historians of this persuasion found little to praise in men who spent a life saying "no" to inflation, "no" to government protection of corporate enterprise, and "no" to the politics of the spoilsman.

The historical pendulum has gained the patrician liberals a few apologists, but their accord has been limited to the position of a link in the chain of slipping status that ultimately gave the nation its Progressive movement. Commemorated for their custodial service to the "mind in American politics," they have been honored for their commitment to individuality. "What finally justified the Mugwump to himself and justifies an enduring

---

1. Eric Frederick Goldman, *Rendezvous with Destiny: A History of Modern American Reform* (New York: Alfred A. Knopf, 1952), p. 25.

place for him in the history of his era," wrote a friendly historian, "was his insistence on his own autonomy."[2] The pendulum may eventually gain the liberal reformers more than apology. As the nation once again moves into an era in which corruption, inflation, and artificial restraints in production become the stuff that animates politics, a new appreciation has been acquired for men who were as much concerned with the means in which power was exercised as its ends. Of greater consequence has been the growing tendency to abandon a compartmentalized treatment of the patrician liberal. The genteel reformer of New England, like his Bourbon counterpart in the South, is now being regarded as an integral part of a much broader nineteenth-century liberal movement—a movement that has much more than a passing connection with twentieth-century reform.

Part of the bad press given the "best men," both North and South, can be laid to their self-imposed isolation from other minority groups. But even here, broader, less compartmentalized interpretations, have correctly insisted that the "outs versus ins" mentality forged a bond between these patrician reformers and less fortunate ethnic minorities, a kind of brains and brawn approach to politics. This "Liberal-Democratic" coalition combined free thinkers in religion, men of small property, and advocates of sound money and low tariffs with people who suffered contempt for ethnic identity, as for example southern whites. As such it became a combination of "voting blocs" and an "ideology," the one not necessarily compatible with the other.[3] These diverse groups were joined by a common view of the enemy. They saw Tories in England and Republicans in America as people who identified the nation with themselves, people who cultivated notions of superior religions, were contemptuous of the common folk, and promoted rule by oligarchy. Moreover, they manipulated government to their own advantage through a skillful use of corruption, and they encouraged economic policies which contravened the principles of laissez faire, thereby leading to imperialistic ventures in foreign policy. With this shared view of the dominant party, the "outs" were to be found coalescing behind "Gladstone in England, George Brown and Alexander Mackenzie in Canada, and Tilden and Cleveland in America."[4]

Dawson fit quite comfortably in the Liberal-Democratic fold. Like E. L. Godkin of *The Nation*, Dawson "spoke with the voice of Manchester to the

---

2. Geoffrey Thomas Blodgett, *The Gentle Reformers: Massachusetts Democrats in the Cleveland Era* (Cambridge: Harvard University Press, 1966), p. 46. The best known application of the status thesis is found in Richard Hofstadter, *The Age of Reform: From Bryan to F.D.R.* (New York: Alfred A. Knopf, 1955), p. 137.

3. Robert Lloyd Kelley, *The Transatlantic Persuasion: The Liberal-Democratic Mind in the Age of Gladstone* (New York: Alfred A. Knopf, 1969), p. 408. An early interpretation comes essentially to the same conclusion. See Earle Dudley Ross, *The Liberal Republican Movement* (New York: Henry Holt, 1919), pp. 237–39.

4. Kelley, *Transatlantic Persuasion*, pp. 408–412.

New South."[5] In the years immediately following restoration, the Charleston editor was able to devote more time and attention to the issues that gave life and substance to this political philosophy. He urgently sought to clean out the channels of politics through civil service reform and a general restriction of the suffrage. He lent a sympathetic pen to such various causes as Irish home rule, Chinese immigration, woman's emancipation, and labor. At the same time he favored sound money and free trade, sought to protect the rights of property and the inviolability of contractual obligations, and gave much support to the preservation of law and order through licensure laws directed at pistols, whiskey, and gambling. Not infrequently Dawson took contradictory positions on the major questions of the day, but they were more often than not contradictions inherent in the philosophy he espoused.

Dawson was most alert to the idea that means should not subvert ends in political life. His experience with the restoration of home rule in South Carolina made him painfully aware of the dangers arising from revolutionary reform. In preparing a speech for the Reform Club of New York, the editor came to his "objective point" in a discussion of the revolution of 1876. "There was and there is," he warned, "too little regard for the character of the channels through which the broad current of reform should find its way."[6] For most of Dawson's northern audience this meant civil service reform, but in South Carolina the conduit of reform was more elemental. It was the electorate itself, and Dawson labored long to perfect democracy by clearing out the illiterate and uneducated debris which clogged its channels.

South Carolina whites were generally agreed that the black vote should be restricted. Their only differences involved questions of just how far the proscription should be carried out and by what methods. Dawson's principal motivation came from his recognition that a white minority bent on white supremacy would forever subvert the democratic process. Taking his cue from an admission by Hampton in April, 1881, that irregularities had occurred in past elections, Dawson sprang to the attack. "The 'irregularities,' or whatever else we please to call them," he wrote, "were justified and justifiable—just as revolution or rebellion is permissible when there is no escape from tyrannical government under which neither life nor property are safe." Dawson concluded that it was "manlier to rest on the right of revolution, whatever form it takes, than on denials which do not carry convictions, and on evasions which deceive nobody worth deceiving."[7]

The only way to make the whites behave was to eliminate the black voter as a factor in South Carolina politics, but Dawson's commitment to

---

5. C. Vann Woodward, *Origins of the New South, 1877–1913,* A History of the South, vol. 9 (Baton Rouge: Louisiana State University Press, 1951), p. 146.

6. MS copy in Dawson Papers, Duke University Library, cited hereafter as Duke.

7. *News and Courier,* April 23, 1881.

democratic forms made only one route acceptable. Literacy qualifications would bar approximately seven Negroes for each white while at the same time honoring the principle that laws should apply equally to both races. Other solutions were considered offensive. When the South Carolina legislature discussed a small registration fee, the *News and Courier* objected on grounds that any property qualification was obnoxious to a democratic society. When the legislature proposed the infamous "eight box" law to confound the supposedly illiterate and ignorant black voter, the *News and Courier* objected on grounds of basic fairness. When the legislature persisted, Dawson tried for a reduction in the number of boxes to no more than four. "The trouble about it," reasoned the editor, "is that there are a good many white voters . . . who are likely to be confused and lose their votes, when the election machinery is too complicated."[8] Dawson felt sure that the legislature could arrive at a registration law that would both secure white civilization and be just and equitable to all, and he warned, "the people of the United States (who have already proved themselves more than a match for South Carolina) will not continue to acquiesce in revolutionary processes, and will not consent to have us represented, in Congress, by modes which have been hitherto indispensable in the conduct of our State affairs."[9]

So intent was Dawson on literacy qualifications that he was willing to cheat on the principle in order to gain its adoption. For those whites who feared disfranchisement under the same provisions, Dawson offered irrefragable proof that white supremacy would always preserve "with equal exaction, the natural difference between the two races." For whites who remained unimpressed by tautological statements of their own supremacy, Dawson conceded that the impact of the law on white people might be mitigated by permitting those who had voted for twenty years or more to continue that privilege without registering. "The 'Stalwarts' will call it a new form of bulldozing," Dawson acknowledged, "but the intelligent opinion of the country will be with us, and we shall save our State, our own people, and our own civilization."[10]

The General Assembly of South Carolina responded with an election law in early 1882 which contained, not only the simple literacy features, but other provisions which clearly invited fraud. A special house committee inserted one measure requiring "the election manager, on demand of the voter, 'to read to him the names on the boxes.'"[11] The possibilities for

---

8. Ibid., November 25, 1881, and January 18, 1882.

9. Ibid., November 25, 1881.

10. Ibid., February 6, 1880. See also editorials of May 5 and 16, 1881.

11. William J. Cooper, Jr., *The Conservative Regime: South Carolina, 1877–1890*, The Johns Hopkins University Studies in Historical and Political Science, ser. LXXXVI, no. 1 (Baltimore: The Johns Hopkins Press, 1968), pp. 101–2.

fraud in such a procedure were legion, but the *News and Courier* swallowed the entire package. While Dawson could no longer defend South Carolina's suffrage restriction on the high grounds he had hoped for, the editor was not loath to adopt the more traditional argument *tu quoque,* that the North was just as bad.

The other approach Dawson took to purify democracy owed its inspiration to the father of Yankee ingenuity in democratic politics, Elbridge Gerry. Again it was to stop the "desperately hard work in divers ways" with which South Carolina won its congressional seats from the black majority that Dawson advocated gerrymandering the congressional districts.[12] Prophetically, when the Radicals took similar steps in 1876, Dawson called for them to do their worst, for "the Democrats can stand gerrymandering now better than Radicals can stand it hereafter."[13] The opportunity to return the favor came when the census of 1880 gave South Carolina two additional seats in Congress.

Dawson and the newly elected congressman from the Charleston district, Samuel Dibble, took the arrangements in hand. On March 30, 1882, the *News and Courier* began calling for a special session of the legislature. The General Assembly was urged to adopt a plan which would give the whites six districts and leave one for "the ex-convicts and scalawags." At the same time Dawson worked closely with Dibble and Congressman George Tillman in Washington to develop an acceptable proposal. N. G. Gonzales, then the *News and Courier*'s young Washington correspondent, described Dawson's role in the redistricting effort. In a letter home, Gonzales explained, "The *News and Courier* . . . does not 'obey Washington orders.' The re-districting was the only thing to save us four members next fall, and the Congressmen solicited the paper, they did not order it." With a touch of pride in the man Gonzales otherwise thought was a bit too overbearing, he asserted, "Dawson came to his opinion alone, and so satisfied are the Solons that the *News and Courier* could secure the re-districting, that they give themselves no more concern about it."[14]

The plan worked out by Dawson and Dibble called for massing the black votes into one district by ignoring county boundaries, and it won overwhelming approval. Dawson defended the action by claiming it was far "better to gerrymander the State than to encourage fraud and violence at elections."[15] Gonzales was more specific. "The day of the tissue ballot is

---

12. Dawson to W. L. [*sic*] Rosecrans, May 14, 1882, Dawson Papers, Duke.

13. *News and Courier,* March 15, 1876.

14. N. G. Gonzales to his aunt, April 9, 1882, Elliott-Gonzales Papers, Southern Historical Collection, University of North Carolina, cited hereafter as SHC.

15. *News and Courier,* June 14, 1882.

gone," he confided in a letter. "The law forbids them, and the Government would raise Cain if they were used again. As to the Edgefield way of killing opponents," concluded Gonzales, "I don't believe in it, and the people, even in that county, would not practice it again."[16] Such testaments to the quieting effect notwithstanding, the New York *Tribune* could find nothing "in the way of gerrymandering that will compare with South Carolina's effort in that direction 'for pure Dibbletry.'"[17]

If Whitelaw Reid's *Tribune* could not appreciate the rationale, Dawson's soon-to-be Mugwump friends did. "They reasoned," wrote the historian of northern Republicans and the southern Negro, "that the Negro was inferior and uneducated; that his ignorance made him an easy prey for voracious and unscrupulous machine politicians; that Reconstruction had proven the folly of colored rule; and that measures like the Force bill would unduly increase the authority of the central government at the expense of local and state authorities."[18] Dawson's efforts, aimed directly at the Negro, to restrict suffrage and to gerrymander in favor of whites were not inconsistent with this Liberal-Democratic persuasion. That creed simply affirmed that "minority groups should be given equal status within the nation—always with the exception of the Negro—and local self-government should be the basis of the Constitution."[19] In that light, Dawson was justified in believing that home rule and suffrage restriction served to advance his political philosophy.

During this period Dawson's relationship with northern liberals became much more active. In January, 1881, he received a letter from Richard Louis Dugdale, secretary for the Society of Political Education (SPE), asking him to become secretary for the Southeast and a member of the executive committee.[20] The SPE was the most ambitious effort ever undertaken to organize liberal reformers nationwide. By disseminating information on political economy, they hoped to convert a million Americans to the cause of free trade and civil service reform. The original promoters were David Ames Wells, Charles Francis Adams, William Graham Sumner, and Horace White. The Society's weekly bulletin, *Million,* carried "the latest intelligence on civil service and tariff matters to a distinguished, exclusive membership."[21] Dawson accepted the invitation of Mr. Dugdale and actively advised the SPE on programs and approaches to advance the organization's goals.

---

16. N. G. Gonzales to his aunt, April 9, 1882, Elliott-Gonzales Papers, SHC.

17. Quoted in *News and Courier,* August 11, 1882.

18. Stanley P. Hirshson, *Farewell to the Bloody Shirt: Northern Republicans and the Southern Negro, 1877–1893* (Bloomington: Indiana University Press, 1962), p. 252.

19. Kelley, *Transatlantic Persuasion,* p. 46.

20. R. L. Dugdale to Dawson, January 28, 1881, Dawson Papers, Duke.

21. John Gerald Sproat, *The Best Men: Liberal Reformers in the Gilded Age* (New York: Oxford University Press, 1968), p. 56.

Throwing himself into the work of the Society with a will, Dawson constantly kept its mission before the people of South Carolina and urged widespread membership. The SPE was addressing the live issues of the day, and nowhere was this enlightenment more needed than in the South. Southern people knew little about economic questions and seemed to care less. "They have depended too long," he wrote, "upon their favorite leaders, (themselves often as ignorant in reality as the constituents they would enlighten) for instruction in such matters." The reluctance to acquire wisdom was explained by the fact that "every Southern white man knows . . . that he is better than 'a Nigger' and that Radical is only another name for Rogue, but 'in round numbers' this is about all he does know."[22]

A few days before receiving Dugdale's invitation, Dawson was already busy at the work of enlightening the unwashed multitude. For his first lecture Dawson chose Henry George's *Progress and Poverty* and proceeded to give it an unprecedented five-day editorial review. Declaring it "one of the most remarkable books published in this generation," he admired its close reasoning and deep feeling inspired by a "love of mankind, and trust in God." Dawson saw the book as an argument against those who would take an examination of prevailing conditions and construct a brief for communism. George demonstrated that poverty need not be a concomitant of progress. His book rejected the Malthusian doctrine that poverty was the inevitable function of population growth and the "niggardliness of nature." The book's real value lay in its proof that the problem was an unequal distribution of wealth, that "the Malthusian theory gratuitously attributes to the laws of God results which really spring from the mal-adjustment of men."[23]

Having satisfied himself that society's ills could not be attributed to natural laws, Dawson broached without blanching George's suggestion that the government may one day have to appropriate land. Despite his liberal precepts, Dawson conceded that George may have grasped a greater truth. "What George has done," concluded the editor, "if he has correctly solved the problem, is to unite the truth perceived by Adam Smith and Ricardo to the truth perceived by Proudhon and Lasalle; to show that *laissez-faire* (in its full true meaning) 'opens the way to a realization of the noble dreams of socialism; to identify social law with moral law, and to disprove ideas which, in the minds of many, cloud grand and elevating perceptions.'" Dawson felt that while final judgment should be suspended, no one could begin to think about the great issues of the day without consulting this seminal work.[24]

---

22. *News and Courier,* August 20, 1881.

23. Ibid., January 22, 24, 26, and 27, 1881.

24. Ibid., January 27, 1881.

There was no indication of what the people of South Carolina felt about their first lesson in political economy, but Henry George read the editorials and found in them a new friend. In a letter to Dawson he proclaimed the review to be "the best statement of my argument which I have yet seen." His feeling for the Carolina editor was "like that of one who struggles in the breach, to the strong comrade who comes up beside him." Whatever reservations Dawson may have entertained on certain points, George predicted, "From henceforth you and I are enlisted in the same cause. You can no more help it than can I."[25]

A second letter from George and the editorial reply it provoked testified to the depth of Dawson's apprehension that heroic solutions might indeed be required for the world's problems. In his letter George waxed even more enthusiastic about the groundswell for reform and enclosed his pamphlet on the "Irish Land Question," written in order "to radicalize the Irish movement," which in turn would stir the masses both in America and England. He was particularly anxious that it achieve wide circulation in England, for it was there "that the great fight is to be made, and English thought reacts most powerfully on this country."[26]

George next proceeded to an enumeration of the reasons why he had so much hope for the future. First was the "rapidly strengthening radical feeling among the most active of the intelligent classes." This new feeling could be seen in the press where the conservatism of the men who owned the journals was not shared by "the men who do the journalism." Second, the working classes were falling under the spell of "socialistic ideas." The various land leagues and the greenbackers were doing much good work in that direction, though he admitted to sharing Dawson's suspicions about "greenbackism." Third, the Democratic party was dead and would find new life in the discontent arising from "the growth of corporations, the increase in large fortunes, [and] the tendency towards concentration everywhere apparent." Fourth, the debate over taxation and the tariff would serve as "a great means of popular education."[27]

Finally, Henry George believed men like Dawson held the key to unleashing the forces of reform. The single taxer ended his long letter with an idea as to how his new world would be born.

> If I mistake not, both in Europe and in this country events will move very fast. The great work, is the work of education. I do not conceal from myself the difficulties and dangers. I have on the contrary a much more vivid appreciation of them than most men have. Nevertheless, I have hope, for I find everywhere there are men like yourself, men who have the ability, and

---

25. Henry George to Dawson, January 31, 1881, Dawson Papers, Duke.
26. Henry George to Dawson, March 18, 1881, ibid.
27. Ibid.

who are in the position to be leaders of men, who are carefully considering all
these questions, and who are animated by that spirit which removes moun-
tains. My faith is rather in the intelligence and devotion of such men than in
the intelligence of the masses.[28]

Moved by these words, Dawson responded a week later with a highly
favorable review of the "Irish Land Question." He reported without
criticism George's view that the "American system is really worse for the
tenant than the Irish system: 'for with us there is neither sentiment nor
custom to check the force of competition or mitigate the natural desire of
the landlord to get all he can.'" Perhaps Dawson saw the influence of
George Fitzhugh in such pleadings, but whatever the motive the editor was
inspired to launch his own views on the Irish question. He argued that the
people of Ireland should boldly assert home rule, for the struggle was not
"between Irishmen and Englishmen, but between all men and the system."
"True radicalism (the end of private property) was true conservatism."
Dawson ended the editorial doubting that it was possible to read George's
pamphlet and *Progress and Poverty* without "being impressed with the
painful conviction that the extent of the social disease is not exaggerated,
and that no other peaceful remedy than that which is proposed gives equal
promise of a complete and lasting cure." For Dawson it was "the greatest
question of the age." In Henry George there was "no taint of the
'Commune,' of free-love, of infidelity," and the *News and Courier* hoped
that those "who reflect on the anomalies of our civilization, with its
extremes of riches and misery . . . will read his works themselves and form
their own conclusions."[29]

Dawson's intellectual friendship with Henry George proved a certain
independence from men like Godkin who believed reformers of George's
stripe to be "utter scoundrels [and] participants in the great conspiracy
against property and order."[30] The questions raised by the new industrial
society found Dawson torn between an implicit faith in the natural laws of
Adam Smith and utopian social schemes. As an Idealist, Dawson was
prepared to concede the truth in each competing political philosophy,
believing that such concessions, no matter how antithetical, would produce
an ultimate synthesis for reform.[31] He wanted to believe that Henry
George had found the golden mean between Adam Smith and Proudhon, a
grand scheme that promised true laissez faire, true conservatism, and
confirmed the justness of God's law. At the same time Dawson was

---

28. Ibid.

29. *News and Courier,* March 26, 1881.

30. Sproat, *Best Men,* p. 245.

31. Perry Gilbert Eddy Miller, ed., *American Thought: Civil War to World War I,* with
intro. by Perry Miller (New York: Holt, Rinehart and Winston, 1954), p. xiii.

frightened by men and women who, struggling in the sweat of their own misery, grasped for solutions that fell short of the clean precision of a single tax. Thus, caught somewhere between hope and fear, Dawson came willy-nilly under the influence of men whose "reasoning was bound by virtually the same premises as the classical theory. Unable or unwilling to destroy it as a piece, they sought some loophole that would allow American society to make its sudden leap into heaven instead of hell."[32]

Because Dawson conceived of few economic alternatives beyond the chimera of more cosmic schemes, he always fell back on his traditional grounding in Smith and Ricardo. All efforts to avoid the consequences of the "invisible hand" were frowned upon. Organizations like the National Greenback Labor Party were natural communists. Their program to fiat sufficient per capita currency, regulate interest, forbid corporate use of public lands, develop natural resources to guarantee jobs, and to oppose all servile labor raised the specter of the commune. The National Party was offering only a short cut to ease while ignoring the real problems of the country. Instead of "showing that honest and economic administration and the shattering of the Washington Rings [would] put the country on its legs again," the Greenbackers made war on capital. Until that far-off day when common property became a fait accompli, labor's interest was best served by encouraging "the circulation of capital and [making] it safe."[33]

Behind all unnatural tamperings with Smith's law Dawson saw the bugbear of inflation. "They who start out with inflation and the denunciation of capital," he warned, "will end by camping in the dark tents where waves the Red Flag of the Commune."[34] To guard against such an unhappy ending, Dawson said no to free silver and yes to free banking. The editor's objections to silver, like fiat money in general, were couched in terms of honesty of the most basic sort. He charged that those who favored silver were expecting "to reap thereby some peculiar advantage, not wholly compatible with old-fashioned honesty." Their object was to discharge public and private obligations through inflation, and thus they violated the sanctity of the contract. Not averse to redundancy when assailing the enemies of capital, he prophesied that opposition to Resumption (returning to the gold standard) was the breach in the wall through which the Communists would pour.[35]

Dawson did not simply ignore the problems of currency. He favored a repeal of the national bank law which operated to make the currency inelastic. Noting that the national banks were disposed "to contract their

---

32. Robert Huddleston Wiebe, *The Search for Order, 1877–1920,* The Making of America (New York: Hill and Wang, 1967), p. 137.

33. *News and Courier,* April 23, 1878.

34. Ibid., May 9, 1878.

35. Ibid., September 19, 1877, and May 8, 1878.

circulation at the very time that it should be expanded," he urged repeal of the 10 percent tax on state bank notes. He argued that state currency need not circulate beyond state boundaries and that maximum issue could be regulated by law. Within these limits state banks would always have the power to give relief in stringent seasons.[36] Dawson's position on banking contained sufficient economic truth to lend an air of plausibility. His was a solution that had appeal for a capital-starved region, but it also appealed to older and higher principles. As in the case of sound money, Dawson's economic philosophy owed much to the Jacksonian belief that money had certain moral properties and that economic power invited corruption. Well might Dawson ask, "How much more dangerous are 2,000 National Banks than was the one National Bank that Jackson denounced?"[37]

Accompanying Dawson's orthodox views on currency was an equally traditional commitment to laissez faire. Free traders all over the country frequently sought Dawson as a speaker or an organizer, and in 1885 the Charleston editor was honored with election as a vice president of the American Free Trade Association. Like so many low tariff men in the South, Dawson was not so orthodox as to abandon incidental protection for southern manufacturing. In a letter to Richard Dugdale of the SPE, Dawson spoke of the exemption of cotton manufacturers from taxation in South Carolina, "which exemption is in the nature of protection and has undoubtedly led to the starting of many Factories which otherwise would never have been projected."[38] One historian accurately described such inconsistencies when he noted that beneath the flowing ties and courtly gestures of the "so-called 'Bourbon' leaders of the South . . . lurked an eminently practical attitude toward the relationship of politics and business."[39] None, save doctrinaire free traders, would quarrel over the modest contradiction between a tariff for revenue only and incidental protection.

Dawson's adherence to laissez faire also led him to favor government regulation of the larger corporations whose power threatened the free flow of commerce. He advised Dugdale that the SPE should educate the public to "the difference between such business as transportation and telegraphing and such as Baker, Corn Factor, etc." Such a distinction would bring out the reasons "why regulation by the Government is necessary for the former and not for the latter group."[40] Dawson further believed that only the national government could regulate practically the powerful

---

36. Ibid., February 7, 1878.

37. Ibid., September 26, 1878.

38. Dawson to R. L. Dugdale, March 30, 1881, Dawson Papers, Duke.

39. John Ralph Lambert, *Arthur Pue Gorman,* Southern Biography Series (Baton Rouge: Louisiana State University Press, 1953), p. 89.

40. Dawson to Dugdale, March 30, 1881, Dawson Papers, Duke.

interstate corporations, that "in a few years there [would] be little or no trace, on the Statute books, of the famous Granger movement against railroads." National legislation, he believed, would avoid the evils of local antagonism to railroads and would at the same time "put an end to the railroad wars, which cost the shareholders so much, and in the end, are injurious to trade and industry everywhere."[41]

Despite his belief that only national regulation could rationalize the new industries, Dawson supported South Carolina's efforts to establish a strong independent regulatory commission for railroads. During the four years from 1878 to 1882 in which such legislation was agitated, the *News and Courier* sustained every action in a progression that led to rate-setting itself.[42] Local conditions prompted this inconsistency in Dawson's general attitude. The powerful Richmond and Danville syndicate, under the direction of Tom Scott and later William Pancoast Clyde, had virtually cut Charleston's commercial throat by diverting rail traffic in a north-south direction. The strong 1882 law, however, was gutted a year later in a legislative spectacle that saw Clyde sitting in the South Carolina General Assembly while his henchmen bribed legislators into amending the law. The *News and Courier* itself made such a dramatic reversal during the December legislative session that charges of its being bought were not difficult to believe.[43]

Six days later, N. G. Gonzales, then the paper's Columbia correspondent, described the whole sorry mess. In a letter to his uncle, he wrote:

> Never, never was there a more disgraceful spectacle in a white Legislature in S.C. than the manner in which this bill was carried through. Leading opponents of the bill were bought in with railroad attorneyships, etc; the negro vote—which carried the day in both houses—with free passes, and, doubtless, other inducements, and men on our side were spirited off and made so drunk with railroad champagne that we had to send carriages for them and haul them to vote. Clyde stayed in both Houses when the fight was going on and watched it with millionaire insolence . . . . The whole thing was disgusting and demoralizing. I tried to expose it but was muzzled. The paper flopped, also, in the nick of time.[44]

41. *News and Courier,* April 3 and June 13, 1878.

42. For a history of the South Carolina Railroad Commission see Albert Neely Sanders, "The South Carolina Railroad Commission, 1878–1895," (MA thesis, University of North Carolina, 1948), and idem, "State Regulation of Public Utilities by South Carolina, 1879–1935" (Ph.D. diss., University of North Carolina, 1956). See also Cooper, *Conservative Regime,* pp. 126–33.

43. *News and Courier,* December 17, 1883.

44. N. G. Gonzales to his uncle, December 23, 1883, Elliott-Gonzales Papers, SHC.

That same day Gonzales wrote to his nephew saying, "It is very disgusting, but I can't help it, and can only hope that a kind Providence will enable me to leave this unthankful, bloated and insincere journal before many months."[45]

The 1883 amendment which emasculated the South Carolina Railroad Commission, passed by only two votes indicating that the *News and Courier*'s reversal may well have been decisive—certainly influential. To a startled public, the *News and Courier* suggested that they should have little difficulty in distinguishing fickleness from "changes of conduct which are the result of study and inquiry and the comparison of theory with practice."[46] The public might have been better enlightened had Dawson simply argued that his avowal of state regulation was his inconsistency, that he had all along maintained serious reservations about the effectiveness of state action. Dawson needed no interpreter to explain the economic theory behind his action. A letter which reached his desk a few weeks later, if published, would have resolved any doubt. "It is of the utmost importance," wrote Clyde, "that the people of South Carolina should learn to regard this matter of capital and its rights from a common sense standpoint."[47] Men who believed in the immutable authority of the "invisible hand" could hardly be more specific. Another letter from Clyde seemed to punctuate the matter. "It is simply a question of supply and demand," Clyde wrote, "and one which the unalterable laws of commerce will regulate more quickly than anything else in these days when capital where it is untrammelled enters so vigorously into competition for any business which yields an unusual profit."[48]

The compulsive craving for order, manifest in Dawson's reluctance to tamper with classical theory and his efforts to restrict suffrage, was softened and balanced by the editor's ability to appreciate the social dynamics described by a Henry George. Working in the midst of this tension, Dawson developed a reformer's sympathy for disadvantaged groups in the new industrial order—a sympathy which, for the reasons discussed above, was never translated into positive programs for redress. Dawson resisted efforts to restrict immigration, resented any discrimination based on a man's religion, rebuked the nation for its shabby treatment of the Indian, fought zealously for Irish home rule, and felt that labor often got a raw deal. When the summer of 1877 erupted in the country's first great strike, Dawson scolded Godkin and his magazine for suggesting that labor should be willing to accept less. "There is no real comparison between a reduction which lops off luxuries and a reduction which cuts into

---

45. N. G. Gonzales to his nephew, December 23, 1883, ibid.

46. *News and Courier,* January 8, 1884.

47. W. P. Clyde to Dawson, January 14, 1884, Dawson Papers, Duke.

48. W. P. Clyde to Dawson, September 8, 1884, ibid.

the necessities of living." No "worthy man should be contented with such a life."[49] Unable to find meaningful solutions, Dawson's frustrations often led him to condemn the same groups for their understandable restiveness. They became a threat to order.

No group, excepting of course blacks, received more attention from Dawson nor better illustrated the editor's reform instincts than did women. Unfortunately Dawson has been remembered solely for the collection of stories, written by women, which he compiled and published under the title *Our Women in the War*.[50] From these tales and his declaration that women were the "soul" of the Confederacy, it has been argued that Dawson sought to return women to their antebellum pedestal. "Thousands of Daughters of the Confederacy float before our eyes!" wrote one historian of southern women. "But what Dawson, even in the eighties, married to a woman who had turned newspaper columnist after the war, did not comprehend was the thoroughgoing social change which the war had precipitated among southern women."[51] Few readers of the *News and Courier* would have accepted that judgment.

Dawson's early correspondence with Sarah was a constant source of encouragement for her to overcome a lack of self-confidence and to develop her talents as a writer. During their courtship and after, Frank urged Sarah to write for the *News*, paid her the going rate for articles, and advised her on matters of style and subjects but never dictated content. Part of Dawson's success as a newspaperman came from an ability to recognize talent, and his earnest solicitation of Sarah's work was no exception. When one of her early articles came down rather harshly on widows, he urged her to do a piece on widowers and to "be as hard on the men as you can." Another subject that needed writing concerned "the 'Employment (or want of employment) for Women,' that is, their difficulties of making a livelihood & need of throwing open to them more ways of living." On another occasion he enclosed some material for an article "about female clerks" and indicated that "one good point in the Federal administration" was the increasing number of women in clerical jobs.[52] To

---

49. *News and Courier*, August 22, 1877.

50. Compiled from the *News and Courier*, *"Our Women in the War"*: *The Lives They Lived, The Deaths They Died* (Charleston: *The News and Courier* Book Presses, 1885). Dawson also delivered a speech titled "Our Women in the War," February 22, 1887, to the Fifth Annual Reunion of the Association of the Maryland Line, in the *News and Courier*, February 23, 1887.

51. Anne Firor Scott, *The Southern Lady: From Pedestal to Politics, 1830–1930* (Chicago: University of Chicago Press, 1970), p. 102.

52. Numerous letters from Dawson to Sarah, ca. March–November, 1873, offer advice and encouragement. Quoted material from letter ca. March 16 and another dated March 18, 1873, Dawson Papers, Duke.

these encouragements, Sarah responded with a remarkable series of essays in which she spoke boldly to the degradation of women as second class citizens. Indeed, it would seem that Sarah and Frank worked together much as did Harriet Taylor and John Stuart Mill.[53]

Dawson's interest in the condition of women continued throughout his career as a journalist. One of his most brilliant editorials, and one which attracted an unusually large amount of correspondence, was written in 1879 on the subject of what it was like to be "Only a Woman!" The question posed concerned the future of the little girls and winsome women who today bore man's affection but tomorrow had to provide for themselves. He asked why one-half of all women could not find congenial work when they needed it most, and why they were not properly paid for the work they could get.[54]

To these queries, the *News and Courier* suggested several answers. First, society had little use for a woman once she ceased "to be diverting." Moreover, man treated "woman as a divinity as the readiest way of putting her on the shelf." When man could not claim the best jobs for himself or could not bar woman altogether, his "pride demands that, for the same quantity of work and kind of work, a woman receive less than is given a man." Equal pay for equal work was "simple justice," but simple justice was about the last thing society accorded women "outside of the region of pretty speeches and trifling compliments."[55]

All around were bookkeeping and clerical jobs which women could perform with equal ability, but men kept these easy jobs, leaving agricultural and manual pursuits neglected. While slamming the door in woman's face, men would "unhesitatingly give her their seat in a car, lend her an umbrella, or put themselves to direst inconvenience in buttoning her glove or picking up her handkerchief. What is pleasant to themselves they permit; what is useful to her they prohibit." The evils of job denial reached into the home itself, for unable to support herself and fearful of societal scorn, women were forced to make husband, housekeeping, and babies her end. "Absorbing if not elevating!"[56]

The root of the problem was man's reluctance to admit that women were equal. Dawson found unreasonable the fear that independence would make a woman less "womanly," for "no one is debased by the consciousness that independence is within reach, a consciousness that women yearn

---

53. Dawson kept Sarah's editorials in a scrapbook which he later presented to her. The scrapbook is in the Dawson Papers, Duke. For the Taylor-Mill relationship see Alice S. Rossie, ed., *Essays on Sex Equality: John Stuart Mill and Harriet Taylor Mill* (Chicago: University of Chicago Press, 1970).

54. *News and Courier*, March 29, 1879.

55. Ibid.

56. Ibid.

for and rarely possess." Dawson realized that woman's emancipation would be a long time in coming, but the good work would have begun when "everybody who reads these words shall ask himself the question, 'How shall this cherished daughter, whose sweet kisses greet me this fair morning, maintain herself, in honor, when, in God's providence . . . she must apply herself to such work as women can perform or eat the bitter bread of calculating charity."[57]

For his work Dawson was greeted "as the one in a thousand among men who dares use his pen or open his mouth to declare the injustice (amounting to oppression) exercised against that being they affect to defend and support."[58] But again Dawson's appreciation for a social problem was not matched by an ability to find solutions. He remained curiously ambivalent on the subject of woman's suffrage, even to the point of indulging occasional slights which denied his professed belief in the fundamental equality of the sexes. Again his fear of social disorder interfered with his sense of social justice. Admitting that the "emancipation of women" had far the better advocates on its side, he nonetheless saw the struggle as "an indication of a radical discontent with the principles which have heretofore regulated human government, and promises to be a fruitful source of disturbance in the immediate future."[59]

No discussion of reform would be complete without considering efforts to control the public vices which threatened the moral fabric. In South Carolina the chief evils were whiskey, gambling, and pistols. Like many latter-day Progressives, Dawson did not favor absolute prohibition, but rather supported efforts to place vices beyond reach of the vicious elements. Dawson believed that licensure laws were the best method for discharging the fiduciary obligation the better elements owed the working class. "Whiskey makes a brute of the white man," noted the *News and Courier,* "but it makes a ravening, ferocious beast of the colored man. These colored people are our wards, and their position as the laboring class makes it our interest to care for and protect them."[60]

---

57. Ibid.

58. Ibid., April 12, 1879. For a sample of the letters prompted by the editorial, see also ibid., April 3, 5, 25, and 26, 1879.

59. Ibid., October 4, 1879. Dawson's objection to suffrage extension rested principally on his apprehensions concerning Negro women who had always been "more violent than the men." He believed that "refined and delicate women would refuse to avail themselves of the privilege, and the already ignorant majority would be reenforced . . . by a horde of women depraved and infuriated."

60. Ibid., November 27, 1880.

Of the three sins, the deadliest was the gun-toting habit which had become as prevalent as military titles. On coming to Charleston in 1876, A. B. Williams expressed some pride in his "silver mounted twenty-eight calibre six-shooter" which "had been regarded in Virginia as quite a formidable weapon." His pride quickly melted when a South Carolinian warned, "Sonny, if ever you shoot any gentleman in this part of the country with that thing and he finds it out, he'll take it way from you and beat you with it for insultin' him." Such sentiments prompted Williams's remark that "the really well-dressed man wore a forty-four."[61] So ardently did Dawson work to put an end to hip-pocket justice in South Carolina that William Watts Ball could write, "The keynote of Captain Francis W. Dawson's policy. . . until his death in 1889, was 'law enforcement,' especially the enforcement of the law against duelists, lynchers, all men of violence."[62]

Dawson favored a registration law for hand guns and a complete prohibition of concealed weapons. When opponents cited constitutional scruples, the *News and Courier* replied, "We cannot admit that punishment for carrying concealed weapons will disarm the people, or deprive them of the right to carry arms. The Constitutional right is 'to keep and bear arms for the common defense,' and, if this is to be construed to authorize the citizen to buckle a pistol around his waist or dangle a sword at his heels, it cannot be stretched to cover a right to hide a pistol or dagger so that murder is made easy."[63]

As South Carolina struggled to achieve a reputation for law and order, nothing, apart from lynching, was more embarrassing than the Code *Duello*. Before the War it had been a symbol of aristocratic integrity, but after that great divide, the code passed increasingly into the hands of the swashbucklers who liked to honor themselves with self-conferred brevet promotions. While Dawson opposed the code on moral and religious grounds, most of South Carolina's *viri boni* opposed it because they saw the ancient combat being declassed.

The issue reached the boiling point on a summer day in 1880. Sometime between the hours of one and three o'clock on the afternoon of July 5, two parties drew up on the highland above Dubose's Bridge in Darlington County. The men quickly assembled, and after some discussion all but two withdrew to the side. Separating by an honorable distance, the determined men awaited the shot that would signal the commencement of their mortal combat. Three shots shattered the silence in quick succession. The first two

61. Alfred B. Williams, *Hampton and His Red Shirts: South Carolina's Deliverance in 1876* (Charleston: Walker, Evans & Cogswell, 1935), p. 64.

62. William Watts Ball, *The State That Forgot: South Carolina's Surrender to Democracy* (Indianapolis: Bobbs-Merrill, 1932), p. 171.

63. *News and Courier*, December 15, 1880.

shots fell harmlessly. The last, erupting from the gun of Colonel Ellerbe Boggan Crawford Cash, tore into the body of Colonel William McCreight Shannon. Shannon staggered, dropped to one knee, then fell under the weight of a tradition that was to expire with his last breath. In the bitter recriminations which followed, Cash wrote of the man he had killed, "I was fond of him, and the feeling seemed reciprocal. God forbid that I should now seek to cast reproach upon his memory. Most honorably has he settled account with me, and we have passed receipts as to the affairs of this world."[64]

The duel at Dubose's Bridge split South Carolina society along the lines that had been drawn since the campaign of '76. Senator Butler joined Dawson in condemning the duel, while Martin Gary came to the aid of Cash. The soon-to-be-governor, Johnson Hagood, and Wade Hampton sought to mediate the quarrel. Most of the ruling hierarchy refrained from condemning the code itself, but expressed indignation at the style in which the duel had been carried out. Senator Butler spoke for the rest when he wrote Dawson saying, "In former days the most punctilious decorum and chivalric courtesy distinguished the conduct of gentlemen in 'affairs of honor,' and coarse ribaldry and gasconade in correspondence was as odious as the brand of cowardice; but now the 'swashbuckler style' seems to be fashionable."[65]

Dawson launched a campaign to diabolize Cash in an effort to get tougher anti-duelling legislation. The editor's task was made easy by Cash's reputation. He was said to rule Chesterfield County much as if it were a feudal barony. Elected a colonel at the outset of the war, Cash soon fell out of favor with his men and returned home in 1862. For the duration of the war, he was exceedingly kind and generous to the needy, the wounded, and the families of soldiers, but among his detractors he "was never considered a South Carolina GENTLEMAN." His son was said to have behaved like a western desperado, periodically terrorizing towns, and the Colonel himself gained a reputation for numerous lynchings and cavalier shootings of his "niggers." An extreme Straight-outer in '76, he became a devoted follower of Martin Gary. Already anathema to the Conservative regime, Cash committed final apostasy by going over to the Independent Greenback Party in 1882.[66]

---

64. Ellerbe Boggan Crawford Cash, *The Cash-Shannon Duel*, with appendix by Bessie Cash Irby (Boykin, South Carolina, 1930), first printed (Greenville: *The Daily News* Job Printing Office, 1881), p. 5. For Shannon's side of the story see S. W. Henley, *The Cash Family of South Carolina* (Wadesboro, North Carolina: *Intelligencer* Print, 1884). For a complete description of the duel see Harris H. Mullen, *The Cash-Shannon Duel* (Tampa: Trend House, 1963), and idem, " 'Make . . . Arrangements for a Hostile Meeting' " *South Carolina History Illustrated* 1 (May, 1970), pp. 26–31, 62–63.

65. M. C. Butler to Riordan and Dawson, July 13, 1880, quoted in Cash, *Cash-Shannon*, p. 19.

66. Henley, *Cash Family*, passim.

The embittered Gary, now only months from his death, wrote Cash saying "I have no respect for the opinion of F. W. Dawson, who, I am informed is a bastard, and who I know to be a liar, a bribe-taker, a coward and a blackguard." Gary also described Dawson as a man who would be proscribed in every "civilized country," and whose "influence in this state is due alone to the countenance and support of such men as Hampton and Butler."[67] Not to be outdone, Cash described the editor as "a Yankee vagabond who 'guessed' at his father's name" before coming South as a spy. The Colonel conceded Dawson's "energy and decided smartness, for although his intimate and villainous connection with the Radical party and 'my dear Josephus,' and his shameless cowardice and utter disregard for truth have been thoroughly ventilated, he is now master of the situation and more completely rules poor, emasculated, Yankee-ised South Carolina, than did our immortal Calhoun."[68]

Butler did not escape the venom of Cash and Gary either. Gary thought Butler should be the last one to act a "censor morum" in the matter of duelling. The punctilious Butler had always recognized the code and had sent and carried challenges. The acknowledged leader of the "Hamburg Massacre," the Senator now denied it, "thereby adding perjury to the crime of murder." Gary further charged Butler with seducing and abducting the daughter of a neighbor.[69] Cash, now totally consumed with hate, wrote Gary asking for all the details on the aforementioned charges as well as some information on the rumor that Butler had been advertised in Washington as a "whore house rowdy." The vindictive Colonel concluded, "I wish to know every dirty trick he has been guilty of which is *publicly known* and *generally believed to be true*—Damn the proof—I need no proof for any charge I will make against him—*I hold all trumps on that point*."[70]

The vituperation of Cash and Gary was no doubt aggravated by their inability to get a free press and stood as suppressed testimony to the awesome power of the *News and Courier* to silence enemies of the Conservative regime. Cash complained of being "forced to go to Republican newspapers to obtain a right denied me by my own party." Such political ostracism could even excite the sympathy of a good conservative like A. B. Williams, who by that time had left the *News and Courier* to become editor of the Greenville *Daily News*. As a result Williams published Cash's pamphlet, but its effect may not have been all that the

---

67. M. W. Gary to E. B. C. Cash, August 3, 1880, quoted in Cash, *Cash-Shannon*, p. 26.

68. Ibid., p. 18. Cash remarked that Dawson already controlled the press and the legislature and that "when Hagood has retired I apprehend he will assume a dictatorship over the Executive Department."

69. M. W. Gary to E. B. C. Cash, August 3, 1880, quoted in ibid., p. 26.

70. E. B. C. Cash to M. W. Gary, January 25, 1881, M. W. Gary Papers, South Caroliniana Library, University of South Carolina.

Colonel could have wished.[71] "I was in sympathy with the dirty old villain until I read this effusion," wrote N. G. Gonzales, "but I now believe that R. & D. knew him better than I did and that he deserved hanging."[72] The *News and Courier* continued its systematic diabolization of Cash, and so successfully that ministers used him as exemplar of the devil incarnate. Cash complained pathetically of his anguish at seeing "Southern gentlemen trying to mimic Henry Ward Beecher and acting as buccaneers and shoulder-hitters for the *immaculate* firm of 'Dawson and Butler.'"[73]

After an extended trial, Colonel Cash was acquitted of the murder of Shannon by a jury of his peers. The *News and Courier* accepted it as another Scotch verdict of "Not guilty, but don't do it again," for the legislature had in the meantime given Dawson his tough anti-duelling law. Three years later the beleaguered Cash saw his son hunted down by a posse for the murder of the sheriff of Chesterfield County. Cash himself was tried as an accessory, and the trial revealed the colonel to be "a wretch *mentally, morally,* and *physically.*" The state's attorney wrote Dawson saying, "Cash I regard as a broken down old man who has lived to see the evil day indeed. Let us sincerely trust that a better day is dawning upon the country, now that the 'gentlemen' desperados are passing away."[74] In justice to Cash, even his enemies conceded that he had many friends and sympathizers which was "evidence that there is something in the make-up of the man of a meritorious nature," and to this day passions of loyalty can be stirred for Cash as well as for Shannon when memories of the duel at Dubose's Bridge are revived.[75]

For his efforts to end duelling, Dawson was knighted by the Catholic Church and was acclaimed throughout the country as a leading proponent of law and order. Belton O'Neall Townsend, whose criticism of violence in the campaign of 1876 brought a stern rebuke from Dawson for betraying his native state, praised the editor for his "liberal & progressive attitude on public questions, &, more particularly for [his] sterling work in attempting to revolutionize South Carolina public sentiment in regard to the spilling of human blood & taking of human life."[76]

---

71. Cash, *Cash-Shannon*, pp. 5, 18.

72. N. G. Gonzales to his brother, August 1, 1881, Elliott-Gonzales Papers, SHC.

73. Cash, *Cash-Shannon*, p. 21.

74. H. H. Newton to Dawson, May 29, 1884, Dawson Papers, Duke.

75. Henley, *Cash Family*, p. 5. For a recent even-handed treatment of both families see John Kennedy Dubose, Jr., "'Necessary Arrangements for a Hostile Meeting'" (Paper delivered at the Winter Meeting of the Camden Historical Society, Camden, South Carolina, 1978), and idem, "A Fateful Encounter," Camden *Chronicle*, March 8, 1978.

76. Dawson became a Knight of the Order of Saint Gregory the Great. This order was founded by Pope Gregory XVI on September 1, 1831, as a reward for zeal and devotion in an age marked by religious opposition and indifference; see note signed B R W, Dawson Papers,

As a liberal reformer Dawson saw government as the only real threat to liberty. His unquestioning faith in the natural laws of classical economic theory blinded him to the slavery it too could produce. Like a good Jacksonian democrat, he believed that concentrations of power should be dismantled, but also like a Jacksonian democrat, he was helpless to prevent the consequences of individual power in an acquisitive capitalistic society. What natural law had joined together, it ill behooved man to put asunder.

Being an active political editor Dawson had little time to reflect on these anomalies, but one editorial did capture the essence of his social philosophy. Appropriately titled "Individuality," the editorial lamented the great wave of "scientific materialism" that was sweeping the world. The new sociology argued that man was a product of cumulative forces of atoms and molecules set in motion long before his birth. Dawson believed the difference between this paganism and that of an earlier time was its suggestion that our work lives on in the race and thus further subordinated man to society.

> The creed is a cheerless one, and it is not surprising that the most vigorous protests against it have been uttered by those natures which still retain faith in motives and sanctions beyond the sphere to which Materialism would confine humanity. The political economist who sees that the triumph of such a doctrine means a deadly blow to the stability of the social order; the statesman who sees that the problems of government must be seriously complicated when the poorer classes shall have become persuaded that their only chance for enjoyment is to be found in this present life, and must be wrested from the minority which controls capital; the divine who perceives that the religion which he preaches has lost its hold upon consciences which no longer believe either its threats or its promises—all must perforce unite in trying to stem the current and to re-establish the bulwark of Individuality which is the surest safeguard against the flood of materialistic communism, whose God is Humanity, and whose hope is personal annihilation.[77]

In the hands of socialists, agrarian demagogues, and communist agitators the doctrine of materialism was especially dangerous, all the more so "because it really contains a certain truth." But to be partially true was not enough. "The age seems still to be far away from that larger synthesis," lamented Dawson, "which shall combine and reconcile that truth with others no less important, between which and itself an unnatural antagonism has been created." Exploitation of this antagonism was unconsciona-

---

Duke. Dawson's brother, Father J. W. Reeks, was instrumental in bringing Dawson's deeds to the attention of the Church. See Bishop of Southwark, petition to the Pope, May 1, 1883, MS copy, ibid. Quoted material from B. O. Townsend to Dawson, May 10, 1884, Misc. Letters, SHC.

77. *News and Courier,* August 2, 1879.

ble. "If the world in the Twentieth Century," concluded the editor, "shall prove to be an uncomfortable habitation for any but a *sans-culotte,* the Social philosophers of the Nineteenth will have to bear the blame."[78]

One historian of the American mind seemed best to describe Dawson when he wrote, "The Idealist was confident that in the climax of his argument he could resolve every contradiction, every objection, into an all-inclusive and affirmative synthesis, and therefore was generously prepared, in the opening portions of his discourse, to acknowledge to the limit the seeming evils of existence." In so doing the Idealist could celebrate "the enduring verities of religion and morality."[79]

---

78. Ibid.

79. Miller, ed., *American Thought,* p. xiii.

Chapter VI
1884: On Top Again

The year 1884 was a high-water mark for reformers in the Gilded Age. The inconsistencies and ambiguities that plagued men who sought to make the old order square with the new were temporarily laid aside. The presidency itself seemed within reach. After a generation of men like Johnson, Grant, Hayes, Garfield, and Arthur, reformers sensed a chance to restore the ancient probity of the early Republic. Enthusiasm abounded, but it differed, at least qualitatively, from the exuberance that had borne the last great Democratic president, Andrew Jackson, into the White House. Noting the difference between 1828 and 1884, Allan Nevins wrote, "But his [Jackson's] age was gone, and a prosperous, settled democracy is always cautious in dealing with policies, though often violent in its enthusiasm for a new spirit."[1]

If Republicans and Tories displayed a penchant for oligarchic rule, elements of the Liberal-Democratic persuasion looked for the strong man to unite them in all their diversity behind a common cause. Politics for them "was a drama . . . in which the degradation might be, if only for a few hours or days, assuaged in the leaping sense of victory that came when the chosen leader came out on top."[2] In casting about for a leader, reformers were to stumble onto an unlikely candidate in Stephen Grover Cleveland. Elected mayor of Buffalo in 1881, Cleveland's principal attributes were a reputation for honesty, a 250-pound frame topped off by a walrus mustache, and a propensity for still greater obesity. Within three years Cleveland was drafted from relative obscurity to serve first as governor of New York and finally as the twenty-second president of the United States. So sudden was the draft that people marveled at its unique place in American history. Woodrow Wilson wrote, "In him we got a president as it were . . . by immediate choice from out of the body of the people, as the Constitution has all along appeared to expect."[3] More than anything else, Cleveland's meteoric rise reflected the ability of the out party to cash in on the nation's general disgust with corruption. The Democrats almost succeeded on that issue in 1876, only to have returning

---

1. Allan Nevins, *Grover Cleveland: A Study in Courage* (New York: Dodd, Mead & Co., 1933), p. 189.

2. Robert Kelley, *The Transatlantic Persuasion: The Liberal-Democratic Mind in the Age of Gladstone* (New York: Alfred A. Knopf, 1969), p. 404.

3. Quoted in ibid., p. 295.

prosperity numb the sense of revulsion by 1880. With hard times again sweeping the land in 1884, the country was at last ready to repent its sins and resolve to lead an upright life, to give up mammon for Grover Cleveland.

Known as the veto governor, Cleveland commended himself to the American people by the enemies he made. John Kelly and Tammany Hall were contemptuous of the ex-sheriff from Buffalo, but for liberal reformers, such contempt was tantamount to an endorsement from the burning bush. The governor's philosophy, if one could call it that, also meshed nicely with the Liberal-Democratic credo. His commitment to individualism led him to praise small government and negative legislation, while his almost fatalistic sense of mankind's limitations "made him suspect reformers who talked either of equality or charity." He was not unsympathetic with the less fortunate, but he believed "a man of talent moved up; a man without talent could not claim society's help."[4] For the nation, Cleveland's negativism had a kind of religious quality about it, an experience of abnegation and ablution in which a sense of outrage served to purify the body politic. "In a real sense," wrote one historian, "Cleveland was to be a Liberal-Democratic leader more in the Gladstonian and Jeffersonian tradition, for he was fundamentally a moralist."[5]

Emerging rapidly "from out of the body of the people," Cleveland carried to prominence men who were fortunate enough to see a star on the horizon. Almost alone among southern editors and politicians, Dawson early cast his fortune with the New York governor, and it paid off.[6] The editor's position as member of the Democratic National Committee may have helped in sounding the political waters, but, whatever the reason, the News and Courier seemed to be keeping a Cleveland watch. On his election as governor, the paper observed political significance in the fact that "the men who give Cleveland his enormous majority in New York are not Democrats." When Cleveland pontificated that winning in 1884 depended on whether Democrats could "show the country that their present success means reform of abuses and good government," the News and Courier found "Presidential timber in such talk as that."[7]

But other candidates laid greater claim to the affections of Dawson's constituents. The neighboring Atlanta Constitution was strong for Tilden,

---

4. H. Wayne Morgan, *From Hayes to McKinley: National Party Politics, 1877–1896* (Syracuse: Syracuse University Press, 1969), p. 194.

5. Kelley, *Transatlantic Persuasion*, p. 294.

6. A clipping from the Cincinnati *Graphic*, 1885, observed, "The *News and Courier* was the first Southern newspaper of prominence to advocate the nomination of Gov'r. Cleveland . . . and . . . it was largely due to the influence of that paper that Mr. Cleveland received the Southern support which insured his nomination" (Dawson Papers, Duke University Library, cited hereafter as Duke).

7. *News and Courier,* November 9 and 10, 1882.

while South Carolina's leading patriarch, Wade Hampton, was a staunch supporter of Delaware's Senator Thomas Francis Bayard. Dawson was not temperamentally disposed to support either of these men. He believed both to be weak and scored them for failing to prosecute their candidacies (and, perforce, the causes they espoused) with vigor. He felt that Tilden's inaction permitted the election of 1876 to be stolen, and on meeting the sage of Greystone, Dawson described him as a man "who looks and speaks like a galvanized mummy."[8] Bayard was similarly berated. Dawson went to the Cincinnati Convention in 1880 with great hopes for the Delaware senator, but disappointedly wrote home, "Bayard has no bureau, no barrel and no boom. Providence is expected to take care of him, apparently, and there is a sad lack of push and activity." Furthermore, Bayard's greatest claim to southern support was a political liability that would not down. In 1861 the senator had given his famous Dover speech in which he denounced the use of force in restoring the seceded states. Dawson was correct in assuming that Bayard's candidacy would make the issue one of loyalty rather than reform.[9]

Thus the Charleston editor had good and sufficient reason to endorse Grover Cleveland, but a more personal motive was also involved. Dawson was never an uncritical admirer of Wade Hampton and was not reluctant to take an occasional editorial swipe at South Carolina's first citizen. The editor's grievances dated back to the campaign of 1876 and what he perceived to be rebuffs at the hands of Hampton and his lieutenants. The tension between the two men mounted when Hampton refused to support Dawson's candidacy for national committeeman in 1880. The editor won the election anyway, largely because Senator Butler was already Dawson's alter ego and because Johnson Hagood, soon to be governor, remained "true as steel."[10] After Cincinnati the *News and Courier*'s attitude toward Hampton became icy.

By March, 1881, Hampton was writing General James Conner expressing concern over "the animus of the N. & C." Disagreeing with Conner's impression that Butler had something to do with it, Hampton recommended treating the matter with "silent contempt." The senator suspected Dawson of "wanting to rule the whole State," and by May his complaints reached the editor. Dawson expressed "great surprise . . . that you now

---

8. Dawson to his wife, July 14, 1880, Dawson Papers, Duke.

9. *News and Courier*, June 21, 1880. For Dawson's assessment of Bayard's liability see ibid., June 12, 1884. As Morgan observed in *Hayes to McKinley*, p. 189, "Senator Bayard wanted lightning to strike, but hesitated to raise any rods."

10. Dawson to his wife, ca. June 21, 1880, Dawson Papers, Duke. See also Record Book, p. 104, in the box labeled "Drama, Poetry, and Accounts," ibid. The Record Book indicates that Hampton favored General John Bratton of Fairfield. Other relevant correspondence include Bratton to Dawson, May 26, 1888, ibid., and Dawson to Bratton, June 1, 1888, Hemphill Family Papers, Duke.

regard 'The News and Courier' as hostile to you," and told the senator of the great esteem in which he was held. Hampton accepted the expression of goodwill, but not without indicating that he was not alone in sensing the antagonism of the Charleston paper.[11] The wound closed but did not heal. A year later, N. G. Gonzales ventured an opinion of Hampton not inconsistent with that of his employer. Writing from the nation's capital, Gonzales declared the senator to be a "nonentity" in Washington and a man who, "living on his old reputation," often "puts on airs." Moreover, Hampton manifested "great contempt for journalists in the abstract but is careful to come to me when he wants anything put in which will show him off."[12]

During the early part of June, 1884, the *News and Courier* showed proper respect for Hampton's friend Bayard, but when Tilden opened the field by withdrawing his name, the voice of South Carolina's Conservative regime came out strong for Cleveland. Seeing this, Hampton wrote Dawson asking him to "go slow on Cleveland & not furl our Bayard banners until we can have a consultation with our northern friends in Chicago."[13] Dawson ignored the plea and continued to cultivate the state for Cleveland. Playing a little loose with the facts, the *News and Courier* got the bandwagon rolling by claiming Georgia and North Carolina solid for Cleveland and by listing the newspapers from Newberry, Orangeburg, Clarendon, Camden, Anderson, Winnsboro, and Kershaw as lining up behind the New York governor. The crescendo was carefully orchestrated to climax with the opening of the state convention on June 26.

The convention marked a personal triumph for Dawson. A clear majority favored Cleveland and opposed including congressmen in the delegation to Chicago. One delegate was reported as not questioning "the integrity of our Congressmen" but thinking "it better not to send them as delegates . . . on account of their profound preference for Bayard." Senator Butler wisely withdrew his name from consideration, but Hampton did not. The big test came on the selection of the four at-large delegates. Hampton was among those nominated. What happened next was a jolt to the South Carolina Democracy. A delegate rose to suggest that the senator be nominated by a "rising vote" of the convention, only to be greeted with shouts of no. A vote was then taken with the ayes carrying by a large majority. Another member then moved that the nomination be

---

11. Wade Hampton to James Conner, March 1, 1881, James Conner Papers, South Carolina Historical Society, Charleston. Dawson to Hampton, May 14, 1881; Hampton to Dawson, May 30, 1881; and Dawson to Hampton, June 18, 1881, Dawson Papers, Duke.

12. N. G. Gonzales to his aunt, March 1, 1882, Elliott-Gonzales Papers, Southern Historical Collection, University of North Carolina, cited hereafter as SHC.

13. Hampton to Dawson, June 17, 1884, Dawson Papers, Duke.

made unanimous, which the chair was forced to rule "so ordered" in the midst of a deafening silence.[14]

After disposing of the Hampton nomination, the convention proceeded to fill the other at-large positions, giving Dawson the highest number of votes. The Hampton forces then moved to have the delegation instructed to vote as a unit in Chicago—a wise move in that Hampton's presence could be expected to sway some of the delegates in Bayard's favor. The pro-Cleveland forces countered with an amendment calling for the delegation to bind itself to the will of the state convention. These motions were eventually tabled, but as the convention adjourned, the *News and Courier* counted fourteen votes for Cleveland and four for Bayard. In a letter to Sarah, Dawson virtually crowed, "you would have been delighted with the way in which I was treated by the Convention. I had the highest vote. There was such opposition to W Hampton that his election, by acclamation, was rushed through. Even then 70 or more delegates voted against him."[15] Hampton would have his turn in Chicago.

The atmosphere in Chicago was heady with convention excitement. Dawson arrived on the fifth of July and immediately found himself in the midst of a howling mob of "Beast" Butler's supporters. "The 'Siege of Paris' paranoia is here," he wrote Sarah, "such as we saw in Paris, & Gettysburg in the same way." In another letter he boasted of all the people who wanted to see and talk with him and described himself as "merry as a cricket."[16] The chirping stopped, however, when Hampton and the Bayard forces went to work on the South Carolina delegation. Leroy Franklin Youmans, attorney general under Hampton, was asked to present a seconding speech for Bayard, and the delegation's Cleveland majority began to melt. It turned out to be a poor trade for the Delaware senator, for Youman's speech was incredibly dull and was followed by the convention's most stirring appeal for Cleveland.[17] But Dawson was counting votes, not listening to oratory, and the results of the first ballot left him shaken. At midnight of the tenth, he wired Charleston reporting that the situation was "perplexing," the opposition to Cleveland bitter, and the prospects bleak.[18]

---

14. *News and Courier*, June 26 and 27, 1884.

15. Ibid., June 27, 1884. 151 ballots were needed to elect. Dawson received 191; Chris H. Suber of Newberry, 186; and Leroy F. Youmans, 145. As next highest, the convention simply declared Youmans to have a majority. See also ibid., June 30, 1884. Quoted material in Dawson to his wife, June 27, 1884, Dawson Papers, Duke.

16. Dawson to his wife, July 5 and 7, 1884, Dawson Papers, Duke.

17. Charles Callan Tansill, *The Congressional Career of Thomas Francis Bayard, 1869–1889*, Georgetown Studies in History (Washington: Georgetown University Press, 1946), p. 331.

18. *News and Courier*, July 11, 1884.

As balloting began on the eleventh, the cloud lifted. Cleveland's count began to inch forward as defections occurred in the Bayard ranks. A Bayard lieutenant wired his chief, saying, "They are all now trying to get the eye of the chair to change—Cleveland is probably nominated on this ballot—great confusion."[19] South Carolina held faster than most states, shifting from a ten-eight Bayard majority to a similar majority for Cleveland. Dawson was happy with victory but not a gracious winner. Of the Delaware Senator, he wrote, "His friends caused his praises to be sung *ad nauseum* by Southern men, and with few exceptions his votes came from the South. This sent him to the rear in short order." Back home the *News and Courier* was, if anything, less charitable. Vaguely hinting at reprisals, the paper declared, "The South Carolina delegates who turned against Cleveland (who is admitted here to have been the choice of the State Convention) are loudly by many people, and by some bitterly, criticised for not more fully representing the sentiment of the State."[20]

Hampton's support for Bayard was built on more than sentiment and revealed the general to possess, contrary to Gonzales's opinion, genuine political sagacity. Hampton believed that without Kelly's Tammany Braves the Democrats could never win New York, and he correctly observed that Cleveland's election as governor was more the product of Republican weakness than the candidate's strength. It took no astute observer to see that Cleveland's courting of the Independent Republicans cost him dearly in the wards of New York City, while Bayard, also claiming reform support, maintained a working relationship with Tammany. Hampton sensed that a successful campaign organization could not be constructed if the party ignored its mudsills. Bayard expressed this same *realpolitik* in a letter to the reformer David Ames Wells shortly after the convention. Bayard was alarmed at the manner in which the "Independent Press" was abusing John Kelly. "Wisely or other wisely," he warned, "the male inhabitants over 21 years of age are entitled to vote—and as the Independents have had their way in choosing the candidate, why should they not desire him to receive all the votes possible?—This heckling of Kelly, and caricaturing him in company with Blaine & Butler may sting him into opposition—and then where are the 30,000 voters needful to carry New York?"[21]

Hampton and Bayard represented a sensible middle course in an election that transcended compromise—a campaign that "took on the quality

---

19. Telegram, G. H. Bates to Bayard, July 11, 1884, Thomas Francis Bayard Papers, Library of Congress, cited hereafter as LC.

20. *News and Courier*, July 12, 1884. The assessment of sentiment in South Carolina was made by N. G. Gonzales reporting from Columbia.

21. Hampton to Dawson, June 17, 1884, Dawson Papers, Duke, and Bayard to D. A. Wells, July 25, 1884, Bayard Papers, LC.

of a great moral crusade."[22] Condemned by Dawson and the Independents for trafficking with ward heelers, they were equally scored by followers of Benjamin Franklin Butler who represented the labor-agrarian-greenback wing of the Democracy. One upset Butlerite wrote his old commander about dispatches from Chicago indicating "that while Wade Hampton cannot lift his finger, or turn his head without 'tremendous cheers' greet him, you by the same crowd 'were hissed.'" Another Butler Democrat wrote saying that if Wade Hampton's views on wages were Democracy, then "good Lord deliver us."[23] Old line party professionals were selling at a discount in 1884.

Despite the appearance of being above it all, Cleveland was represented by some of the most astute political managers to be found. In New York the editor and financier, Daniel Manning, along with William Collins Whitney, scion of a wealthy New England Democratic family, welcomed machine opposition for the reputation it would give Cleveland and then shrewdly maneuvered to get Tammany's votes. By keeping a stiff upper lip they waited Kelly out, and on the twelfth of September Tammany Hall endorsed the ticket. As one historian put it, "By September, Kelly knew that Blaine might carry the Irish wards, and once in office could easily keep them Republican in national elections, whatever they did in local affairs. The city organization was discovering that it had no real independence in national affairs outside the party."[24]

While Manning and Whitney took care of New York, Arthur Pue Gorman of Maryland took over the national campaign. The titular head of the campaign was William Henry Barnum, ex-senator from Connecticut and "a political hack of low reputation." The party was saddled with Barnum out of respect to Tilden and Barnum's large financial contributions, but Gorman, as chairman of the executive committee, planned strategy "with the wine glass and soft touch."[25] Dawson was privy to these arrangements and wrote a friend in South Carolina "that it was better to go in with Barnum, taking care that he should have about him such men as would assure wise political management." Dawson assured his friend that in Gorman the Democrats had "one of the most astute managers in the United States." Cleveland's biographer agreed, saying that in Gorman,

22. Nevins, *Grover Cleveland,* p. 156.

23. J. A. Whitaker to B. F. Butler, July 10, 1884, and William Hunt to Butler, July 1, 1884, Benjamin Franklin Butler Papers, LC.

24. Morgan, *Hayes to McKinley,* p. 212.

25. The assessment of Barnum comes from Nevins, *Grover Cleveland,* p. 160; that of Gorman from Morgan, *Hayes to McKinley,* p. 213. For a general discussion of Gorman's role in the campaign see John Ralph Lambert, *Arthur Pue Gorman,* Southern Biography Series (Baton Rouge: Louisiana State University Press, 1953).

Manning, and Whitney the governor had "three of the ablest political organizers of their generation."[26]

Dawson's early work for Cleveland gained him quick access to the party's campaign apparatus. Reelected to the Democratic National Committee, Dawson left Chicago and went on to New York. There, on the twenty-second, he had an informal conversation with Governor Cleveland and was "profoundly impressed with his simplicity of character, his earnestness & the entire absence of charlatanry & conceit in his composition." On Friday the twenty-fifth he wrote Sarah, saying that he had "become of so much importance apparently" that he was required to stay over until Tuesday for the committee meeting in Albany. At the meeting Dawson was appointed a member of the executive committee and assigned responsibility for conducting the campaign in the South Atlantic states. The next day he served on the notification committee for Thomas Andrews Hendricks, the vice presidential nominee and nostalgic holdover from the Tilden ticket of 1876.[27] Dawson soon left New York for Charleston, but not before his activity generated rumors that the editor was eyeing Hampton's seat in the Senate. "It is due to myself to say that . . . Senator Hampton deserves to be, and will be, his own successor," Dawson wrote, "and that, furthermore, I am not a candidate for any public office . . . and will not accept any such, at this time or hereafter."[28]

Arriving in Charleston, Dawson immediately set about the work of the campaign. Serving on Dawson's subcommittee for the South Atlantic states were Patrick Walsh of Georgia, Matt Whitaker Ransom of North Carolina, H. D. Semple of Alabama, and Samuel Pasco of Florida. After ascertaining their status, Dawson wrote Manning, indicating that all was well and offering advice on what the party should do about the Buffalo scandal. The scandal involved an illegitimate child which was the product of an early affair between Cleveland and one Maria Halpin. At the very least the scandal tarnished the impeccable image Cleveland had struck and promised excellent campaign material for the supporters of James Gillespie Blaine. Dawson joined the chorus of those calling for candor and complete disclosure. "The truth when plainly told and vouched for," Dawson advised, "will not hurt him in the least but the uncontradicted lieing of the Blaine organs may do some harm."[29]

26. Dawson to Daniel Sullivan Henderson, August 11, 1884, Dawson Papers, Duke; and Nevins, *Grover Cleveland*, p. 160.

27. Dawson to his wife, July 23, 25, and 29, 1884, Dawson Papers, Duke. See also John W. Holcombe and Hubert M. Skinner, *Life and Public Services of Thomas A. Hendricks with Selected Speeches and Writings* (Indianapolis: Carlon and Hollenbeck, 1886), p. 359.

28. MS note, New York, July 31, 1884, Dawson Papers, Duke. The note was published in numerous newspapers in both South Carolina and Georgia.

29. Dawson to Daniel Manning, August 11, 1884, ibid.

While the campaign degenerated into general mudslinging, Dawson and the executive committee developed more practical concerns with carrying a solid South which, combined with Indiana, New York, New Jersey, and Connecticut, was to send "pa" to the White House. Dawson's intelligence indicated that the South Atlantic states were safe with the exception of Florida and South Carolina. Florida presented two unique problems. First, the state had a large population of northern immigrants who, while voting Democratic in local contests, still tended to vote Republican in national elections. Second, a recent court ruling made it mandatory that Florida voters be registered during the month of October, a fact of considerable importance in terms of voter eligibility for the coming election. To overcome the former, Dawson called for campaign material from national headquarters which would exhibit the public record of Cleveland, believing that the "considerable body of Northerners" in Florida would be subject "to those influences and considerations which bring over to us so many Republicans in the North." In the matter of registration, Dawson urged men like Zebulon Baird Vance of North Carolina to make appearances during the month of October. So anxious was the national committee about Florida that Dawson had to write saying, "I beg you to believe that I have not neglected this Florida business, and that I would go instantly to the scene of action if my presence there seemed to be necessary." Later he wired for money explaining that the situation was "serious" and concluding, "I am in hot water." Cause for alarm was more apparent than real, and Dawson, working through men like Senator Wilkinson Call, could report a comfortable margin in November.[30]

South Carolina had her problems too, not the least of which was apathy. On numerous occasions Dawson expressed fear that the failure of blacks to run a state ticket would lull the whites into a sense of false security about the national elections. Other causes contributed to the general lack of concern. The new registration law had been featured as a sure way to reduce sharply the number of black voters, while redistricting made six congressional seats absolutely safe. Furthermore, home rule had given the white community eight years to solidify its supremacy. The old scare tactics were no longer effective. So when Dawson issued the traditional call for mass meetings, it was not surprising that many South Carolinians simply yawned. William Mauldin of Greenville wrote, "We held a mass meeting here on Monday. . . . Gov. Thompson, Sen. Butler & others spoke— crowd not very large, but attentive." By mid-October Dawson was writing the state chairman saying, "It is very plain now that we must depend

---

30. Dawson to W. H. Barnum, August 17, 1884; Dawson to A. P. Gorman, August 28, October 2 and 6, 1884; Dawson to Wilkinson Call, August 16 and November 8, 1884; Dawson to Z. B. Vance, September 3, 1884, ibid.

hereafter for our success on organization and not the evanescent enthusiasm of mass meetings."[31]

Another problem was the lingering threat of an Independent movement. In South Carolina the Greenback-Labor party reached its peak in 1882, but Dawson still felt it necessary to write his subcommittee asking if there were any sizable Greenback, Labor, or Prohibition sentiment in the respective states. In North Carolina, Dawson urged a coworker to assure the "working people" that the Democrats would continue "such protection as the tariff gives them."[32] But Dawson's real fears were more the product of labor and ethnic blocs at home. In early August rumors spread through Charleston that there was considerable disaffection among the "working men" and that the "Irish Democrats were organizing a Blaine Club." With some relief Dawson wrote headquarters, "I have made careful investigation, and can hear of only 3 Irishmen who talk Blaine, and they will either vote for us on election day, or not vote at all. Some of the working people have a squint towards Butler, but before the election the pressure will be so great that they can be depended on . . . to fall in line." Later Dawson warned South Carolinians that "opposition to the Democratic party in this State will, indeed, be alarming when a strong body of white Democrats, seeking political independence, shall give cohesion and energy to the colored masses."[33]

The black majority presented a unique problem in 1884. Gerrymandered out of their congressional seats, the Negroes held a 20,000-vote majority in South Carolina's Seventh District—a majority that could prove extremely embarrassing in the presidential sweepstakes. Though the blacks had been tacitly promised no opposition on their reservation, it soon became obvious to Dawson and his friends that the absence of opposition would allow the Negroes to mass all their votes for Blaine. The explanation was simple. Under the "eight-box" law, two boxes were designated as federal—one for congressional contests and the other for presidential electors. Without opposition at the congressional level, the illiterate and ignorant blacks could simply put votes for presidential electors in both boxes and thus insure that at least one vote for Blaine would find the right box. The

---

31. Description of the Republican strategy in Dawson to W. H. Barnum, August 9, 1884; and Dawson to G. T. Graves of Jacksonville, Fla., September 27, 1884, ibid. Evidence on mass meetings comes from Dawson to J. Q. Marshall of Columbia and Dawson to A. P. Gorman, October 11, 1884; and Dawson to James F. Izlar, October 14, 1884, ibid. Mauldin's observation is in the William Mauldin Diary, October 5, 1884, Southern Historical Collection, cited hereafter as SHC.

32. Dawson to Patrick Walsh, August 13, 1884, and Dawson to R. K. Battle, September 7, 1884, Dawson Papers, Duke.

33. Dawson to M. W. Ransom, August 13, 1884; Dawson to W. H. Barnum, August 17, 1884; and "Address of the South Carolina Democratic Executive Committee to the People of the State," September 1, 1884, written by Dawson, ibid.

Democratic solution was to find an opponent for the Negro congressman, Robert Smalls, thereby creating enough confusion so that black votes could be rejected. With election managers empowered to give assistance to the illiterate voter, every one knew that a little friendly assistance in the wrong direction would invalidate a vote.[34]

That Dawson intended to reduce the black majority by fraud was unmistakable. By mid-August he was convinced that opposition to Smalls was essential. By late September the congressional executive committee for the state's Democrats issued a call to convene for the purpose of making a nomination in the Seventh. Dawson hoped all along that an Independent Republican would emerge with whom they could cooperate, but failing in that, he believed that the next best strategy was to run a popular white Democrat. He wrote Gorman, "The purpose of the Committee in ordering the Convention is to insure opposition to Smalls . . . so that it will not be easy to circumvent our two-box law by voting for electors in each of the two boxes." He explained that it would be "an expensive business" and asked for $5,000.[35] Three days before the convention assembled, Dawson again wrote Gorman. "I do not wish to seem importunate, but I assure you that there is terrible need of extra-ordinary measures which cannot be carried out . . . without the assistance I asked for." He warned that "the action of the Congressional Convention . . . will probably be governed largely by what I hear from you." The assurance was forthcoming, and the Democrats nominated Colonel William Elliott of Beaufort.[36]

The money came in two installments, the last being received on the twenty-fifth of October. On that day Dawson revealed what he meant by "extra-ordinary measures" or "heroic remedies." Thanking Gorman for his cooperation, he noted that the "unaccustomed soil" of the Seventh was about to be "tickled with the political plough, [and] it is expected to bring forth a big crop of Democratic voters." To get the planting started, Dawson authorized associates throughout the black district to draw $250 on sight. Each letter ended with the suggestion, "If you need more than this, and can put it to good use, I will try to increase the appropriation. There are divers ways in which the money ought to be useful, which will no doubt occur to you."[37] And no doubt each correspondent knew what "divers ways" meant. Dawson himself offered a literal interpretation of the euphemism the following year. Advising his old commander, Fitzhugh

---

34. Dawson to S. H. Rogers, August 19, 1884; Dawson to Gorman, September 27, 1884; and Dawson to Samuel Dibble, January 26, 1885, ibid.

35. Dawson to Gorman, September 27 and October 6, 1884, ibid.

36. Dawson to Gorman, October 16 and 25, 1884, ibid.

37. Letters from Dawson to M. P. Howell of Walterboro, W. H. Cuttino of Sumter, Thomas M. Gilland of Kingstree, A. J. Hydricks of Orangeburg, and Thomas Talbird of Beaufort, all on October 25, 1884, ibid.

Lee, on how to win the gubernatorial contest in Virginia, Dawson called on his experience in South Carolina and ventured the following proposal:

> I hardly like to make any additional suggestions about the campaign, but there were many indications . . . that it was thought useless to make such a fight in the colored counties. Allow me to say that these counties are the very place to save votes. You can reach the white people in the white counties by argument, by persuasion, and by drawing the color line, perhaps, but in the colored counties you can save votes, if you cannot win votes in *divers ways*. The bed-rock of the whole thing is to make the colored people understand that the respectable white people of Virginia intend to rule the State. Make them understand this, and you will have no trouble. Black majorities will disappear as the snow melts before the sun. I am satisfied myself that the simple appearance of a band of red-shirts in each colored county, as a proclamation that the elements which control South Carolina, Georgia, North Carolina and the other states have made up their mind to control Virginia likewise, will do the business. There need not be a blow, nor even a harsh word. Satisfy 'Cuffy' that you are in earnest and he will abstain from voting.[38]

Martin Gary would have been proud.

Such herculean efforts must have induced a wave of revulsion among men like Congressman Smalls, especially when after Cleveland's election the *News and Courier* sought to reassure the black citizenry. Somewhat sanctimoniously Dawson wrote:

> But the colored people, to be reassured, need more than is given in legislation, or in declarations of political parties and public meetings. They who cannot read the Statute books are quick enough in observing the conduct of the white people around and about them. They who cannot hear the fervid declarations of the orator are keenly alive to the harsh words or threats of those who come in contact with them. Far more, we are confident, can be accomplished by personal kindness, by exact justice in the dealings of every-day life, by a settled determination to take no advantage of their ignorance, by indulgence toward their weakness and their prejudice, than can be accomplished by any law that the Legislature can enact. . . . This it is the part of the white people to do, because they are the white people—the superior and ever dominant race. It is the part of the white people to do it . . . because justice and right, and every law, human and divine, require it and command it.[39]

All the above applied only if Negroes abstained from exercising the Fifteenth Amendment. Black citizens of the Seventh would surely have

---

38. Dawson to Fitzhugh Lee, August 14, 1885, ibid. Italics added.

39. *News and Courier,* November 14, 1884.

entered a demurrer when Dawson wrote Gorman saying, "it is good for the country, is it not? to have the South on top again."[40]

Dawson's star rose with that of the South. Newspapers were quick to see that the Charlestonian's early support of Cleveland gave him a unique position among southern politicians and editors. Ruling Hampton and Butler out, the Atlanta *Constitution* concluded that "Captain Dawson would prove an admirable dispenser of federal patronage" and indicated that anyone wanting office "would do well to apply to the editor of the Charleston *News and Courier.*" The Columbia *Daily Register* was bitter. Clipping a notice from the Cincinnati *Time Star* which put forward Major Burke of Louisiana and Dawson as "Cleveland's chief advisers in the South," the *Register* vowed to expose "the aspiring South Carolina boss . . . even though the shadow of this Captain Dawson and Major Burke should cross our path." The Columbia paper noted that this same sort of thing "transpired after the Chicago Convention, in which this same Captain Dawson was trotted out to the front as the great leader of South Carolina, whilst Wade Hampton was noticed as a man of waning influence."[41]

In point of fact, Dawson honored his commitment to civil service reform and exercised restraint, with one exception, in taking advantage of his special relationship with the administration. He contented himself with a few supporting recommendations and general editorial suggestions that more women ought to be hired and that public offices ought to be for the public. For example, one editorial observed that not an occasion passed in South Carolina when a speaker did not say, "But for the interest manifested by the women, but for their zeal in urging father, brothers, sons, husbands and lovers to do their duty, but for the encouragement of their presence 'on this auspicious occasion,' but for 'the sunlight of their smiles, &c., &c., (see old files of *The News and Courier*) 'all would have been lost.'" Dawson then recommended patronage jobs as an excellent way of paying off a debt "so generously and so generally confessed to be due our gentle and efficient allies."[42]

The one exception to Dawson's general abstemiousness at the pork barrel proved to be disastrous. As a favor to Sarah, Frank submitted the name of James Morris Morgan for Consul-General of the United States, at Melbourne, for the British Australian Colonies. It was truly a labor of love, for Dawson never cared much for his capricious brother-in-law. Only months before Frank had written Sarah complaining that "Jimmie has been to see his friends at Bar Harbor & enjoying himself hugely while you

---

40. Dawson to Gorman, November 18, 1884, Dawson Papers, Duke.

41. Clippings from the Atlanta *Constitution,* dateline Charleston, November 21, 1884, and the Columbia *Register,* November 26, 1884, ibid.

42. *News and Courier,* May 18, 1885.

have been making yourself ill & me miserable by worrying about him. There is never a time that he cannot have his round of gaiety, no matter what others may suffer." Dawson could only conclude, "What waste of life it is to think of curing what is incurable."[43]

The obstacles to Morgan's appointment were truly formidable. Normal procedure dictated that the appeal be made to Secretary of State Bayard, whose presidential aspirations Dawson helped thwart, and through Senator Hampton, whose position in South Carolina was not always properly respected by the editor. To make matters worse, appointments of the new administration, particularly those from the South, met trenchant Republican opposition, and in South Carolina, Democrats proved reluctant to grant a favored plum to a man like Morgan who had spent so little time in the state. Hampton himself did not resist Dawson's efforts, but public reaction in South Carolina made it difficult for him or for Senator Butler to press the action with much vigor. It soon became clear that Dawson would have to cash in on his favored position with the president, and Cleveland proved willing to sustain his able lieutenant from Charleston. Morgan's name was submitted shortly after the inauguration, and when Bayard seemed to be dragging his feet on the application, Dawson went to the president, who requested that Bayard give the matter his earliest consideration. Two days later, April 17, the appointment was determined and the commission conferred.[44] Dawson's troubles were only then beginning.

The first storm broke over a pamphlet which Morgan had written the year before entitled *America's Egypt*. The pamphlet strongly commended Blaine for his conduct of foreign policy and seemed to endorse his presidential aspirations. When Bayard was given a copy, the secretary turned livid with anger and summoned Morgan to his office on the twenty-second of April. Accompanied by Senator Butler, Morgan sat through a virtual "torrent of abuse." Realizing nothing could be gained at the State Department, Morgan proceeded to the White House where he was greeted by Cleveland's customary scowl for office seekers. Jimmie described what happened next.

> He [the president] opened the interview by saying: "Mr. Morgan, do you really believe Mr. Blaine to be as able a man as you describe him in this article?" I replied: "I most assuredly do, sir." Mr. Cleveland's eyes twinkled and a humorous smile passed over his face as he said: "I am very glad to hear

43. Letters from Dawson to his wife, ca. September 16, 1884, Dawson Papers, Duke.

44. For evidence of Bayard's reluctance to move quickly see Robert M. Larner, Washington correspondent for the *News and Courier*, to Dawson, April 7, 1885, Dawson Papers, South Caroliniana Library, cited hereafter as SCL. Information on Dawson's personal visit with the president and Bayard's subsequent action on the nomination is in the *News and Courier*, April 25, 1885.

you say so, for if you did not regard Mr. Blaine as an able man I am doubtful if you would have the capacity to fill the important position I am sending you to. I wish you a pleasant voyage. Good-bye!"[45]

Jimmie wired Dawson, "Have seen the Prest and Secretary / it is all right."[46]

While Morgan was somewhat cavalierly parading through interviews, Dawson labored to convince his friends and the public that his brother-in-law was a loyal Democrat and that the pamphlet merely advocated a "spirited foreign policy."[47] The situation was all the more vexing because Dawson knew the defense to be a lie. When the article was first published, Frank wrote Sarah saying, "Jimmie has sent me his pamphlet, but I have not yet read it all—it is merely an argument for a 'spirited foreign policy' & Blaine on that account." A month later he wrote, "I am mortified at his Blaine talk . . . but I have no right to interfere, & will not." All this occurred at about the time Jimmie was being "a swell at Bar Harbor, in the train of a 'rich widow.'"[48]

The first storm did not compare for embarrassment with the second that struck. Republicans had resurrected the disabling clause of the Fourteenth Amendment in order to badger southern appointments. This section provided that anyone who had previously taken an oath of office, civil or military, to uphold the Constitution of the United States and who subsequently engaged in an act of rebellion against the same would be barred from holding any federal office unless said disability were removed by act of Congress. One of the early cases was that of General Alexander R. Lawton of Savannah who had been appointed consul-general to Russia. Cleveland's attorney general, Augustus H. Garland of Arkansas, worked hard to build a case which argued that the Fourteenth Amendment did not operate retroactively to overturn President Johnson's proclamation of pardon, dated July 4, 1868. The *News and Courier* could not agree and felt that the language of the amendment combined with subsequent action by Congress made it clear that it was retroactive and not simply a device to cover future rebellions.[49] Nonetheless, Garland's decision became the

---

45. James Morris Morgan, *Recollections of a Rebel Reefer* (Boston: Houghton Mifflin, 1917), pp. 427–28.

46. Morgan to Dawson, April 22, 1885, Dawson Papers, SCL.

47. Dawson to Bayard, April 22; to M. C. Butler, April 23; to Daniel Lamont, Cleveland's private secretary, April 25; and to Hampton, April 30, 1885. Each letter protested Morgan's loyalty to the Democratic party. The letter to Bayard is located in the Dawson Papers, SCL, and the others in the Dawson Papers, Duke.

48. Dawson to his wife, June 30, August 12, and September 16, 1884, Dawson Papers, Duke.

49. *News and Courier*, April 6 and 10, 1885.

policy of the administration and Lawton's appointment failed only because the general wanted "to relieve the administration entirely."[50]

It soon occurred to Dawson that Jimmie might suffer the same disability, having been an acting midshipman at Annapolis when the war broke out. Allaying Frank's concern, Jimmie wrote on April 13 denying that he had taken the oath either on entering Annapolis or when the acting midshipmen were moved to Newport. With this assurance the matter lay quiet until the first of May. On that day Secretary Bayard, receiving reports that Morgan had in fact sworn an oath, immediately wired Dawson. Within minutes the secretary had a reply. "I pledge you my word," Dawson telegraphed, "that I investigated fully the matter of his eligibility before recommending him to you and the President for appointment. Will telegraph you a full statement of the facts tonight." True to his word, Dawson wired a night message which related substantially the facts Jimmie had supplied and added that Morgan's resignation before graduation meant that he could not have been an officer. Swallowing hard, Dawson concluded that even if none of the above were true, Morgan was still eligible under the attorney general's ruling in the Lawton case.[51]

Working hurriedly Dawson sent counsel to Washington and called on the assistance of Sarah's brother-in-law, Richard Coulter Drum, the Adjutant General of the Army. The next morning, May 2, Drum went to the State Department and informed Bayard that he had personally "examined into Mr. Morgan's status in the Navy and found that he had not taken an oath on entrance or before leaving it." At the same time Dawson sent a seven-page letter to the secretary rebutting Bayard's reasons for seeking a delay in Morgan's departure and introducing his counsel, George Dwight Bryan of the Charleston bar.[52] By noon of the second, all seemed to be going very well indeed.

But even then Drum was rushing to a dispatcher with the following message. "I have seen a copy of the oath taken by Morgan in which he swears to support the Constitution. This will certainly cause rejection. Had he not better be delayed or return?" Despondent, Dawson returned to his desk and looked back over the seven-page memorandum he had drafted for Bayard. He then wired Drum, "Must be some mistake unless you have

50. A. R. Lawton to Bayard, May 4, 1885, Bayard Papers, LC.

51. Morgan to Dawson, April 13, 1885, Dawson Papers, SCL. Telegram, Dawson to Bayard, May 1, 1885, Bayard Papers, LC. Night message, Dawson to Bayard, May 1, 1885, Dawson Papers, SCL.

52. Telegrams, Dawson to R. C. Drum, May 2, 1885, Dawson Papers, SCL; Drum to Bayard, May 2, 1885, Bayard Papers, LC. The letter introducing Bryan to Bayard was written by Dawson, May 2, 1885, Bayard Papers, LC, while a MS copy of the seven-page memorandum is in Dawson Papers, Duke.

seen his signature to oath. . . . If upon receipt of my statement to Bayard you are satisfied to ineligibility, he had better return and resign."[53]

The next day, May 3, Drum was again in the dispatchers office. "I have seen the oath signed by Morgan. There is no question as to its authenticity." But Dawson had already determined his course. Ignoring the position of the *News and Courier* on the Lawton case, Dawson vowed to force the administration's hand. He knew Garland could not rule against Morgan "without making fish of him and fowl of Gen. Lawton." "Accepting the oath as a fact," Dawson wired Drum, "Morgan is not disqualified, and I shall make the fight in his behalf to the end." To Sarah he wrote, "It is an awful slip up on the oath, but never [fear] Jim is eligible. . . . Our aim is to get the question before the Attorney General & we can corner him. Don't allow Jim to halt or return. *Like Nelson, he need not see* the signal of recall. In the winter we can fight it out in the Senate." For his part Bayard was only too happy to turn the mess over to the attorney general, and Dawson could wire Jimmie on the seventh, "Enemy making devilish fight since you started, but telegrams from our counsel today after week's work allow you to sail in peace and hope. A dieu!"[54]

The Morgan appointment was but one episode in a federal patronage struggle that had little rhyme and not much more reason. Cleveland strove manfully to steer a middle course between the Scylla of a party starved by twenty-five years exile and the Charybdis of Mugwumps whose pretensions were no less demanding. The confusion made a mockery of planning and resulted in Cleveland's seeing "patronage as a way of avoiding factional fights by creating an element loyal to him. . . . He vaguely thought office holders should favor the government over their party . . . but loyalty to Cleveland became the acid-test of fitness." Under these circumstances Cleveland could appreciate a letter from Dawson that read, "At the bottom it is nothing more than a concentrated movement to condemn the Administration for recognizing the claims of leading Democrats, and, as I believe, to weaken me personally in my own state in support of you and your administration."[55]

Back home the struggle took no less toll on the Charleston editor. In a letter to Gorman, Dawson complained about "my friends in South Carolina who believed in any body but Cleveland, and who have always hated me because I have been successful in politics and otherwise, and have lived

---

53. Telegrams, Drum to Dawson, and Dawson to Drum, May 2, 1885, Dawson Papers, SCL.

54. Telegrams, Drum to Dawson, and Dawson to Drum, May 3, 1885, Dawson Papers, SCL. Dawson to his wife, May 4, 1885, Dawson Papers, Duke. Dawson to Morgan, May 7, 1885, Dawson Papers, SCL.

55. Morgan, *Hayes to McKinley,* p. 249. Dawson to Cleveland, May, 1885, Dawson Papers, Duke.

only about twenty years in the State."[56] David Wyatt Aiken, congressman and formerly the agricultural reporter for the *News and Courier,* led the denunciation of the Morgan appointment. The upshot was a call by the Blackville Democratic Club to consider resolutions critical of Dawson's action. Convening on Saturday the twenty-fourth of May, the citizens of Blackville were surprised to find the accused editor of the *News and Courier* personally on hand to defend himself. After an eloquent appeal, the Democratic Club gave Dawson a clean bill and adjourned. So disgusted was the *News and Courier*'s reporter, Carlyle McKinley, that he sarcastically suggested the investigation should have been more thorough and extended "so as to include an inquiry into the important question whether Morgan ever lived in a State that was ruled by a Republican Governor, whether he ever received a letter from the hands of a Republican postmaster, and, finally, whether he ever lived in the same town or county with a Republican."[57]

The bitterness reached into the family itself. Sarah's oldest brother, Philip Hickey Morgan, the only Unionist of the four Morgan brothers and a Republican, could not retain his consular post in Mexico "while Jim, who turned Republican, in hope of office, & was blatant, as alleged, for Blaine, is palmed off as a democrat, & gets a soft place." Dawson could only sigh to Sarah, "As I told you from the first, you are punished (or honored) because I, being unable to do the impossible for the elder brother, did what I could for the younger."[58]

Jimmie's appointment was not finally confirmed by the Senate until August 4, 1886. When Senator Butler wired Dawson saying the appointment would go through, Frank wrote a note to Sarah, who was then in France. "So the agony is over. . . . There is one happy woman in Europe to-day; and one very happy man in Charleston. It has been a weary, weary fight for me; and a very costly one too." As an after thought he scribbled, "Horay! Hip! Hip! Hurrah!"[59]

It had been a strange year. Beginning with the struggle for Cleveland's nomination against the wishes of the state's acknowledged leader and hero, passing through an arduous campaign which brought that "leaping sense of victory . . . when the chosen leader came out on top," and ending with "the costliest act of kindness I have ever done," the year was anything but dull. In light of Morgan's controversial status as an acting midshipman, it was ironical that Dawson's only personal reward from Cleveland was appointment to the Board of Visitors for the United States Naval Academy.[60] Still, it was good to be riding the crest.

---

56. Dawson to A. P. Gorman, May 3, 1885, Dawson Papers, Duke.
57. *News and Courier,* May 25, 1885.
58. Dawson to his wife, May 3, 1886, Dawson Papers, Duke.
59. Dawson to his wife, July 30, 1886, ibid.
60. Dawson to his wife, ca. July, 1886, and W. C. Whitney to Dawson, May 28, 1886, ibid.

AUSTIN JOHN REEKS, age 19, London, 1859 *(Manuscript Department, William R. Perkins Library, Duke University)*

LIEUTENANT F. W. DAWSON (NEE REEKS), age 22, Richmond, 1862 *(Manuscript Division, William R. Perkins Library, Duke University)*

DAWSON, Charleston, November 1874 (*Manuscript Department, William R. Perkins Library, Duke University*)

The Dawson house at 43 (now 99) Bull Street *(Manuscript Department, William R. Perkins Library, Duke University)*

SARAH FOWLER MORGAN DAWSON, age 44, Paris, 1886 *(Manuscript Department, William R. Perkins Library, Duke University)*

News and Courier offices, 19 Broad Street *(Manuscript Department, William R. Perkins Library, Duke University)*

The staff of the *News and Courier,* 1886. (From left to right)
FRONT ROW: Roswell T. Logan, John L. Weber, James Armstrong, Carlyle
McKinley, Matthew F. Tighe. BACK ROW: R. M. Solomons, John A. Moroso,
R. A. Smith, Francis W. Dawson, J. C. Hemphill, Yates Snowden, D. L.
Selke. *(South Caroliniana Library, University of South Carolina)*

CAPTAIN F. W. DAWSON, age 48, 1888 *(Manuscript Department, William R. Perkins Library, Duke University)*

SARAH DAWSON with grandchild, ca. 1900 *(Manuscript Department, William R. Perkins Library, Duke University)*

Chapter VII
Of Fathers and Sons: The New South

The *News and Courier* always reserved the first day of September to publish its annual review of Charleston's commercial and industrial activity. The review for 1886 proved a little less sanguine than those of previous years, and for good reason. Charleston's gross trade had fallen almost a million dollars from the total of the previous September. Dawson blamed it on the failure of Charleston to control a single railroad in South Carolina and on the inability of her people to recognize that there were "changes in the modes of transacting business which are incompatible with the easygoing methods of the fathers and grandfathers of the present generation." But there were also some encouraging signs. More and better houses, more carriages and horses, more traveling than before, a better grade of goods displayed in the various shops, and a marked advance in real estate values—all pointed to better times if "no tidal wave of prosperity."

And so a casual reader of September 1, 1886, would have been exhorted to build better for the future. But there were no casual readers of the *News and Courier* that day, for every Charlestonian was already painfully aware of what appeared on the eighth page of that edition. "A TERRIBLE EARTHQUAKE—CHARLESTON SHAKEN FROM CENTRE TO CIRCUMFERENCE—The Whole City Injured—Sad Loss of Life—Five Successive Shocks—Scenes and Incidents—The Most Disastrous Event in the City's History." How those headlines came to appear on the eighth page of the *News and Courier* formed one of the more dramatic episodes in Dawson's journalistic career.

On the evening of August 31 Dawson retired early from his office. The ability to get most of the work done in advance was one of the good things about the annual commercial review. With Sarah and the children in Europe, Captain Dawson had a chance to catch up on some personal items in his home study. He was in his third floor room enjoying the summer evening quiet when a soft rumbling noise quickly rose to a terrific roar. The great Bull Street house "seemed literally to turn on its axis." Dust and debris choked the room as the ceiling cracked scattering plaster all over. A huge tank in the attic burst, flooding the bedrooms and sending water cascading down the spiral staircase. Statues and lamps were wrenched from their bases and hurled to the floor. The large porch with its massive pillars and solid marble steps "was swept away as though it had been shaved off with a razor."[1] The time was 9:51.

---

1. *News and Courier,* September 1, 1886. For a vivid description of Dawson's actions following the quake, see Miriam Dupre to Sarah Dawson, September 1, 1886, Dawson Papers, Duke University Library, cited hereafter as Duke; and M. Dupre to Mrs. J. C. Hemphill, September 27, 1886, Hemphill Family Papers, Duke. Miriam was Sarah's sister.

Dawson rushed into the street. The air was full of wails and shrieks. "From every side in that quiet neighborhood came the cry, 'God help us!' 'God save us!' 'Oh, my God!'" For a moment it was like the war all over again, only this time it was "worse than the worst battle of the war." The terror heightened as shocks followed in rapid succession at 10:09, 10:14, and 10:30. In the midst of this horrible din, Dawson started for the *News and Courier* building. Already a salamandrine glare arched above the city as fire began to do its deadly work. By the time Captain Dawson reached the offices on Broad Street most of the staff had fled.[2]

Working quickly, the editor rounded up enough help to get out a shortened eight-page edition. As a result of these labors, Charlestonians, cut off from the rest of the world by a disastrous earthquake, were able to read of their own destruction from the pages of their own newspaper only hours after it happened. It was a remarkable feat of journalism. The admiration expressed on all sides may have momentarily turned Dawson's head, for he felt compelled to apologize when too few compositors showed up to produce an edition the following day. In a letter to Sarah he noted that she would "find that *The News and Courier* was only suspended for one day, and that was not because of any injury to the establishment, but because of the cowardice of the compositors." Conceding that he was perhaps a bit too harsh in calling it cowardice, he nonetheless begrudged their thinking "more of running to their families than sticking to their posts." For sometime thereafter the staff of the *News and Courier* was goodnaturedly divided into "quakers and non-quakers."[3]

The continued publication of the newspaper served as a steadying influence for Charlestonians during the crisis, and Dawson's reputation rose as he assumed a commanding role in efforts to relieve the city's suffering. He served on the more important committees, was instrumental in making contact with charitable sources at the North, and daily encouraged and directed the stricken citizenry through the agency of the *News and Courier* . "As a rule every great emergency develops its hero," wrote the Augusta *Chronicle,* "and in this instance Capt. F. W. Dawson has become master of the situation."[4]

---

2. *News and Courier,* September 1, 1886. See also Robert Molloy, *Charleston: A Gracious Heritage* (New York: D. Appleton-Century, 1947), pp. 266–71; and David Duncan Wallace, *The History of South Carolina,* vol. III (New York: American Historical Society, 1934), pp. 333–35.

3. Dawson to his wife, September 19 and 27, 1886, Dawson Papers, Duke. Though the paper was not published on the second, Dawson forwarded his story to the New York *World* where it appeared under the same date.

4. Augusta *Chronicle,* September 15, 1886. Dawson described his activity in letters to his wife, September 5, 8, 10, 19, 20, 24, 26, and 27, 1886, Dawson Papers, Duke.

For Dawson it was a personal triumph. "Perhaps nothing less than the Charleston earthquake of August 31, 1886," wrote Jonathan Daniels, "could have made his acceptance final among his neighbors." After turning "to the English-born editor for leadership," the representatives of the oldest families were only then willing to give this "newcomer (by Charleston standards) the accolade of their appreciation and acceptance."[5] On the morning of November 10, as Dawson came down to breakfast, he was surprised to find a beautiful silver service on the table before him. Attached to the silver was a note signed by twenty-six friends and leading citizens of the community. In the quiet of the dining room (Sarah and the children were still in Europe) Dawson read:

> It is today exactly twenty years since you first came to Charleston and cast your lot with its citizens. In that period have happened, in quick succession, events which will always be counted as among the most momentous in the history of Charleston. In the narrative of all these events, your name will appear as one of the chiefest actors, and always in the part of striving for the weal of our city and its citizens.[6]

As he laid the note back on the tray, Dawson no doubt remembered the letters to his mother during the war, filled with pledges to succeed in his adopted land. He must have wished that she, more than anyone else, could have been with him at that moment.

Francis Dawson was not the only man whose reputation was enhanced by the earthquake which racked the southeastern seaboard. One hundred and fifty miles away, Henry Woodfin Grady felt the tremors and, like Dawson, rushed to his office to take charge. After reading the dispatches which were pouring in, Grady realized that only Charleston remained silent. The next morning brought alarming reports of death and destruction. Grady's intuition told him it was "the most important news event in the South since the surrender of the Confederate armies," and he made plans to go immediately to the scene of the disaster.[7] That decision would catapult the young Atlantan into national prominence.

Grady reached Charleston on the evening of September 2. Within hours he was sending vivid descriptions of the devastation to newspapers all over the country. He toured the city, interviewed the principals in the drama, including Dawson, and returned to Atlanta with still more material for

---

5. Jonathan Daniels, *They Will Be Heard: America's Crusading Newspaper Editors* (New York: McGraw-Hill, 1965), p. 201.

6. Friends to Dawson, November 10, 1886, and Dawson to his wife, same date, Dawson Papers, Duke.

7. Raymond Blalock Nixon, *Henry W. Grady: Spokesman of the New South* (New York: Alfred A. Knopf, 1943), pp. 3–7.

publication. Published over his full name, these articles brought instant fame and an invitation to address the New England Society of New York on the subject of the New South. "That one brief talk, described by Champ Clark a generation later as 'the most famous after-dinner speech within the memory of any living man,' established Henry W. Grady as the acknowledged spokesman of the Southern spirit of progress and goodwill."[8]

Grady made his stirring address on the evening of December 22, 1886, at Delmonico's. Borrowing lines from Benjamin Harvey Hill, he proclaimed, "There was a South of slavery and secession—that South is dead. There is a South of union and freedom—that South, thank God, is living, growing every hour." In words which would later win countless oratorical contests throughout the South, Grady gently interred the Old South and resurrected the New with an assertion that the nation had at last produced a "typical American"—a man who embodied the virtue of a diverse people and united what stern custom parted wide. The audience assembled at Delmonico's that evening burst into a frenzy of sympathy when Grady declared that "the first typical American, the first who comprehended within himself all the strength and gentleness, all the majesty and grace of this republic, [was] Abraham Lincoln."

With few exceptions the speech was praised throughout the South, and what objections were voiced came from free-trade journals not liking Grady's protectionist views. Compared with the general reaction, the criticism raised by the Charleston *News and Courier* seemed personal, vindictive, and churlish. The motive was likely jealousy, along with pique at imagined slights, and Dawson felt them with childlike intensity. Yet the resulting journalistic skirmish between the *News and Courier* and the *Constitution* did much to reveal Dawson's thinking on the New South.

Six days passed before Grady's speech appeared in the Charleston paper, and the editorial reply never mentioned his name or his famous speech. Dawson denied "absolutely that among thoughtful Southerners there is any such thing as an intelligent recognition of Mr. Lincoln as a typical American." The South was willing to give him credit for "his shrewdness, his knowledge of men, his loyalty, his perserverance," but "he was never a typical American, unless such an American must necessarily be coarse while kindly, vulgar though good-hearted, ill-bred while acute, awkward while amiable, and weak in act while strong in word." Though unwilling to praise Lincoln as a model American, Dawson did perceive traits that made him "a typical western man," or "perhaps a type of new class who are rising into prominence in parts of the 'New South.'"[9]

The most damning characteristic of this "new class" of men was their seeming willingness to adopt what one South Carolinian termed "policy

---

8. Ibid., p. 7.

9. *News and Courier,* December 29, 1886.

and expediency as standards."[10] They appeared all too eager to admit Garfield's dictum that the North was "eternally right" and the South "eternally wrong" in an effort to gain economic concessions from the North. Again with Grady in mind, Dawson agreed with the Augusta *Chronicle* that "conversions under excitement and enchantment" led to this kind of cowardly confession in the midst of "post-prandial pledges," and he condemned those who by the "witchery of pen or voice" would seek to extinguish "the principle of the 'Old South.'" Dawson reminded those who would be expedient or politic that "it is not for the sons to apologize for their fathers, whose homes and honors they inherit."[11]

In responding to the *News and Courier*'s splenetic treatment of its hero, the *Constitution* accidentally stumbled onto the pique that seemed to motivate Dawson's editorials. The Atlanta paper observed that while Mr. Grady was in New York striking a "note of harmony and fraternity," Charleston alone gave it no notice, even though "at the very moment the speech was made Charleston was enjoying the benefit of $800,000 contributed by the stingy and puritanical North." The reference was to earthquake relief, and such an obvious attempt to cast Dawson and his paper in the role of ingrates angered the Charleston editor. In a now-that-you've-mentioned-it editorial, Dawson charged that Grady's articles from Charleston, off which he had won acclaim, actually belittled the significance of the earthquake, thereby limiting the contributions that would otherwise have flowed freely from the North. The editor went on to suggest that the response of the American people to the Charleston earthquake, much more than Grady's speech, proved the harmony existing between the sections. Dawson accused Grady of being a latecomer to the field of sectional reconciliation and compared the Atlantan to "a leaf on the bosom of a broad river. As a leaf, he partakes of the flow of the mighty stream without directing or influencing it."[12]

Dawson was so envious of Grady's success that he accepted two invitations to address national audiences, even though—as he confessed to Sarah—it would mean being burdened with an "awful o-r-a-t-i-o-n to write; & I can't orate." The first speech was delivered on January 12, 1887, at the Cooper Union Hall in New York on the subject of free trade. The second address was prepared for the eighth annual reunion of the Association of the Maryland Line, a Confederate survivors' association, and was delivered in Baltimore on the evening of February 22. Concerning both invitations Dawson wrote that "as Henry Grady had been reaping the

---

10. J. J. Pringle Smith to W. P. Miles, June 29, 1877, William Porcher Miles Papers, Southern Historical Collection, University of North Carolina, cited hereafter as SHC.

11. *News and Courier,* December 30, 1886.

12. Ibid., January 1, 1887.

harvest of reconciliation & praise from the seed that I had been amongst the first to sow, I thought it advisable to keep to the front myself."[13]

Dawson was overly modest about his abilities as a speaker, but even so, the speeches were no great success. The Cooper Union address was numbingly dull, containing much of the servile language that had become stock-in-trade for New South orators confronting northern audiences. The Baltimore speech was equally tedious, but because it was prepared for a more empathetic audience, the address had its moments of brilliance, particularly when Dawson sought to praise where others apologized. He told the survivors:

> It is well enough to cover our wounds and hide our scars. But never let it be denied—that the scars and wounds are there; that they are there, not to rankle or to irritate, but as signs and tokens of the days that are dead, the glories and disasters whose memory we could not blot out if we would, and would not if we could! Too much history has already been written for us. Too little has been written by ourselves, and for the justification of our people. It is, then, but meet and right that, on such an occasion as this, the truth shall be told, and the whole truth, even if it hurts the feelings of "our friends, the enemy."[14]

The private reaction to Dawson's Baltimore address expressed more clearly the line dividing his conception of a New South from Grady's. The letters to Dawson, coming largely from "professional southerners," men whose chief ally seemed to be "inertia,"[15] made Dawson appear more a patron of the "Old South" than he was in reality. One South Carolinian wrote that a recent trip North made him feel "even more keenly than before, the false position we were sought to be placed in by the utterances of Henry Grady, and it was therefore with additional pleasure that I read the antidote so promptly and efficaciously applied by you the other day." The correspondent also mentioned referring to Dawson's editorials while North "as evidence that his [Grady's] ideas by no means meet with universal acceptance."[16] Another writer, praising the speech as "one of the most valuable contributions to the history of the 'lost cause,'" commended Dawson's courage not to indulge in "weak and cowardly concessions to the dominant sentiment and the repudiation of principle for the sake of

---

13. Dawson to his wife December 26, 1886, and February 8 and 11, 1887, Dawson Papers, Duke.

14. *News and Courier,* February 23, 1887.

15. Edd Winnfield Parks, ed., *Southern Poets,* American Writers Series (New York: American Book, 1936), p. xiv.

16. Philip E. Chazal, to Dawson, February 26, 1887, Dawson Papers, Duke.

securing policy."[17] William Gordon McCabe, founder of the University School at Petersburg, expressed similar sentiments, while Charles Colcock Jones, Jr., critic of the New South and staunch defender of the faith, found the address truly "admirable" and promised to circulate copies among his friends.[18]

Francis Dawson was in no danger of giving up hope in the promise of a New South. He simply believed that reconciliation with the North could not be bought at the expense of forgetting or apologizing for the past. He was convinced that the history of the War for Southern Independence had to be written by southern writers. He argued that sectional pride preceded sectional reconciliation, that "the vindication of the South, at last, is the vindication of a part of the Union, and it will be to the honor and strength and glory of the whole Union that that vindication shall be full and complete as it surely will be."[19] If Grady were taking his cue from Abe Lincoln, then Dawson seems to have had his ear cocked in the direction of Jeff Davis.

Several explanations can be offered for Dawson's having place in the pantheon of New South prophets while receiving the praise of those who sought to preserve Old South virtues. Unlike some apostles of the New South, Dawson did not seek to establish a continuous thread between the old and the new—to fashion, as it were, a "vital nexus" between the past and the present.[20] For Dawson the war was more cataclysmic. It severed the thread of history. On one side of that dividing line lay the southern conception of a constitutional republic that was no less valid for having been defeated. On the other side lay a new constitutional necessity, whose rectitude depended on the existing secular power and faith in the beneficence of Providence. Such a view of history lacked the easy certainty of those who made the past more usable by forging links to the present. Nor did it advance arguments made understandable by an unbroken, linear view of history. In Dawson's words it was enough to teach the children "that it was might which triumphed over right, in order that the ways of Eternal Providence should be made manifest—for our good in the end, for the good of the sinning and the sinned against."[21]

Dawson's separation and embrace of both the past and the present was made easier by neutralizing the moral issue of slavery. He objected to

---

17. W. L. T. Prince of Cheraw to Dawson, June 28, 1887, ibid.

18. W. G. McCabe to Dawson, June 13, 1887; and C. C. Jones, Jr., to Dawson, June 7, 1887, ibid.

19. *News and Courier,* February 24, 1877.

20. For a discussion of the New South effort to fashion a usable past, see Paul Morton Gaston, *The New South Creed: A Study in Southern Mythmaking,* ch. 5, (New York: Alfred A. Knopf, 1970), "The Vital Nexus."

21. *News and Courier,* November 30, 1882.

assertions by men like Grady that slavery had been the central issue of the war. The English-born editor much preferred the view that led him to enlist on the side of the South to begin with—a view which transformed the war into an aggravated constitutional dispute between the proponents of centralization and those of home rule. Slavery itself, Dawson argued, was a doomed institution. England's experience proved that the advance of civilization and the institution of slavery were incompatible. Thus, by removing the moral issue of slavery, by neither condemning nor defending the institution, Dawson was able to find "no incompatibility between the obligations of the living present and the fragrant memories of the days that are not."[22]

Other elements went into making up the differences which distinguished Dawson's New South from that of Henry Grady's. As an alien, Dawson took the history and prejudices of his adopted land much less for granted. The need to sink roots and to prove loyalty, especially in staid old Charleston, was a compelling force in shaping Dawson's career. Another difference was age. The Charleston editor was ten years older than his Atlanta counterpart—years which were more like a full generation, for they made one man a veteran while the other was still a schoolboy. Walter Hines Page captured the dramatic implication of this age difference when he said of those who survived the war:

> It gave everyone of them the intensest experience of his life and ever afterward he referred every other experience to this. Thus it stopped the thought of most of them as an earthquake stops a clock. The fierce blow of battle paralyzed the mind. Their speech was a vocabulary of war, their loyalties were loyalties, not to living ideas or duties, but to old commanders and distorted traditions. They were dead men, most of them, moving among the living as ghosts; and yet, as ghosts in a play, they held the stage.[23]

Though overdrawn when applied to a man like Dawson, there is yet some truth to Page's insight that no veteran could outlive his baptism by fire.

Still another element, contributing to the more apparent differences between the two editors, was Dawson's public style. As Broadus Mitchell put it, "Dawson was not an orator, and had none of the flourish of Grady." Dawson's attack was "direct and concentrated," too prosaic to fire the imagination. Yet on the more practical concern of bringing cotton mills South, Mitchell continued, "In this thinking . . . the *News and Courier* preceded the *Constitution* by ten years."[24] All these factors—historical

22. Ibid. See also issues of the *News and Courier,* November 15, 1881; and February 25, 1882.

23. Quoted in Burton Jesse Hendrick, *The Life and Letters of Walter H. Page,* vol. I (New York: Doubleday, Page, 1922), pp. 90–91.

24. Broadus Mitchell, *The Rise of the Cotton Mills in the South* (Baltimore: Johns Hopkins Press, 1921), p. 114.

perspective, alien birth, age, and style, not to forget pique and envy—made Dawson more prone to rhapsodize a romantic past while Grady penned odes to a new breed of men.

More important than all the above, however, was the fact that the New South creed was written for an urban religion. Grady's apostolic role was made all the more congenial by living and breathing the ebullient spirit of Atlanta, while Dawson sang his incantations of a New Departure from a city which increasingly prided itself on its quaint difference. After his death, the Columbia *State* recalled that Dawson had done "as much for his city and his State as Grady ever did for his. Nay, more—for while Grady's light task was to aid in a rapid development, Dawson's was the hard one to arrest decay." If Grady were "the apostle of peace," concluded the *State,* then Dawson should be remembered as "the herald of hope."[25]

Dawson himself marveled at the bustling air of progress which seemed to permeate Atlanta. Returning from a visit there, he wrote:

> It is hardly an exaggeration to say that the city enlarges under the eye of the casual visitor. The houses outrun the streets. Building lots command high prices, and the demand does not abate. The whole city is throbbing with life and energy. Stately buildings for business purposes and costly and tasteful private residences spring up on every side. The trains on the network of railroads of which Atlanta is the centre rumble night and day. . . . Atlanta is indeed a phenomenal city![26]

It was this spirit which, no doubt, prompted the *News and Courier* to subtitle Grady's New York speech, "The New South from an Atlanta Standpoint."

By contrast Dawson found his own city lacking in the essential ingredients of progress, and the discovery was frustrating in an age that called for the booster to claim pluck and energy on all sides. When the Baltimore *American* chided Charleston for being a city "where the sentiment 'I am an American' has lost its meaning," the *News and Courier* could not muster a sharp denial. Quite the contrary, Dawson conceded that Charleston was "not overflowing with life and activity." The city was entirely "too sensitive to criticism," or put another way, the people were not "mixed up enough." Charlestonians were too much caught up in the old way of doing things to join the American success story. A survey of developments in the postbellum period suggested that many hard lessons were necessary "to teach business men that new conditions were incompatible with old systems." Such faultfinding lent credence to the self-aggrandizing assertion of the Columbia *Register* that "the old City by the Sea has been the stumbling

25. Quoted in *News and Courier,* October 29, 1891.

26. Ibid., March 20, 1880.

block of the State from the time she failed to carry out the dead Hayne's glorious dream of railroad connections with the Great West."[27]

Though overly sharp in its criticism, the *Register* may have correctly dated the onset of Charleston's decline. "No doubt," one writer observed, "a close socio-political history of Charleston could trace, in the years immediately preceding the Civil War, indications that the city's civilization was already betraying signs of having reached a kind of Spenglerian saturation point." It had become a city where the grandeur of the Greek revival revealed all its pretentiousness by being placed against a backdrop of slums and a general "down-at-heel look."[28] But one also gets the impression that while there is some agreement as to when Charleston's decline set in, the explanations for the decline have been too facile. Historians have emphasized Spenglerian saturation points or the existence of a closed society. They have pointed to the work of the South Carolina Railroad and Canal Company and the nation's first operational locomotive, "The Best Friend of Charleston," as a kind of last great push in the twenties and thirties after which permanent decay set in.[29] Yet the facts do not square.

In the period 1783 to 1850 the city accumulated a debt of only $338,000 which included a subscription of $200,000 to the South Carolina Railroad and Canal Company. By contrast, the decade of the fifties alone found Charleston making subscriptions totaling $2,750,000 in an effort to establish railroad links with the West. None of the schemes succeeded and all eventually "passed out of the hands of Charleston interests in the course of time and became absorbed into North and South railway systems, the interests of which were diametrically opposed to the development of Charleston."[30] But at the very time Charleston was supposedly turning in on itself and becoming the archtypical home of an effete aristocracy, she was doing more than ever to achieve Robert Young Hayne's dream of a route to the West.

These expenditures, coupled with war and depression, left Charleston in serious financial difficulty. The municipal debt which stood at $338,000 in 1850 climbed to $4,700,000 by 1880. By the latter date, the South Carolina Railroad had defaulted in payment of the interest on $6,000,000 worth of securities, the bulk of which were held by Charlestonians and the city

27. Ibid., December 10 and January 1, 1880; and January 11, 1883.

28. Molloy, *Charleston*, p. 95.

29. Ibid. A more recent study focuses on the manner in which Charleston society turned in on itself. See George Calvin Rogers, Jr., *Charleston in the Age of the Pinckneys*, Centers of Civilization Series (Norman: University of Oklahoma Press, 1955), p. 34.

30. Robert Goodwyn Rhett, *Charleston: An Epic of Carolina* (Richmond: Garrett and Massie, 1940), pp. 312–21; and John Ford Stover, *The Railroads of the South, 1865–1900: A Study in Finance and Control* (Chapel Hill: University of North Carolina Press, 1955), p. 34.

government. Securities worth another $6,000,000 had already been "blotted out for practical purposes." Under this kind of pressure the municipal government itself was forced to suspend payment of interest and the *News and Courier* could count a loss to Charleston of nearly a million dollars, the major portion of which was "a direct subtraction from the fixed income of persons in extremely moderate means who cannot make up for it by speculative enterprise, or by increased activity in business."[31] The great leap forward, which was expected to come with the restoration of home rule in 1876, was being dragged back by past liabilities which bore heavily on the present.

Compounding the depressed conditions were the recurring business failures. Summing up the commercial year in September, 1878, Dawson felt confident that the failure of a number of business houses which had been staggering under old indebtedness boded well for the future. "The few rotten spots have been cut out," was the surgical claim, "and the constitution of the mercantile body is vigorous and powerful." Unfortunately, the report for the following year was even gloomier. The number of failures rose from thirty-eight to sixty with an attendant increase in liabilities from $513,561 to $681,220. Included in the list for 1879 was the important commercial house of James Adger and Company in which a large amount of capital was invested by the principal banks.[32]

Failure in the mercantile community was of no greater consequence than the failure of individuals to meet their public obligations. The problem became so acute that the city was forced to auction the property of 1,200 citizens for back taxes. This dire circumstance prompted the *News and Courier* to ask, "Of the sixty thousand inhabitants of Charleston how many of them to-day are producers? How many of them are to-day non-producing consumers, who are entirely dependent upon the owner of some piece of real estate, the rental of which (if fortunately it may be rented) is barely enough to pay the taxes and insurance upon it?"[33] The newspaper apparently thought it answered the question by having to ask it.

All these difficulties were intimately bound to the crisis in railroading. By the late seventies both the South Carolina and the connecting Greenville and Columbia railroads were in the hands of receivers. Again and again the cry went up to get the roads out of litigation. It was estimated that settlement of the South Carolina Railroad problem alone would mean an immediate interest payment of three to four hundred thousand dollars for Charleston. Moreover, the crisis extended directly to the lower classes as well as the large investors and the municipal government. One of the

---

31. *News and Courier*, January 1, 1879.

32. Ibid., September 2, 1878; and September 1 and 27, 1879.

33. Ibid., December 11, 1878.

first acts of the South Carolina Railroad upon going into receivership was to declare its "fare-tickets" unredeemable. These two-dollar freight and passenger tickets had been circulating as a medium of exchange since 1873. The *News and Courier* itself accepted the fares in payment of all dues, whether for advertising or subscription. When the courts ruled them worthless as an unsecured debt, the newspaper protested, "They are mostly held by shopkeepers and workingmen who can ill afford to lose a penny in these tough times, and we shall be only too glad to do what we can in pressing the payment of the 'fare-tickets' to the last farthing."[34] Charlestonians, rich and poor, simply could not escape the growing debt problem, at the heart of which lay the broken railroads of more ambitious dreams.

The cumulative force of these financial difficulties had an enormous impact on public policy. There were two alternatives for settling what had become the municipal embarrassment. One was to repudiate the debt outright, and the other was retrenchment. In the best redeeming spirit, Dawson opted for the latter. Repudiation was first proposed by Mayor William W. Sale in December, 1878. Sale had been an ardent supporter of Gary's straight-out policy and was viewed by his supporters as a defender of the little man against the power of the Broad Street clique. Failure of the "better elements" to get organized in the municipal elections of 1877 forced them to acquiesce in Sale's election for the sake of party unity. Thereafter the *News and Courier* followed the Sale administration with patronizing advice which never concealed the paper's contempt for the mayor.

Looking to the city charter, Sale found no authority to contract debts except for the general care of the city. He believed that "the whole railroad debt so-called" was "without authority of law, and foisted upon the people (ever confiding and unresisting) by a set of rings and cliques." Dawson flashed back, "Mayor Sale is no Bourbon. He forgets everything, and learns nothing." The editor doubted whether there was "any other white man in Charleston of average intelligence who is unaware that this whole question had been tried and adjudicated by the highest tribunal in the State."[35] Whereupon the *News and Courier* proceeded to give its unrefined mayor a gratuitous lecture on *stare decisis*.

The day before his tactless rebuke of Sale, Dawson had outlined clearly his thinking on the subject. "It is right and desirable that Charleston should be improved and even beautified," advised the editorial, "provided that her people can bear the necessary taxation." Yet the city government was being maintained on "a scale that is adapted to the requirements of a City with four or five times the population of Charleston." Rather than repudia-

---

34. Ibid., May 19, 1879, and October 2, 1878; and Samuel Melancthon Derrick, *Centennial History of the South Carolina Railroad* (Columbia: The State Co., 1930), p. 243.

35. *News and Courier*, December 12, 1878.

tion, which would be an act of dishonesty and would destroy faith in the public credit, the *News and Courier* entered a plea for halving the municipal budget.[36]

The election of a true-blue Conservative, William Ashmead Courtenay, in December, 1879, meant the fulfillment of the Dawson plan. Budgets were slashed, portions of the debt retired, and taxes cut—all of which the newspaper attributed to "the application of sound business principles to government." Of greater moment, however, was the decision of the Courtenay administration to amend the charter with respect to the future acquisition of debt. At the insistence of the city government, the General Assembly acted favorably on an amendment to prohibit further debt unless approved by two-thirds of the city council and a like fraction of the registered voters at a special election. Though the measure applied only to liabilities in excess of the city's current annual income, the *News and Courier* was correct in its assessment that the new act was "equivalent to the absolute prohibition of any new debt of any kind."[37]

The real tragedy was that the cost-accounting mentality of pay-as-you-go won out at the very moment when the main current of government promotion for internal improvements and railroading was flowing back to localities. Though a final expedient, local governments were used extensively for that purpose in the eighties and illustrated "the importance of the 'booster' spirit in American economic development."[38] Francis Dawson could still call for private subscription, but the city of Charleston, taking counsel of its fears, could no longer match ambition with money and withdrew from the race. Thus ended thirty years of desperate, even herculean, efforts to make of Charleston a metropolis.

The policy of retrenchment did not preclude Dawson's indulging in the rhetoric of the booster. Not a year went by that the *News and Courier* was not found nurturing some new scheme to harvest the trade of the Great West. Charleston was constantly put forward as the natural South Atlantic outlet for western produce. The resulting competition, it was argued, would force New York prices down and the whole nation would benefit. Direct trade with Africa and the markets of Europe were advanced as realistic goals. Nor was the ancient idea of a passage to India without an audience in Charleston. The *News and Courier* could declare, "So ambitious are we that we shall not be satisfied until Charleston has, in addition, the export and import trade of the mighty and populous East. Our policy is Pacific, and there is scope enough for Savannah and Charleston—and for Port Royal to boot!"[39]

---

36. Ibid., December 11, 1878.

37. Ibid., February 9, 1881, and February 15, 1882. See also Rhett, *Charleston*, p. 313.

38. Carter Goodrich, *Government Promotion of American Canals and Railroads, 1800–1890* (New York: Columbia University Press, 1960), p. 289.

39. *News and Courier*, July 19 and October 12, 1878; and September 24, 1880.

To achieve this position of most favored among cities, Dawson constantly repeated what he considered to be the three essentials for Charleston's growth. The list included harbor development, improved terminal facilities, and rail outlets to the West. "Deep water on the bar, carrying the railroads to the water, and direct communication with the great cities of the West and Northwest," summed up one editorial, "are measures which *The News and Courier* has persistently and earnestly advocated." The speedy completion of each would assure the East-West flow of traffic through the old City by the Sea.[40]

Dawson was to be frustrated on all three counts. To get deep water at low tide, the *News and Courier* encouraged a project to build jetties from Sullivan's and Morris Islands to the bar and hoped for completion as early as 1878. However, federal subsidies came in niggardly allotments. By November, 1881, only $754,000 had been spent, and Dawson urged the citizens of Charleston to put pressure on Congress for an additional $750,000 to be allocated immediately. Urgency was dictated by the completion of a similar project that same year in Wilmington, North Carolina. Charlestonians were shocked when Congress proposed only $100,000 and were rendered incredulous when the whole bill was defeated. All had depended upon swift completion, and the report of the Harbor Commissioner for 1883 was anything but encouraging. "This procrastination threatens serious consequences," he noted, "as enough seems to have been done to disturb the natural currents, and not enough to direct them in their permanent future flow." The reports through 1887 related a similar message, and after that year, harbor improvements dropped from the reports for the remainder of the decade.[41]

The second problem was Charleston's antiquated terminal facilities. In a move that would have been commended by present-day environmentalists, Charlestonians in the twenties moved to prevent the construction of rails inside Line Street, which then formed the city limits and had earlier served as the 1814 line of fortifications against England. By the eighties that decision was regretted, for transferring goods from one mode of transportation to another in order to cross the city forced up the cost of doing business in Charleston. The only people happy with the situation were draymen, wharf-owners, and Charleston's rivals along the South Atlantic seaboard. Again prompt action was deemed essential, but again the work dragged on endlessly. During 1882 and 1883 a thousand feet of waterfront facilities were constructed by the South Carolina Railway Company, but it was not until December, 1885, that the legislature authorized the construc-

40. Ibid., August 7, 1879.

41. Ibid., September 3, 1878; August 13, 1879; November 1, 1881; January 25, 1882; February 15 and May 3, 1883. See also the city of Charleston *Year Books,* 1883, 1884, 1886, and 1887 (Charleston: *The News and Courier* Book Presses).

tion of a line along and across the streets of Charleston from the main depot to the wharf.[42]

Equally vexing was the condition of the South Carolina Railroad. It was "the child of Charleston capital" and served as the city's only real hope for a strong commercial future. But declining profits forced the railroad into the hands of a receiver in October, 1878, and it remained there until November, 1881. The road itself was sold for $1,275,000 in July 1881, and though Dawson sought to put the best possible light on the transaction, he personally sold 200 shares of stock the day before on the apparent belief that prompt action would prevent an even heavier loss. Even though the road was reorganized as the South Carolina Railway company, conditions did not materially improve for the remainder of the decade. By October, 1889, the railroad had gone under again, and the court-appointed receiver was none other than the ubiquitous Daniel Henry Chamberlain.[43]

Thus it came to pass that Charleston entered the eighties with her hands tied. It was all the more tragic, for these years would mark the takeoff period for postbellum southern railroading. "While the 1870's had been years of receivership and failure," wrote one historian of the movement, "the next decade, that of the 1880's, was a period of record-breaking prosperity and expansion. Railroad building was extremely rapid through the 1880's and consolidation and merger became the general rule." During this time, the ten southeastern states nearly doubled their rail mileage, but South Carolina lagged far behind, slipping from seventh to ninth in relative rank and ending the decade next to last in increase of percentage.[44]

It is problematic whether, given favorable conditions, Charleston could have gained her outlet to the West. The new mergers and combinations seemed intent on bending trade in a North-South flow which redounded to the benefit of Atlanta. First Tom Scott's Southern Security Company and later William Clyde's Richmond and West Point Terminal Railway and Warehouse Company worked to turn rail traffic away from the coastal cities. Mergers and combinations which seemed to offer some hope for Charleston in 1880 and 1881 were frustrated as Clyde's Richmond and Danville syndicate moved relentlessly to buy up South Carolina's railroads and to convert them into North-South feeders.[45]

William Mauldin of Greenville, prominent in South Carolina railroading circles, kept a diary which reflected the enormous power exercised by

42. *News and Courier,* March 31, April 1, August 26, and November 18, 1879; and Derrick, *South Carolina Railroad,* p. 260.

43. Derrick, *South Carolina Railroad,* p. 250; *News and Courier,* July 29, 1881; and Dawson to T. B. Myres, July 27, 1881; and Dawson to J. J. Higgenson, July 27 and August 2, 1887, Dawson Papers, Duke.

44. Stover, *Railroads of the South,* pp. 186, and 191–93.

45. See Maury Klein, *The Great Richmond Terminal: A Study in Businessmen and Business Strategy* (Charlottesville: University Press of Virginia, 1970).

Clyde and his syndicate. Returning from a directors' meeting of the newly created Greenville and Laurens Railroad, he wrote:

> Good feeling manifested but the chance of building the road to our commercial advantage is very slight now. The Richmond and Danville monopoly controls all the lines of Rail Road in the upper part of the state & well nigh formulates public sentiment. Exercising large pecuniary power, they are able to so act as to shape in a large degree the *political* policy of the State. It will in time develop into a contest between the people and the monopolists.

A few months later, Mauldin wrote, "We are hemmed in on all sides by the R & D—and the whole country is under the control of monopolies."[46]

Mauldin was not alone in his fears. Dawson, representing Charleston's merchant community complained, "It really would seem that the Richmond and Danville Octopus touches nothing that it does not injure."[47] Such expressions as these made it all the more paradoxical when Dawson and Mauldin dodged their golden opportunity to strike at the monopolists. In the spectacular legislative session of 1883, which witnessed Clyde's henchmen buying up legislators at every hand, both Dawson and Mauldin capitulated to the interests of the Richmond and Danville and supported the gelding of South Carolina's strong regulatory commission. Mauldin was the only member of the Greenville legislative delegation to vote with the Clyde forces.[48]

Dawson's alternately hostile and friendly attitude toward the Richmond and Danville led to charges that the *News and Courier* could be bought,[49] but the truth of the matter was that Charleston's weak commercial position

---

46. William Mauldin Diary, September 26 and November 7, 1881; and June 22, 1882, SHC.

47. *News and Courier,* October 14, 1882.

48. Ibid., December 17, 1883; and William Mauldin Diary, December 25, 1883, SHC.

49. In letters to his uncle and nephew, December 23, 1883, N. G. Gonzales complained of being "muzzled" by Dawson when he tried to expose the machinations of the Clyde syndicate, Elliott-Gonzales Papers, SHC. Four years later when the *News and Courier* was criticizing the Richmond and Danville, John C. Haskell, local attorney for the railroad, wrote his superiors, saying that the paper was trying "to force us to bribe it," and that while he had never "personally engaged in buying it," he knew "it to be done with great success." Haskell to T. M. Logan, June 6, 1887, J. C. Haskell Letter Book, South Caroliniana Library, University of South Carolina, cited hereafter as SCL. Haskell's tale is doubtful. He was an old Hampton lieutenant who never liked Dawson. Moreover, none of his correspondence with Dawson at this time even vaguely hints at a deal, and Dawson ultimately settled his differences with the railroad by corresponding with senior officials, not Haskell. The evidence is found in letters, all dated 1887, from Haskell to J. C. Hemphill, June 6, to T. M. Logan, June 6, to Dawson, June 10, and to [?] Thomas, June 13, J. C. Haskell Letter Book, SCL; and Dawson to J. C. Haskell, June 8, to Peyton Randolph, June 14, and to T. M. Logan, June 27, Hemphill Family Papers, Duke.

made any consistent editorial policy on the subject impossible. The Dawson realized that the Richmond and Danville posed the most serious threat to Charleston's commercial future, but he also recognized that it was the major agency of northern capital in the state. To punish the Clyde syndicate would not alter that company's policy, but it might damage the state's ability to attract other sources of capital. It was a dilemma from which there seemed no escape. Any consistent policy would so expose the city to one horn of the dilemma as to make commercial death certain.[50]

The condition of railroads in South Carolina also forced Dawson to deviate from the more traditional economic alignments of the New Departure. The outstretched arms of the South Carolina Railroad were immovable tracks to an improbable future. They forced Charleston to seek commercial independence by breaking through the North-South barrier in search of connections with Louisville, Cincinnati, Chicago, and St. Louis. So compelling was this half-century-old dream that Dawson was constrained to oppose what became a crucial article in the hidden compromise of 1877, Tom Scott's Texas-Pacific Railroad. While southern brigadiers were flocking to the siren calls of Scott's organization, Dawson cried out that the scheme would ruin the region. It would dry up the South's credit with the national government while favoring Philadelphia and points North rather than southern ports. The *News and Courier* was convinced that Tom Scott had "hoodwinked many well-meaning Southern men who ought to know better."[51] Dawson continued to oppose the Texas-Pacific even as it was becoming a part of the quid pro quo of the Compromise of 1877. He argued that the North would perceive the South as attempting to recover its war losses by raiding the federal treasury and asserted that if the South opposed Scott's scheming it would make "the 'Confederate Brigadiers' a blessing, instead of a menace, in the eyes of the Northern people."[52] It is safe to say that regard for northern feelings was the least of Dawson's concerns.

Yet Dawson could not help but sense that his own city was outdoing the brigadiers when it came to self-deception. He knew the South was depen-

---

50. Dawson's seeming inconsistency on how much authority should be given the railroad regulatory commission led one historian to charge duplicity, William James Cooper, Jr., *The Conservative Regime: South Carolina, 1877–1890*, Johns Hopkins University Studies in Historical and Political Science, ser. LXXXVI, no. 1 (Baltimore: Johns Hopkins University Press, 1968), p. 132. Yet in only one year of the six in which regulation was agitated in South Carolina did Dawson support more than advisory powers for the commission, and in that year Dawson answered to the will of his constituents. Very frank letters on this subject may be found from Dawson to W. P. Clyde, December 7, 12, and 13, 1884, Dawson Papers, Duke.

51. *News and Courier*, November 30, 1875. See also C. Vann Woodward, *Reunion and Reaction: The Compromise of 1877 and the End of Reconstruction* (Boston: Little, Brown, 1966), pp. 90–94.

52. *News and Courier*, January 18, 1877.

dent on the financial centers of the East. Standing at the fork in the road to reunion, it took little prescience to see that "the natural alliance of the South, as a borrowing section, is with the East, not with the West."[53] Thus, Charleston might propose her future on the long nourished dream of Robert Y. Hayne, but the East would dispose. Such a situation did not bode well for that future.

Francis Warrington Dawson and the *News and Courier* stood as proof that Charleston's economic decline was not accomplished without protest. The old City by the Sea did not wither on the vine because of some fatal flaw in her character, some aristocratic hubris in an age gone mad after yankee success. From 1850 to 1880 the city made valiant efforts to rescue herself from commercial oblivion. The aristocratic pretensions which failed to prevent Charleston from being the first city in the United States to place a steam locomotive into operation similarly failed to stop the city from bleeding her reserves dry in an effort to share in the nation's general opulence. The list of broken and failing railroad schemes staggered the imagination. As a consequence of these dashed hopes, Charleston entered the eighties a debt-crippled city with no returns on the investment. She was incapable of deepening her harbor and painfully slow in improving her port facilities. She remained unattractive to the larger commercial forces at work—a neglected stepchild of her imperial mistress.

By the time the earthquake struck in 1886, it was already apparent that Charleston was not to partake of the urban prosperity which fueled most of the New South bombast. Having watched the city try and fail, it was not surprising that Dawson took umbrage when Henry Grady described the earthquake-torn city as "the last citadel of the old regime."[54] The desperate struggle to bring his city into the economic mainstream left Dawson ill-disposed to accept the consolation of visitors who described Charleston as a place where "the old traditions are held fast with a sense of age and of history which give to the society an individuality and a charm to be found no where else in our shifting time."[55] But after the disastrous quake of August 31 and the leaping fame it brought the young editor from Atlanta, Dawson veered in the direction of a more rhapsodic view of the old order. The seeds of such an approach were there from the beginning, but it took the events of late 1886 to bring them to fruition. More than ever, Dawson was made aware that his city occupied an ancillary position in the new order.

Dawson's disassociation from what was becoming the Grady position had one other effect: it sharpened his ability to criticize the more unrealistic claims of the New South evangelists. In 1885 Dawson had defended the

---

53. Ibid., January 22 and 23, 1878.

54. Quoted in Nixon, *Henry W. Grady*, p. 6.

55. "Charleston Revisited," *The Nation* (February, 1882), p. 94.

South's leading propaganda organ, the *Manufacturers' Record,* against charges of falsifying evidence of southern progress. But in the controversy following Grady's speech, the *News and Courier* reversed itself and indicted the Baltimore paper for gross manipulation of the numbers. Dawson now concluded that "the statements of the *Manufacturers' Record* are shown to be erroneous and misleading. They are wrong in principle, and fatally defective in their application. Their only effect is to delude those who cannot think for themselves, and to cause premature elation to newspapers which have not the patience to construct statistics on their proper account."[56] These manufactured records were no better than the false prophecy of a Henry Grady who pointed to "local affluence" (Atlanta) and proclaimed "general prosperity."[57] Though accused by the *Constitution* of denigrating the South's accomplishments, Dawson was beginning to perceive what men like Walter Hines Page and Lewis H. Blair would later observe more clearly, "that the New South writings were that fuzzy medley of strong belief and personal experience out of which social myth emerges."[58]

56. *News and Courier,* May 21, 1885, and February 1, 1887.

57. Ibid., January 8, 1887.

58. Gaston, *New South Creed,* p. 202.

Chapter VIII
Lord of the Rings

By general agreement of friend and foe alike, Captain Dawson was a powerful, if not the most powerful, figure in South Carolina politics during the 1880s. Having no personal ambition for office, the Charleston editor was content to play the role of Warwick. He was not a public man. He shied away from occasions which called for him to address large audiences, but he relished his work behind the scenes. The executive committee, the convention caucus, and the private encounter were his element. The New York *Times* described Dawson as a man whose head was "cool on all occasions" and whose "merciless application of the party whip . . . frequently prevented a 'bolt' when such an event was imminent."[1] A contemporary could write, "As a leader Capt. Dawson was bold and ambitious. But he was not the politician. . . . He lacked the ruggedness, though not the readiness, of a public man. His manner of speaking was finished rather than magnetic. His voice was sweet and rich with distinct English accent and a slight trace of intonation." The prepared essay was his forte, not "the rough and ready debate of the public hall."[2]

Similarly Dawson did not work with or through South Carolina's most public men. Generals whose gray eminence cast but a shadow of their former authority left the editor singularly unimpressed. He preferred working through county executives, legislative delegations, and men on their way up. The Columbia *Register* was not far from the mark when it denounced Dawson as an adventurer who was "always on the make and always ready with the first occasion to take the back track, whilst he trenched himself about with fifth rate politicians manning the outposts."[3]

To be a power broker, it was necessary for Dawson to encourage the entry of new men into the system, while maintaining the existing structure through which they would rise. By occupying this middle ground, Dawson inevitably antagonized both the Hampton faction who practiced the politics of deference and those outside the existing order who demanded a more active voice in party affairs. In 1885 the editor found the state in much need of "a little iconoclasm," and wrote that it was time "to disregard absolutely the notion that rank in the Confederate army, or

---

1. New York *Times*, March 30, 1880.
2. Augusta *Chronicle*, March 14, 1889.
3. Columbia *Register*, November 26, 1884.

eminence at the Bar, or a long pedigree (of a hundred years or there-abouts) is an all-sufficient qualification for any post of honor and trust."[4]

The appeal for iconoclasm came in response to the search for a new superintendent for The Citadel, but it coincided with a much more pervasive feeling that what South Carolina needed was a "new deal." Articulated first by the Greenville *News,* the call for a new departure soon became an attack on "ring" politics. For Dawson the cry of ring domination was a familiar one, and he called on those making the allegation to expose those forming the cliques and to specify the malfeasance that resulted. Dawson went on to acknowledge "a sufficient reason for a very radical change in official circles" and an "urgent need of more youthfulness," but he refused to concede that ring rule lay at the bottom of the problem.[5]

The call for specificity provoked replies. The Greenville *News* claimed that "a dozen families could be mentioned whose ramified connections really govern the State." The Abbeville *Medium,* in obvious reference to Martin Gary's last encounter with the establishment, said that a ring had existed ever since 1880 when the state executive committee called "the convention out of time and precipitated the nomination of the State ticket." The Aiken *Journal and Review,* seeing better than most, charged Dawson with trying to stir up a debate where none existed so that he might fill the columns of the *News and Courier* in a dull season. Furthermore, declared the country journal, it was foolish for Dawson to ask those calling for a new deal to furnish proof of malfeasance. To do so would be to treat public office like the civil service when every good democrat knew that simple rotation of elected officials was healthy for democracy.[6]

Not surprisingly the most specific charge came from the Columbia *Register.* Edited by John W. R. Pope, a Hampton loyalist who could never tolerate Dawson's irreverence for the general, the Columbia paper blurted that "if there be a ring in the State, it is the executive committee of the State, and that ring is on Dawson's little finger." Burned by this lively spark, Dawson dropped all fruitful discussion of the need for a new deal and spent his time burying the poor Pope in his own verbiage. Dawson cleverly indicated that the only conceivable inference that could be drawn from Pope's accusation was that members of the state executive committee were either dishonest, fools, or knaves.[7]

To his enemies and detractors, Dawson was surely a frustrating enigma. To the Hampton loyalists he seemed to be a backstage manipulator bent on replacing the general's influence with his own, yet he frequently paid

4. *News and Courier,* August 17, 1885.

5. Ibid., August 20, 1885.

6. Comments reprinted in ibid., September 9, 1885.

7. Ibid., September 9, 14, 16, and 18.

editorial fealty to Hampton, particularly when the structure of the regime seemed threatened. To those outside the system Dawson seemed the guiding genius behind an apparatus which kept decision making in the hands of cliques and rings, yet he joined with them in calling for a rejuvenation of the party. For his part, Dawson carried on in the confidence that he was working for a political climate in which only the fittest served.

That rings existed cannot be denied. Ben Tillman later claimed that any town boasting more than 5,000 inhabitants was governed by a ring.[8] Dawson himself acknowledged the existence of one in Charleston but thought it was the inevitable consequence of having only a select group who were qualified to hold positions of public trust. In a letter recommending a young Charleston merchant for the post of railroad commissioner, Dawson warned Governor Thompson that the appointment "would be considered as keeping the public offices too much in the same hands." In fact, the nominee was "the nephew of the Collector of the Port and belong[ed] to the same set in Charleston as Postmaster Huger, Deputy Collector Walker and Messrs King and Pinckney who have received appointments in the Custom House." Dawson concluded that the "hard-fisted Democracy, upon whom we largely depend for our success," would cry ring, but "it would be hard to find among them a proper person for the office of Railroad Commissioner, and fitness for the office must be the prime consideration."[9]

Dawson's commanding position in South Carolina politics can be attributed to several factors, not the least of which was his newspaper. Enemies screamed of being muzzled, winners were grateful, and prospective candidates earnestly solicited notice. Congressman Samuel Dibble, who became a real power in the Charleston district, felt like many another politician when he wrote "to say how great a debt I owe you personally and the *News & Courier.* . . . I shall never forget the personal, as well as party, interest you evinced."[10] Of equal importance was Dawson's influence over the state's patronage. He won the prerogative through a combination of circumstances, beginning with Hampton's gradual withdrawal from an active political role after the nomination of Johnson Hagood in 1880. In truth, the general never wore the mantle of political authority very well. His active years had been spent exercising that authority which flows from being a plantation grandee and military commander, and he never seemed quite comfortable in the political market place of bargain and barter. Not only did Hampton fail to exercise his power, he also declined to designate

8. Ibid., August 29, 1888.

9. Dawson to Hugh S. Thompson, September 9, 1885, Dawson Papers, Duke University Library, cited hereafter as Duke.

10. Samuel Dibble to Dawson, November 10, 1882, ibid.

an heir who could or would. Johnson Hagood refused to run for a second term as governor and was succeeded by Hugh Smith Thompson, a man of great ability and a loyal Conservative, but not one of the original Hampton lieutenants.

In the absence of a dominant politician Dawson's political talents could be used to maximum effect. Serving as a county, state, and national committeeman, he was able to exercise influence at all levels of the party apparatus. They were the only positions he ever actively sought. His enemies accused him of engineering his election to the national committee in 1880, and evidence indicates that in 1888, after Tillmania was beginning to take hold, Dawson expressed great concern lest he lose that post.[11] It was from that position that he won his way into the confidence of the Cleveland Democrats. With Hampton withdrawing and with Dawson successfully supporting the Cleveland candidacy, South Carolina's patronage fell naturally into the hands of the Charleston editor.

Dawson did have one political ally who laid claim to the right social and military credentials. Old soldiers said Matthew Calbraith Butler "had been the perfect cavalryman." An extraordinarily handsome man, he was tall, graceful, and possessed of the manners of a Chesterfield. His courtly ways were matched by a streak of courage that gained him a stump at the battle of Brandy Station. "In the hour of danger," wrote Dawson's brother-in-law, "he was one of the coolest men I ever saw, and he feared neither man nor devil. But with all his beautiful manners, when he wanted to, he could be the most cold-blooded, insolent human being that mortal eyes ever beheld." His strengths and weaknesses blended to create a favorable public image. Whatever else, wrote one historian, "He was enviably popular."[12] Elected to the Senate in 1876, Butler spent eighteen undistinguished years in that body, gaining a reputation primarily for licentious behavior.[13]

Just how Butler and Dawson came to be friends is not clear. Evidence does indicate that as early as 1878 Butler and Hampton were having their

---

11. Dawson to C. S. McCall of Marlboro, May 2 and 9, 1888, Charles Spencer McCall Papers, South Caroliniana Library, University of South Carolina, cited hereafter as SCL.

12. Descriptions of Butler from William Watts Ball, *The State that Forgot: South Carolina's Surrender to Democracy* (Indianapolis: Bobbs-Merrill, 1932), pp. 240–41; James Morris Morgan, *Recollections of a Rebel Reefer* (Boston: Houghton Mifflin, 1917), p. 362; and Francis Butler Simkins, *Pitchfork Ben Tillman: South Carolinian,* Southern Biography Series (Baton Rouge: Louisiana State University Press, 1944), p. 264.

13. M. W. Gary and his friends spoke of Butler's unseemly behavior in Washington. See Gary to Cash, August 3, 1880, quoted in E. B. C. Cash, *The Cash-Shannon Duel,* append. by Bessie Cash Irby (Boykin, South Carolina, 1930), first printed (Greenville: *The Daily News* Job Printing Office, 1881), p. 26. See also E. B. C. Cash to Gary, January 25, 1881, M. W. Gary Papers, SCL. Further reference to Butler's conduct is in William E. Earle to W. A. Courtenay, March 26, 1888, William Ashmead Courtenay Papers, SCL.

differences over the state's debt policy.[14] At the same time Butler was trying to break relations with Martin Gary's outspoken position in the party. Steering a middle course between Hampton and Gary could not have been easy, but it was essential to establishing a measure of political independence. Under such conditions, the logical move for Butler was to the former commander of the fusionist faction, Captain Dawson, who was similarly having trouble with Hampton and Gary. Whatever the reasons, the friends of Gary were referring to the "firm of Dawson and Butler" by 1880, and a year later General James Conner was convinced that Butler was at the bottom of the problems between Hampton and Dawson.[15] Finally, it should be remembered that it was Butler who heeded Dawson's suggestion that congressmen should refuse to stand as delegates to the 1884 Democratic national convention, while Hampton, desirous of aiding their mutual senatorial colleague, Bayard, risked his popularity to go to Chicago.[16]

Some thought that Butler's profligacy and debt problems formed the vital link in the alliance between the editor and the senator. William Earle, a native white Republican turned Washington attorney, wrote William A. Courtenay, Charleston's four-term mayor, that federal appointments in South Carolina were being juggled by the "triumvirate." He went on to observe that Butler was a "small factor" in Washington, that he was "a mere succor of Don Cammeron's [sic]," and that together they were "a pair of licentious creatures whose conduct would destroy any-body's respect for their positions." Earle reached the conclusion that "as soon as Dawson can use him no longer he will drop him quickly." When Courtenay asked Earle to be specific as to whom the triumvirate comprised, he replied, "I think if you will make some cautious inquiry at the Peoples' National Bank, you will find that a note for $2,500 was discounted, just before the earthquake. That Butler got the money but never paid it and that Simonton and Dawson endorsed it." A few months later the inquisitive Earle was wondering where Butler got "the money to buy and then furnish a house here in the heart of the fashionable part of the city?"[17]

Earle's facts were essentially correct, but he was reading more into them than warranted. Actually Dawson had loaned Butler money as early as the

14. See Record Book in box marked "Drama, Poetry, and Accounts," Dawson Papers, Duke.

15. Cash, *Cash-Shannon*, p. 21. Wade Hampton to James Conner, March 1, 1881, James Conner Papers, South Carolina Historical Society, Charleston.

16. Details of the convention are in the *News and Courier*, June 26 and 27, 1884. Reaction to Hampton's decision is in ibid., June 30, 1884.

17. William E. Earle to W. A. Courtenay, March 26 and November 15, 1888, and March 10, 1889, William Ashmead Courtenay Papers, scl. The reference is to Charles Henry Simonton.

May before the 1884 state convention. The transaction Earle had in mind began in June, 1886, when Butler approached Simonton and Dawson to help him secure a loan of $5,000. In a letter to Dawson he complained, "It is devilish inconvenient to be poor and not qualified to steal. The education of my children has been a great strain upon my resources and I have done my best to equip them for life. After this year they will all be thru—then I hope to breath [sic] freer." Dawson and Simonton were able to scrape up the necessary cash and accepted as collateral Butler's life insurance policy, valued at $2,500, along with a draft on the Secretary of the Senate for $2,000. Though occasionally late in his payments, Butler eventually made good on his obligation.[18] Such unregulated loans were common in that day and time, symbolizing friendships and no doubt oiling political relationships. Dawson himself, in his early career as a newspaperman, had benefited more than once from just such loans, and would do so again.

There can be no doubt that rings existed in various forms and at various levels of government to advance the fortunes of a certain class of politician, just as there can be no doubt that Dawson figured prominently in the more important cliques. But it is also true that these rings were little more than loose assemblages of men accustomed to ruling in a deferential society. They believed they had the blessings and assent of the dominant class and that little, in a systematic way, need be done other than to justify their decisions to the "hard-fisted Democracy." Besides, when malcontents complained loudest of ring rule, Dawson and his friends always had Hugh Smith Thompson to serve up as living proof that no rings controlled the Palmetto State.

Thompson was Dawson's kind of man. He was capable, thoroughly conservative, and above all else not a Hampton lieutenant. Before 1882 Thompson served with distinction as the state superintendent of education, and in that year, despite the absence of a distinguished military record, was drafted by a state convention deadlocked between two Hampton men with stars on their collars, Generals John Bratton and John Doby Kennedy. William Watts Ball remembered that "Confederate veterans back home privately expressed disgust when the news of the nomination of other than one of the Generals arrived, but their displeasure soon passed."[19] Thompson went about his business with the cost-accounting efficiency so admired by Dawson and showed some independence of the legislative delegations which traditionally ruled South Carolina. This mild independence even drew comment from *The Nation*, which expressed pleasure at the gover-

---

18. Dawson to M. C. Butler, May 13, 1884; Butler to Dawson, June 21, 1886; Dawson to his wife, August 19, 1886; Butler to Dawson, July 23, 1887. See also notes on the contents of Dawson's private box in the Bank of Charleston, entry dated May 28, 1887, all in Dawson Papers, Duke.

19. Ball, *State that Forgot*, p. 181.

nor's confirmation of over 600 appointments, "a number of which were not recommended by county conventions or delegations." Godkin's journal saw it as proof that civil service reform was taking hold in the South.[20] In summing up Thompson's work, Dawson wrote that the high character of his administration was best exemplified in his leaving office with less personal wealth than when he entered.[21]

Thompson's exemplary poverty was characteristic of the Conservative regime's emphasis on the traditional virtues. The story is told of a clerk in the comptroller-general's office who stole thirteen or fourteen thousand dollars, whereupon the comptroller resigned "in a mistaken sense that he might be blamed because an underling had betrayed him, the custodian of public funds."[22] As far as is known, it was the only evidence of financial peculation attributable to the Bourbon Democracy. Indeed, men who prided themselves on economy were hardly the stuff out of which the traditional rings were built. By its very nature a frugal government limits the rewards at its disposal. Moreover, the truly powerful ring requires an active political chieftain, and yet, as observed earlier, South Carolina was without such a leader in the 1880s. Some believe it was because Hampton failed to name an heir.[23] More likely it came as a result of the belief that none was needed. Those who were qualified to govern already held office. The only real requirement of such a government was that it give a periodic accounting and that it justify its qualifications to hold the public trust. In such an atmosphere the belief evolves that suasion much more than reward is the means for sustaining the established interests, and where the art of persuasion constitutes the principal political stay, who better to turn to than the state's most influential news editor?

Thus, it was with a sense of security, an abiding faith in their own infallibility, that the Conservatives confronted the challenge that would prove their undoing. In fact, the political atmosphere had become so calm in the summer of 1885 it could be argued that Benjamin Ryan Tillman was a welcomed relief from the growing political torpor, a momentary diversion from the routine and commonplace. The setting and occasion for the commencement of the Tillman movement were as unpromising as seemed the chances for political excitement. The summer convocation of the State Grange and the State Agricultural and Mechanical Society was, as usual, to be attended "by intelligent and representative farmers." Gathering at Bennettsville in August weather so hot that dogs dared not venture from

---

20. *The Nation*, January 8, 1885.

21. *News and Courier*, July 18, 1886.

22. Ball, *State that Forgot*, p. 183.

23. William J. Cooper, Jr., *The Conservative Regime: South Carolina, 1877–1890*, Johns Hopkins University Studies in Historical and Political Science, ser. LXXXVI, no. 1 (Baltimore: Johns Hopkins University Press, 1968), p. 81.

under the porch, the farmers sat in the courthouse listening to the customary essays on fertilizers, tobacco planting, and grape culture, while the sawdust-strewn floor soaked up tobacco juice and flies darted in and out of the dust-illumined light which streamed through the too-few windows. On the second day of the convention, after hearing an essay on land drainage and assurances from the commissioner of agriculture that farmers were not growing poorer though "they did not prosper as they should," the weary planters were greeted by "a long and rambling speech containing many hard truths, mingled with a great deal of dry humor."[24]

In many ways the speaker was as unconventional as his speech. He was not a state chemist, a commissioner, or some professor. He was a farmer "whose appearance was a mixture of the plain and the uncouth and whose one eye flashed ominously."[25] Nor could he boast that his cyclopian glare came as a result of engaging the enemy at some critical juncture in the war. Indeed it was an abcess in his left eye, the result of a freak accident, that prevented him from casting his youthful lot with the Confederate armies. Here was a new man with a new deal, but all his audience knew was that the younger brother of Congressman George D. Tillman of Edgefield was rumored to have something out of the ordinary to say.

After giving the typical self-effacing apologies expected of a speaker who takes pride in being of humble origin, Tillman launched into an arraignment of the traditional evils of the southern farm system and a not-so-traditional charge that politicians and "lawyers in the pay of finance" were the root of the problem. The agricultural department in the South Carolina College, which was designed to lift the veil of ignorance from the benighted farmer, was accused of using the farmers' money instead to train lawyers and scholars who Tillman equated with "drones and vagabonds." He scolded the farmers for allowing themselves to be duped. He told the story of the poor farmer who finally made it to the state legislature only to emerge one year later a politician, "the contact with General This and Judge That and Colonel Something Else" having awed and corrupted him. Tillman called for resolutions demanding the execution "in good faith" of the federal laws guaranteeing money for agricultural education, the establishment of agricultural experiment stations and farmers' institutes, and the addition of one farmer from each congressional district to the state board of agriculture.[26]

Though four of his five resolutions failed to pass, Tillman left Bennettsville confident that "the farmers did the listening, the politicians the voting,

---

24. *News and Courier,* August 5–8, 1885. See also Simkins, *Pitchfork Ben,* pp. 92–95; and idem, *The Tillman Movement in South Carolina* (Durham: Duke University Press, 1926), pp. 54–60.

25. Simkins, *Pitchfork Ben,* p. 92.

26. *News and Courier,* August 7, 1885.

and that explains why the resolutions failed to pass." After all, he had gone there not "to pass resolutions but to explain to the farmers how they are duped and robbed."[27] For the next three months Tillman remained content to harvest his profitable acres and perhaps to watch with some amusement the reaction of the state press to his unusual speech.

When Tillman did box the public ear again in November, he was to follow the pattern established at Bennettsville. He was no ordinary hayseed; he was a shrewd man who possessed an excellent education, both theoretical and practical. Of greater moment, however, was his intuitive understanding of the requirements for successful agitation. Tillman constantly baffled his enemies. Every move he made seemed sure to be counterproductive; yet his popularity only grew. He abused his followers to their faces, calling them ignorant, imbecilic, backward, apathetic, and foolish. He assailed his enemies with a tongue so outrageous that many believed only the demise of the code kept him alive. He never won a factual dispute, at least as far as the state's press was concerned, and he seemed to have no real program beyond the establishment of a separate agricultural college (which he proved willing to lay aside if there were serious cost objections) and the call for a reorganization of the state agricultural department. All the other issues he raised from time to time were either not uniquely his own or were pushed with whatever inconsistency seemed demanded by the occasion. Despite all this, his movement grew and multiplied, thriving best when the issues appeared either contrived, contradictory, or without foundation.

What Tillman instinctively understood was that the absence of a specific program left him less vulnerable; he had nothing to defend and everything to attack. By flailing his followers he engendered a sense of helplessness, made them feel powerless before the dominant class. In denouncing the Agricultural Society and the Department of Agriculture, he left little doubt that existing institutions were of no consequence in the solution of the ills which beset the farmer. Slowly but surely, Tillman was transforming the impotence of the farmer to achieve his goals into a condemnation of the social order which allowed him no avenue in which to do it. Existing institutions were buttressed by lawyers, merchants, and politicians. What was needed was for the 76 percent of the population who tilled the soil to assume control of these institutions and reform would flow like water from a spring. Tillman needed no program; he needed grievances, and there were enough of those around to fuel a Midianite war of extermination between Us and Them.[28]

---

27. Ibid., November 19, 1885, and Simkins, *Pitchfork Ben*, p. 95.

28. The type of agitation described has been labeled "non-programmatic radicalism" in Robert D. Marcus, "Wendell Phillips and American Institutions," *Journal of American History*, LVI (June, 1969), pp. 41–58. For other commentary on the absence of programmatic issues see Ball, *State that Forgot*, p. 217.

To counter the Tillman insurgency, the Conservative regime relied heavily on Captain Dawson; not because they felt the need for a leader, but because they wanted a defender with a large audience. The Charleston editor carried their case with all the confidence of a general who holds the strategic redoubts and overwhelming numerical superiority. He did not take farmer Tillman for granted. Like many other Conservatives he conceded the grounds for grievance and most of the farmers' demands. His strategy, if it could be called that, was to convince the antagonist that there was plenty of room for change within the system. At first Tillman proved receptive to Dawson's sympathetic and tolerant overtures, but with the same instinct that made him a radical without a program, he soon understood that the editor could kill him with kindness. He realized that tolerance could be repressive and that the fortunes of the movement depended far more on resistance than on acceptance by the established interests.[29]

In the interim between Bennettsville and Tillman's reemergence in November, 1885, the Edgefield farmer busied himself with more than the fall harvest. He corresponded with General Stephen D. Lee, a former South Carolinian who was then serving as president of the Mississippi Agricultural and Mechanical College at Starkville. Out of this correspondence Tillman became convinced that South Carolina needed a separate agricultural college, and on November 19 he launched a letter-writing campaign to the *News and Courier* that continued with only brief interruptions until farmer Tillman reached the governor's chair in 1890. His first letter began by denouncing those who laughed at his Bennettsville speech, continued by advocating the separate college idea, and concluded with the hope that he had "so successfully set the question afloat that it will not be allowed to sink out of sight anymore."

Dawson replied the following day giving Tillman's suggestion a full editorial column and urging the legislature to give the idea "the utmost consideration." Dawson then wrote Tillman asking him to be more specific as to how such an institution could be practically funded and established. When Tillman responded that the state was in all probability too poor at present but that means such as county subscriptions might be used to come up with the necessary $125,000, Dawson waived the objection, declaring that the farmers had exclusive claim on the land script fund and that the legislature should proceed to a consideration of the Tillman plan. On December 21 the *News and Courier* commended the senate for striking a proposal that would have increased appropriations for the agricultural annex at Columbia and gave its first positive editorial endorsement of the separate college.[30]

---

29. See Robert Paul Wolff, Barrington Moore, Jr., and Herbert Marcuse, *A Critique of Pure Tolerance* (Boston: Beacon Press, 1965).

30. *News and Courier*, November 19, 20, 30, December 1, 3, 4, 7, 9, 12, and 21, 1885.

Before leaving for an extended European vacation in early February, Dawson had time to publish Tillman's call for an agricultural convention and to observe that the call would be read "with interest throughout the State and with alarm by the politicians."[31] Dawson observed better than he knew. As he boarded the *Celtic* for Liverpool, he left behind a state on the verge of far greater turbulence than the signs of the time revealed.

Some were more uneasy than others. They saw in the agitation for a separate agricultural college an attack on their beloved institution at Columbia. To them the South Carolina College was not simply a place to equip young men for the professions, but an instrument for the preservation of civilization. No one could better speak for this group than the man who did more than any other to reopen the college after its degradation during Reconstruction. Charles H. Simonton, writing while the first flush of Redemption was in bloom, observed, "The war and the events since the war have demoralized our people fearfully. A whole generation has grown up uneducated. The honor and name of the State are to them, but a dream of their fathers. A new class are coming into control of the State, & a sort of Red Republican agrarian spirit is abroad. The college must check and destroy this."[32] Simonton and his fellow alumni were by no means a majority, even among Conservatives, but they did hold influential positions in the party. As one historian remarked, "A roll call of Conservative leaders read like a roster of the University alumni association."[33] This segment of the party would organize to defend the college against Till-mania, even as they had rescued its classical columns from Radical ruin and defended it against those Conservatives wedded to the church-supported institutions which dotted the state.

While Dawson was in Europe the *News and Courier* took a decidedly querulous posture toward the farmers' movement and its various demands. Always claiming support for the movement, the newspaper missed no opportunity to call into question various facts and assumptions which underlay the farmers' demands. The purpose of this sniping was to convince the farmers that since they were a majority they had no one else to blame but themselves. Again and again the paper cautioned against making the issues political and raised the specter of other classes combining to make their claims against the government. Chaos would result if the farmers went outside regular party channels. These editorials were served up as prelude to the Farmers' Convention which assembled in Columbia on April 29, 1886. The *News and Courier* was apparently satisfied that the farmers had heeded their warnings, for Dawson returned from Europe just

---

31. Ibid., January 28, 1886.

32. C. H. Simonton to W. P. Miles, May 25, 1877, William Porcher Miles Papers, Southern Historical Collection, University of North Carolina.

33. Cooper, *Conservative Regime,* p. 43.

in time to pronounce his verdict that "the State and the Democratic party have been acquitted before a jury of farmers, and upon a prosecution conducted wholly by farmers."[34]

The verdict may have been prematurely judged, for a few days later Tillman wrote Dawson asking why the *News and Courier* had been engaging in such "strange somersaulting of late." Tillman indicated that his friends had warned him against thinking that the Charleston paper was friendly, and he told Dawson that "the 'I told you sos' came thick and fast from many quarters." Always the master psychologist, Tillman went on to add that he had "told them 'Dawson is away & I will not believe he will fight me when he gets back.'" Tillman then asked Dawson if there were any material differences separating them on the issues and suggested that they meet in Augusta to discuss the matter.[35]

This overture was followed by two of the more candid letters that would pass between the men. Dawson expressed some difficulty in seeing just how the *News and Courier* had somersaulted and indicated that he had in no way changed his opinion of the movement or its demands. Admitting that he had had little time to inform himself about the convention proceedings, Dawson confessed that the convention appeared to go "far and away beyond the purposes of your movement as expressed to me in your letters before I went to Europe." He explained that what was in the beginning a proper demand for a college for farmers had suddenly become "an arraignment of the whole State Government, which is equivalent to an arraignment of the Democratic party in South Carolina; or, in other words, an arraignment of the white people of the State." Seeing no justification for such an indictment, Dawson felt constrained to ask again, "What are your purposes?" In concluding Dawson wrote, "Much as you dislike me personally, I cannot bear the idea that any two men who want to do good to South Carolina should get apart, or stay apart, and I count you and me as two such men." As for their meeting, Dawson stated a preference for conferring "within the State in a discussion which relates to South Carolina" and suggested Edgefield Court House "for there is to be a memorial meeting there this month and I have never visited your County Seat before."[36]

Tillman's reply first sought to disabuse the *News and Courier* reporters of the notion that it was "*my* convention." "You can believe me or not as you like," he told Dawson, "but time will prove that this is a deeprooted move on the part of the people & has nothing spasmodic or ephemeral about it." To Dawson's query concerning the purposes of the movement,

34. Editorial campaign in the *News and Courier,* March 9, 16, 19, April 2, 7, 8, 14, 28, 29, May 1, 3, and 4, 1886.

35. Tillman to Dawson, May 11, 1886, Dawson Papers, Duke.

36. Dawson to Tillman, May 13, 1886, ibid.

Tillman enumerated the following: a constitutional convention to abolish useless offices, repeal of the lien law, economy in government, equalization of taxes, primary elections, and a first-class agricultural college. Tillman added that the farmers also seemed pretty dead set against The Citadel as a useless extravagance. He closed saying that Dawson's "frankness" and "friendly interest" had "long since dissipated any [personal dislike] that I will not deny once existed." Tillman again called for a meeting between the two, conceding that while Dawson wielded "more influence than any one man in the state," he had come to inherit as much. "Together I am sure we can accomplish much good for the state," Tillman wrote, "opposed we may succeed in thwarting one another & thus do nothing."[37]

Though the Augusta meeting would eventually take on much political significance, the original purpose of the meeting was to review the issues and to discover what common ground might exist. The fact that the state convention was scheduled for August had little to do with the decision to seek a conference. Neither man was blind to the political possibilities, but the paramount purpose was to learn where each stood, with particular regards to the agricultural college and The Citadel. Tillman proved more willing to talk matters politic and was from the beginning more sensitive to the political implications of their coming together. The fact that the meeting took place in Augusta was a product of this concern. Dawson had suggested either Columbia or Edgefield Court House, but Tillman was intent on Augusta or perhaps Graniteville. The ostensible reason was the need to remain close to his farm, but his rejection of the Edgefield location indicates that he more likely feared the howl that would set up with such a meeting. Tillman was also the only one to make mention of consulting "about a state ticket," telling Dawson that the state must be "rid of the old Bourbon aristocrats & fogies—the 'raddlety-fog-mossites' . . . and inject new blood into the body politic."[38] If Dawson had a motive, other than sounding out the issues, it was more likely than not simple curiosity.

The two men finally agreed on Graniteville for June 1, but a change of gauge on the South Carolina Railway forced Dawson to turn back and arrangements were made to meet in Augusta on the following day. Meeting at the Globe Hotel, the two men dined and talked late into the evening. Dawson no doubt continued his inquiry as to just what the farmers wanted, and Tillman apparently satisfied the editor with his answers. They agreed that Dawson should continue his editorial advocacy of the agricultural college and a greater voice for farmers, while Tillman agreed to help call off opposition to The Citadel, or as Tillman called it, "the Dude Factory." Though they could not have avoided some discussion

---

37. Tillman to Dawson, May 17, 1886, ibid.

38. Tillman to Dawson, May 11 and 17; and Dawson to Tillman, May 13, 1886, ibid.

of political conditions in the state, subsequent correspondence revealed no agreement was reached at the Globe Hotel.[39] Having achieved their purpose, Tillman returned to his farm and Dawson went directly to Annapolis where he was to meet with the Board of Visitors.

Over the next two months Dawson and Tillman corresponded about various matters likely to be raised by the farmers in the coming state convention. Dawson was pleased to see that Tillman had moderated his estimate of the movement's strength, though the Edgefield farmer remained confident of an influential role in the convention. Dawson's major worry was the possibility of the agitation becoming a class movement pure and simple and repeatedly warned Tillman of the dangers in such a course. Tillman made it clear that "the farmers' movement as a class movement [would] return to its legitimate & original purposes only after obtaining political reformation on the lines indicated." Through June and into July the two men made only tentative reference to gubernatorial possibilities, with Dawson mentioning Alexander Cheves Haskell on one occasion and Tillman commenting about Edward McCrady on another.[40]

The talk of candidates did not become serious in any quarter of the state until Governor Thompson's surprise resignation in late June and his departure from office on July 9 to become assistant secretary of the treasury in Cleveland's administration. Tillman was the first to broach the subject, talking favorably about the chances of Lieutenant Governor John C. Sheppard of Edgefield. Tillman observed that he was friendly to the farmers and maintained a commitment both to the separate college idea and to The Citadel—"so you & I can both help him."[41] Dawson had no particular liking for Sheppard and only weeks before had asked the

---

39. Dawson discussed arrangements for the meeting in letters to his wife, May 26, 29, 31, and June 2, 1886, ibid.

40. Historians have overemphasized the political alliance between Dawson and Tillman. Simkins, without benefit of the Dawson-Tillman correspondence, was influenced by their mutual support of Sheppard in the state convention, *Pitchfork Ben,* p. 107. Cooper says that "mention of various state tickets . . . frequently appeared in their correspondence," *Conservative Regime,* p. 178. In fact, none of the correspondence mentions "state tickets," if that is taken to mean a slate of officers. Two letters in June make passing mention of Haskell and McCrady as possible candidates: Tillman to Dawson, June 22, and Dawson to Tillman, June 28, 1886. After the July resignation of Thompson, Tillman mentions his desire to support Sheppard, along with a number of other issues, in letters to Dawson, July 7, and an undated fragment ca. July, 1886. Only by collapsing the correspondence which runs from May 17 to August 24 into one unit can a case be made for a genuine convention alliance. As late as July 29, after they had both decided to support Sheppard, Tillman could write Dawson without mentioning candidates, but definitely promising to say nothing about The Citadel "if you stick to our understanding," the clear implication being that the agreement reached in the summer of 1886 centered on The Citadel and the separate college, and not strongly on much else. All correspondence is in the Dawson Papers, Duke.

41. Tillman to Dawson, July 7, 1886, Dawson Papers, Duke.

president to delay Thompson's pending federal appointment because "the people of the State would look with great aversion upon an act of yours that might promote the Lieutenant Governor."[42] But, despite his misgivings, events of early July made Dawson much more receptive to the idea of working with Tillman for Sheppard.

Rumors began to float that a combination was forming for the purpose of nominating Colonel William Chambers Coker of Darlington for governor, William Mauldin of Greenville for lieutenant governor, and Joseph Haynesworth Earle of Sumter for attorney general. For reasons that are not clear, Dawson strongly favored the renomination of Attorney General Charles Richardson Miles, perhaps because Miles gave Charleston its lone representative in the executive branch.[43] Desiring Miles's renomination and with no particular stake in the gubernatorial race, Dawson now found much more attractive a possible alliance with Tillman for political ends, and there was soon to be added to the rumor mill reports of a combination between Dawson and Tillman to advance Sheppard for governor, C. J. C. Hutson of Hampton for lieutenant governor, and Miles for attorney general.

The so-called combination was hardly worthy of the name. It was poorly organized and marked by less than enthusiastic support. Tillman himself conceded that the farmers were not yet sufficiently organized to control the convention and was even reluctant to openly endorse Sheppard "lest he lose support from other sources."[44] Moreover, by the time the convention came to order, Sheppard appeared to have reneged on his promises to the farmers, and Dawson was frank to admit that Charleston would give little support to the young lieutenant governor.[45] But whether a combination existed in fact was not nearly as important as what the delegates to the August convention thought was happening. On the evening of August 3, as the delegates were assembling, word passed that Tillman and Dawson had agreed to combine for Sheppard. Dawson later declared that the yarns were "told for a purpose."[46] Reacting to this rumor, among other consider-

42. Dawson reported his conversation with the president in a letter to Thompson, June 17, 1886, ibid.

43. Dawson may have had negative reasons to vote against the Mauldin-Earle combination. Mauldin supported the "Greenville idea" which would have apportioned party representation on the white vote, thereby penalizing Charleston. Moreover, the combination was closely abetted by Hampton lieutenants, see Isaac M. Bryan to Dawson, September 15, 1887, Dawson Papers, Duke.

44. Tillman to Dawson, July 7, 1886, ibid.

45. Simkins, *Pitchfork Ben,* p. 108; *News and Courier,* July 29 and August 5, 1886.

46. *News and Courier,* August 9, 1886. It is even possible that N. G. Gonzales was responsible for spreading the rumor. Ball wrote, "It reads a little queer now, but it is the simple truth that N. G. Gonzales . . . furnished the brain and energy for the Richardson candidacy and overcame his chief, Captain Dawson," *State that Forgot,* p. 214.

ations, the convention repudiated the aspirations of Sheppard and gave its support to John Peter Richardson, Clarendon farmer and descendent of a family that had produced four governors. The Augusta *Chronicle* was quick to lay the whole outcome of the convention on the doorsteps of the Globe Hotel. "What they talked about on that clear night," mused the paper, "no one knows, but the rumors growing out of that conference have shaped this convention and changed the personnel of the state ticket entirely."[47]

Neither Dawson nor Tillman felt they had as much at stake as others apparently thought. Writing to Sarah on the day after the convention, Dawson could say, "As a matter of fact, I took no particular interest in anything excepting the renomination of Mr. Miles, and the failure to accomplish that does not affect me in the least. I am on excellent terms with the nominees, and the candidate for governor is already overflowing with affection."[48] The redoubts of the Conservative regime were still secured by the best men.

The convention and the rumored combination did have one significant effect on the future of the state—it taught Ben Tillman a lesson. In the aftermath of the much publicized "Dawson-Tillman Sheppard Combination," the Edgefield farmer wrote Dawson suggesting that it would "be advisable for you once & a while to give me or the 'movement' a punch." Tillman promised to "regard them as 'love licks.'" It was all too reminiscent of an earlier strike for compromise when D. H. Chamberlain was constrained to write that he and Dawson should "not be too good friends." This time it was Tillman coming to the conclusion "that any thing like an 'alliance' between us will kill both. That is, *we* can understand one another but we must NEVER, NEVER, N E V E R, meet again to arrive at such understanding."[49] Tillman had learned, like Chamberlain before him, that while Dawson might speak with an independent mind and while he might have numerous friends, the editor's journal was ultimately the organ of the Conservative regime. For an outsider to be embraced by the *News and Courier* meant certain death among the constituents who gave the outsider his political life.

If Tillman despaired of an open alliance with Dawson, he was nonetheless still naive enough to hope for a combination between his farmers and Charleston against the influences he saw emanating from Columbia. Charleston might remain a good whipping boy for purposes of his rural

47. Augusta *Chronicle,* August 5, 1886.

48. Dawson to his wife, August 6, 1886, Dawson Papers, Duke. See also Dawson to C. S. McCall, August 10, 1886, Charles Spencer McCall Papers, scl. For Tillman's and Dawson's public denials of the combination see the *News and Courier,* August 27 and September 9, 1886.

49. Tillman to Dawson, August 24, 1886, Dawson Papers, Duke.

audiences, but his sixth political sense told him that officeholders, whom he identified with Columbia, were the real cement of the existing order. "Whatever happens," he wrote Dawson, "I hope for the good of the state that Charleston & Columbia will remain at loggerheads." He believed that Charleston now had "a good excuse & opportunity to regain the esteem & respect of the state," and he called on Dawson to lead his city in this political reformation. Something in Tillman made him understand that Charleston was almost as distant from power as were his farmers, that while Charleston had given much to the consolidation of the Conservative regime, she had in fact received very little in return.[50]

Tillman concluded his observations on the state of the state with a plea that Dawson write "a long letter & show your side of the mirror." Whether Dawson ever wrote the letter or reflected on the possibility of reforming the state's political boundaries is not known. The prospects of such an idea would have appealed to his general sense of political independence, but he would have needed time to reflect, and events were fast running ahead of any time for reflection. One week to the day after Tillman placed his letter in the mail, the earth fractured somewhere under the old City by the Sea. The devastation which followed turned men's attention from political reform to the more immediate problems of relief and recovery.

Eight months were to pass before Dawson could find much time for the movement. Preoccupied first with the aftermath of the earthquake, then with his speeches and editorials to counteract Henry Grady's December sensation, and finally with another trip to Europe, the Charleston editor momentarily lost control of the situation. By the time he returned from Europe at the end of April, 1887, the Tillman movement and the alumni of the South Carolina College had locked horns. Moreover, it was axiomatic that when Dawson was away from the *News and Courier* the paper slanted in an anti-Tillman direction. N. G. Gonzales, Carlyle McKinley, and J. C. Hemphill found it difficult to conceal their contempt for the unruly Edgefield farmer.[51]

Dawson did find time to offer some encouragement and assistance to Tillman during the legislative session of December, 1886. But Tillman had decided to abandon, at least temporarily, the separate college idea and to concentrate on a reorganization of the state agricultural department. The end result of such vacillation was bitter disappointment on all counts. To compound Tillman's despondency, the proponents of a university at Columbia seemed to be gaining ground. In fact, the period stretching from

---

50. Ibid. Though Charleston had a capable legislative delegation from 1877–1890, she went virtually unrepresented in the executive branch during that same period.

51. Carlyle McKinley to J. C. Hemphill, August 29, 1886, Hemphill Family Papers, Duke. Tillman complained about the staff in letters to Dawson, July 29, 1886, and January 3, 1887, Dawson Papers, Duke.

September 1886 to June 1887 proved a significant turning point in the fortunes of those Conservatives wedded to the college at Columbia. In September they had feared their college's becoming a "fossilized institution," but by June of the following year the trustees could pass a resolution looking to an expanded university, including colleges of literature, law, and agriculture.[52] Tillman was bitter. He complained to Dawson that "the present legislature has failed most ignominiously to do any thing to give relief or even promise relief." The irate farmer went on to warn that unless something were done to give "my crowd" hope, it would be only "a question of time . . . when the Democratic party will be broken up." He told Dawson to look on the farmer's movement as a "safety-valve" which would prevent the evil day when "the Devil" would tempt "men to use the negro vote to carry their ends." When that day came, the black man would "become the balance of power between the Rich Ruling Bourbons and the poor-feeling & more progressive among our people—I fear this—God grant I am mistaken."[53]

Dawson responded to Tillman's prayer with an editorial declaring that "if South Carolina cannot afford [a farmers' college], it cannot afford to be a State."[54] But the season was not right for agitation. The legislature had adjourned, bleak winter was upon the land, and the contest between Bourbon and farmer would not wax warm again until June. With June temperatures rising, Tillman and the friends of the college began bursting out all over the pages of the *News and Courier*. Paul F. Hammond of Beech Island was the first bloom on the bush with a long letter defending the idea of an expanded university, and Tillman wrote Dawson the same day demanding that the *News and Courier* send one of its correspondents to Starkville for the commencement exercises of the Mississippi college. Tillman observed that any paper that could send a reporter to Liberia could surely get one to Mississippi.[55] Of the two groups, Dawson was still much closer to the farmers on the issue of separate agricultural education. Not only did Dawson dispatch a reporter to Mississippi, but when the South Carolina alumni erupted in celebration on the announcement that their revered president, James M. McBryde, had withdrawn his resignation, Dawson threw water on the celebrants by saying "there was too much gush about this business." Dawson further warned, "It is not to be expected that his [McBryde's] retention will, or should, place the College above criticism."[56]

---

52. Daniel Walker Hollis, *University of South Carolina*, vol. II, *College to University* (Columbia: University of South Carolina Press, 1956), p. 143.

53. Tillman to Dawson, December 23, 1886, Dawson Papers, Duke.

54. *News and Courier*, January 31, 1887.

55. *News and Courier*, June 15, 1887. Tillman to Dawson, June 15 and 25, 1887, Dawson Papers, Duke. The reference was to the *News and Courier*'s sending A. B. Williams to Liberia to report on the Liberian Exodus project for blacks.

56. *News and Courier*, June 24, 1887.

Taken back by such an off handed dismissal of their institution and its president, the friends of the college immediately sent an emissary to Dawson to set matters straight. A. C. Haskell wrote the Charleston editor, saying that McBryde was quite ill and that to continue the *News and Courier*'s criticism of the college might "do fatal personal (I mean physical) injury." Haskell concluded with a request that he be permitted to come in early July to discuss the whole matter, "and if you feel obliged by your convictions to adopt a course antagonistic to the College I give you my word I will tell you as soon as McBryde is well enough."[57] Whether Haskell ever had his talk with Dawson or whether he ever gave the go-ahead is not known. Regardless of what passed between the two men, the *News and Courier* soon commenced a six day, front page, review of the work of General Lee's college at Starkville—the timing of the series clearly indicating that Haskell had been far from convincing. Nor was their any mistaking the caption of the last feature article: "MOSSBACKS IN MISSISSIPPI: WHAT THEY ARE DOING TO CRIPPLE THE FARMERS' COLLEGE."[58]

To give so deliberate offense to the influential friends of the college was curious behavior for the chief defender of the Conservative regime. The probable explanation is that in the summer of 1887 Dawson saw little cause to sacrifice the state's political unity for the sake of a proud and intransigent group of alumni. He still believed that the farmers' movement could be accommodated within the Democratic party as it was then constituted. Furthermore, there were large numbers of denominationalists among the Conservatives, men who had little use for the godless education which proceeded from Columbia. Thus, for the sake of the party, the state, and the white man, it was far better to encourage the numerically superior farmers than to assuage the anxieties of a class of men who had long been accustomed to the homage of a grateful state.[59]

But Dawson was willing to stand by the maverick politician only so long as Tillman remained content to wage a limited war against the established interests. Once Tillman proved willing to move to upper limits in his struggle against the "raddlety-fog-mossites," Dawson called a halt. By the end of September, 1887, the *News and Courier* could no longer countenance the continued intemperance of its erstwhile friend, particularly when Tillman would not stop his endless charges of extravagance and corruption in the state government. In obvious exasperation Dawson wrote, "The government we have is not the most brilliant, or the wisest, in the world; but it is honest and it is safe." By December the editor was convinced that the movement had been seriously "weakened by want of shading and perspective in the speeches and letters of some of its leaders."[60]

---

57. A. C. Haskell to Dawson, June 26, 1887, Dawson Papers, Duke.

58. *News and Courier*, July 7, 8, 9, 11, 12, and 13, 1887.

59. Cooper is correct when he writes that Dawson hoped "to modify Tillman's program and to make him a pillar of the Conservative regime," *Conservative Regime*, p. 177.

60. *News and Courier*, September 22 and December 1, 1887.

The growing alienation from Tillman forced Dawson to reassess his position, and when the board of trustees reported its plan to ask the legislature for a centralized university with an enlarged department of agriculture, Dawson and the *News and Courier* abandoned the farmers' movement. On the third day of December the Charleston paper announced its intention to support the college as it aspired to become a university, and Dawson prepared to do battle with the irrepressible Ben Tillman.

The Edgefield farmer was too wise not to know it was coming, but the feeling of betrayal rankled nonetheless. In a letter to Dawson, Tillman promised an acrimonious campaign against The Citadel along with specifications for his charges "about extravagances & shortcomings of our state government." "You have deserted us," Tillman charged, "just at the critical time when with your steadfast support . . . success would have crowned our efforts." Dawson's reply was calm and reasoned. He explained that three arguments compelled his change of mind. The first two were well known to Tillman—cost and the doubt that people were in a mood to have it passed at this time. The third argument came from "the other side" and persuaded Dawson "that just such practical and scientific education as is given at Mississippi College, *could* be given, and in large measure, is given, at the University in Columbia." Dawson asked Tillman not to despair, for there was no chance of a separate college at present and if the experiment in Columbia should fail, "the separate college will be a necessity."[61]

Dawson's desertion and the subsequent triumph of the alumni in the legislature contributed to a suspect decision by Tillman to retire from an active role in the movement. As usual he sent his announcement to the *News and Courier*. In the covering letter he told Dawson that the announcement was designed to give public notice "that the so called 'alliance' between us is ended." Tillman concluded with an "assurance that I have a much better opinion of you personally than I ever expected when I first wrote you in Nov. 1885, & hoping that the kind feelings I have are reciprocated." For his part, Dawson made a simple observation in the *News and Courier*. "There will doubtless be another farewell," he wrote, "and another and another. As he has not lagged superfluous on the stage, he can with good grace permit himself to come on the scene again."[62]

Tillman's political resurrection was not long in coming and was occasioned by a death. Early in April, 1888, Thomas G. Clemson, son-in-law of John C. Calhoun, died, leaving behind his Fort Hill estate and a cash

---

61. Tillman to Dawson, December 12, 1887; and Dawson to Tillman, December 14, 1887, and January 2, 1888, Dawson Papers, Duke.

62. Tillman to Dawson, January 20, 1888, Dawson Papers, Duke. *News and Courier,* January 26, 1888.

endowment in excess of $80,000 for the purpose of establishing an agricultural college. This turn of events was not unexpected, for Clemson was an old man and had only a short time before conferred with Tillman and others about his wish to aid agricultural education.[63] The friends of the college at Columbia greeted the news with grim resignation. Despite their recent victory in the legislature, they knew that without the cost objection efforts to continue the battle against the farmers' college would seem churlish at best. Dilatory actions were taken, but only to delay the inevitable.

As from the beginning, the separate college was but a symbol of the broader movement, and with the renascence of the symbol, Tillman was prepared to take the larger case to the Democratic state convention in May. In his most vivid language, the unretired agitator described the state government as a place where "putrefaction" had set in and called on the incredulous delegates to adopt a primary system of nominations and thereby end the abuses emanating from Columbia. The News and Courier was delighted with Tillman's performance, believing he had been given rope in plenty to hang himself. "The best cause the world has known," declared Dawson, "would be ruined by an advocate who has no sense of propriety and little self-control."[64] But while Tillman was defeated on the issue of primaries, he succeeded in getting the convention to call for joint debates in each congressional district so that state-wide candidates would have to declare themselves on the issues. Not surprisingly, these joint debates also afforded Tillman the opportunity of stalking the candidates from district to district and carrying his case directly to the people. Red Shirts would remember it as "division of time," only this time it had the sanction of law.

The first meeting was held on the twentieth of July at Hodges Depot in Abbeville County, and Tillman wasted little time in naming the principal villain in the conspiracy against open government. With language to delight his audience, he declared the villain to be "some buzzard who had escaped from the market house in Charleston and gone into the News and Courier office, where it was spewing its slime all over me."[65] He was now calling out the very man who, Tillman conceded, had given him his audience and in whose debt he stood.[66] The sly fox from Edgefield realized that the time had come when there was more to be gained from Dawson's opposition than from his cooperation, and the lion of Broad Street obligingly fell into the trap.

---

63. Hollis, *College to University*, p. 140.

64. *News and Courier*, May 19, 1888.

65. Simkins explains, "At that time buzzards were allowed to hover around Charleston's famous market and eat the refuse," *Pitchfork Ben*, p. 127.

66. Cooper, *Conservative Regime*, p. 146; and Tillman to Dawson, May 11, 1886, Dawson Papers, Duke.

Receiving word of Tillman's personal attack on his character, Dawson hastened to Greenville in hopes of meeting his defamer in the open, but much to his dismay the people of Greenville had not invited the Edgefield farmer. Dawson contented himself with showing how the people might discern between "the true reformer and the false" and with assurances that he would soon force his accuser into the open.[67] In the meantime the *News and Courier* issued calls for Tillman to come to Charleston and for the farmers to abandon their errant leader in favor of the Farmers' Alliance. The paper even promised to become the organ of the Alliance efforts in South Carolina, for that organization had prudently shunned politics.[68]

After Greenville, Dawson reported to New York where the Democratic National Committee was in session, but on learning that Tillman would join the canvass in Charleston itself, Dawson hurried back to observe the spectacle. With torchlights casting their eerie glow over the throng gathered in Washington Square, the various candidates presented their qualifications and were received with polite enthusiasm. The audience was clearly waiting to hear what the agricultural Moses would say, and they were not disappointed. With Dawson present, Tillman threw himself into a performance that foreshadowed the stump politician of the South's future. In the midst of cheers, laughter, and shouts of "Let'er go Gallagher," he alternately abused and amused his audience. At one point he referred to N. G. Gonzales who, in Dawson's absence, had been carrying the commentary on Tillman's antics. With flashing eye and snapping jaw, Tillman cried that he knew the "big buzzard was away, but there was a little buzzard down there who wanted to spew a little slime over me." Apart from this digression, farmer Tillman steered clear of direct references to Dawson and stuck to his stock indictment of state government. Toward the end of his speech a sharp noise sent the crowd scurrying, but Dawson immediately took center stage to restore order. He begged the crowd to give the visiting statesman a patient ear. Moreover, he promised that should Tillman be unable to proceed he "would cheerfully hire the largest hall in Charleston, in which Capt. Tillman should speak as long as he chose and at any time that he might appoint."[69]

When asked later why he had not rebutted Tillman's speech, Dawson claimed that the visiting speaker gave no personal insult and thus any comment on his part would have been superfluous.[70] In fact, Dawson was quite content to let matters stand, confident that Tillman's shrill invective would be the instrument of the farmer's downfall. Dawson's confidence

---

67. *News and Courier,* July 25, 1888.
68. Ibid., July 12 and 13, 1888.
69. Ibid., August 4, 1888.
70. Ibid., August 29, 1888.

was unfounded, for unknown to him the "hard-fisted Democracy" had listened all too attentively to the political pariah from Edgefield. Short days after the August third rally, petitioners were beseeching Tillman to return to Charleston to help them secure "a full, free and fair party vote" and an end to "ring rule." The petition clearly labeled the *News and Courier* as the sinister force behind ring domination. "For years past we have had but one daily paper," declared the plaintiffs, "and this powerful influence in distorting fact and suppressing party information has fostered a political combination, numerically small, but so aided and protected it has largely dominated our county affairs."[71]

Dawson was stunned. He had known for some time that there were grumblings from the Democracy and a lot of loose talk about ring rule, but he also believed that he had met each charge with overwhelming evidence of his and the regime's good faith. Had he not called on the malcontents to prove malfeasance, and had they not remained silent? Had he not time and again asked them to end their complaints by working within the party apparatus, and had they not shown their indifference by failing to attend ward meetings? Now in pontifical language Dawson felt justified in rebuking the petitioners for impugning the integrity of all the good and honorable men who served Charleston. It was his pet response for those who dared challenge the ruling elite. But this time, after invoking the names of the Simontons, the Jerveys, the Dibbles, the McCradys, the Lessesnes, ad infinitum, he concluded by pointing to the gravest fault of all. This time the complainers had gone outside Charleston for counsel, and not to a Hampton, or Butler, or Izlar, or Bratton, but to a "professional agitator—who is looked upon with distrust, if not aversion, by the respectable people of the whole State."[72]

All the editor's righteous indignation was to no avail. Events were hastening with inexorable force toward their denouement, and all the king's men could not silence the steady clink of the sapper's chisel. Tillman was returning to Charleston by invitation, and under an evening sky full of distant lightning and thunder he took his place on the steps of city hall, beneath the spire of St. Michael's. Before he was finished speaking the multitude swelled to three thousand. Again he abused them to their own delight. He called them "the most arrant set of cowards that ever drew the free air of heaven" and was greeted by cheers and laughter. He prayed for mercy on their "pusillanimous souls," and again they shouted their approval. "You are here cringing," he cried, "you are binding yourselves down in the mire because you are afraid of the newspaper down the street." Emboldened by another round of laughter and applause, Tillman compared the editor to the "colossus," with one foot on Georgetown and

---

71. Ibid., August 14, 1888.
72. Ibid.

the other on Beaufort, "while we poor petty men, whose boots he ain't fit to lick, are crawling under him seeking dishonored graves." Cries of "Trot him out" welled up from the crowd.[73]

A Dawson informer darted up the street to the offices of the *News and Courier* where the editor was busy at work. The excited informant told Dawson that Tillman was dragging out all the old charges of printing frauds and Dawson's support of the Chamberlain government, whereupon the editor prepared to meet his accuser. He reached the outer edge of the crowd just as Tillman berated them for not having "killed a nigger" after what the blacks had done at Cainhoy.[74] Dawson's arrival created a sensation, and the crowd parted to let him take his seat on the steps of city hall to await the conclusion of Tillman's remarks. The editor was just in time to hear Tillman explain that "Dawsonism is the domination of that old, effete aristocratic element that clings to power with the grip of the octopod." Having done his worst, Tillman turned the platform over to Dawson who, while not prepared, must have given the possibility of rebuttal some thought.[75]

Dawson opened with an apology lest his voice not reach the entire crowd, for he was "not accustomed to large open-air meetings." The editor early got a chance to display his verbal facility when a shout rose from the audience asking "How about the buzzard?" Dawson paused a moment to let the crowd settle and replied, "There would not be any buzzard if there was no carrion. It is necessary to have scavengers sometimes, and, though I don't like the comparison, when you put the buzzard on me, I can put the carrion on him." As the laughter died away, Dawson proceeded to the same old defense of his actions during Reconstruction that he had employed on countless occasions. When it was over, Tillman left with his escort for the Charleston Hotel, and Dawson, with his friends, retired to the *News and Courier* offices. The following evening a crowd of some two hundred gathered under Dawson's Broad Street window to shout their hurrahs for the editor and to taunt his enemies. The dramatic confrontation between the old and the new was over, but its portents for the future were unsettling. The foundations of the Conservative regime had been badly shaken. The Greenville *News*, which had "looked for a strong debate on pending political issues," could well ask, "What good has been done?"[76]

---

73. Ibid., August 29, 1888.

74. Cainhoy was the site of a political meeting near Charleston during which a riot broke out, leaving one black and four whites dead. The riot occurred in the campaign of 1876.

75. *News and Courier*, August 29, 1888.

76. Ibid., August 29 and 30, 1888. Greenville *News*, August 30, 1888.

A staff reporter who recorded the events of that August confrontation unwittingly betrayed the vulnerable point in the Conservative armor. With the arrogance of those near power, the reporter sought biblical reference to describe the throng that assembled to hear Tillman. Taking his text from the second book of Samuel, he wrote, "And every one that was in distress, and every one that was in debt, and every one that was discontented, gathered themselves unto him; and he became a captain over them." It was an apt description of those who came under the spell of Tillmania. When days later Dawson advocated a "campaign of silence" against Tillman,[77] he was too late. The Edgefield farmer had already assembled his hosts. It was one movement the *News and Courier* would be unable to silence. Dawson was no longer master of a real or an imaginary kingdom.

---

77. Dawson to J. C. Hemphill, September 11, 1888, Hemphill Family Papers, Duke.

Chapter IX
"A Tiger and a Child"

Francis Dawson was two-and-a-half years in the Confederate army before his letters home mentioned the darker-skinned population who figured so prominently in bringing the nation to civil war. Even then the acknowledgment was indirect. He declared to his mother that he "could open the eyes of the abolitionists in England if I had the opportunity." A few weeks later he cautioned his mother not to believe the Yankee accounts of the battles and spoke of northern atrocities, particularly the bayoneting of wounded Confederates by Negro soldiers. His last mention of blacks before the war's end was a casual reference to his "beautiful negro servant" who recently "comforted me with a broiled chicken and some stewed apples," only to turn and take flight with Dawson's prize horse.[1]

It is difficult to account for this lack of focus on so central a theme in southern history. It is true that young Dawson was preoccupied with the excitement of war and his advancement in the ranks, but he made frequent comment on the nature of Yankee aggression still without mentioning their design on the Negro population in the South. It may be that Dawson truly believed, as he declared in his reminiscences, that he was joining a struggle for independence. Like many of his fellow countrymen he "did not believe slavery was the issue at stake. Even Samuel Wilberforce, bishop of Oxford and son of the great abolitionist William Wilberforce, supported Confederate independence."[2]

If Dawson thought the war a matter of home rule, the aftermath of the conflict left him face to face with the issue of race, for the southern people and the nation were turning to the question of who should rule at home. Not long after Appomattox, Dawson told his father that "the negro question is now the great difficulty for solution." Having seen slavery "in every Southern State," he was convinced that bondage was for the Negro "the best condition in every way that has been devised." The young Englishman believed that the planters in Virginia and North Carolina would benefit from emancipation, but he feared that wage labor would

---

1. Dawson to his mother, June 1, 26, and October 13, 1864, Dawson Papers, Duke University Library, cited hereafter as Duke. F. W. Dawson, *Reminiscences of Confederate Service, 1861-1865* (Charleston: *The News and Courier* Book Presses, 1882), pp. 123–24.

2. Dawson, *Reminiscences*, p. 3. Joseph M. Hornon, Jr., "British Sympathies in the American Civil War: A Reconsideration," *Journal of Southern History*, XXXIII (August, 1967), pp. 360–61.

force "women with families and old men [to be] turned adrift by the thousands."[3]

Dawson did find that "in the towns the smart and active negroes are doing very well, but their insolence is beyond all expectation." More than anything else, it was the blacks' assertion of their newly won freedom that pricked the pride of race and drew Dawson into the common understanding of what it meant to be southern and white. He told his father of a mass meeting organized by blacks "to demand right of voting and perfect equality with the whites," and he prophesied that events were "coming to such a pass that either the man of color or the white has to leave this fair Country: the whites will not submit to the insolence of a negro, and so soon as the Yankee troops are withdrawn . . . the negroes will have to be careful how they act and talk."[4]

Dawson's feeling for the Negro alternated between fear and pity, but in either instance his overriding wish was to be rid of the black presence. On one occasion he blurted that his father's "abolition friends who think so highly of Yankee philanthropy" should be made to see the Negroes' "most miserable condition." He saw them "dying by hundreds with starvation and sickness" and could "only hope now as the best thing for them that the whole negro race will soon become extinct."[5] On another occasion pity turned to hate, and he vented his pent-up feelings in a letter to his mother:

> The negroes are protected by the Yankees in everything that they do, and are accorded a thousand privileges that are denied to us. They are permitted for instance to form military companies, they have arms, drill on the public streets, and parade with drums and fifes at any hour of the night. They grow more insolent every day, and unless there is a change in their *status* there must be a collision before long. If so [we will] with God's help kill all the miserable scoundrels and get rid of them once and forever. Were the Yankees but to let us alone the negroes would behave themselves, and they would be treated well, but as it is they are continually taught that they are better than the whites and they naturally think that what is good enough for the whites is not good enough for them. If a war of race once commence, the blacks will be exterminated.[6]

The intensity of Dawson's feeling sprang from a combination of the exhilaration he experienced in war and the deep, sinking sense of betrayal when forced to stand with a defeated army. Throughout the conflict he had been a bitter-ender, arguing against hope that "whatever our disaster the

---

3. Dawson to his father, June 13, 1865, Dawson Papers, Duke.

4. Ibid.

5. Ibid., October 4, 1865.

6. Dawson to his mother, July 28, 1866, ibid.

South can never give up, we must struggle, still struggle to the last."[7] But the desire to continue the struggle was betrayed, and he blamed the planter class with their propertied slaves for the losing of the cause. "You would have supposed," Dawson wrote his father, "that having taken the first step the People wd have been willing to sacrifice every farthing of their property to win success, as that success could bring them a liberty and freedom without which money would be worse than valueless." Bitterly he complained, "They were willing to give their sons and brothers to our Army, saw their lives offered as sacrifices upon the alter of their Country, and still could bear a proud heart amid tears, but the moment their property was jeopardized they became anxious for Peace at no matter what price." The young adventurer concluded angrily that "the majority would I am convinced rather have placed in the Army ten sons than one negro."[8]

Thus, through a strange perversion of the logical processes, Dawson came to believe that the black man by his very existence corrupted the dominant class in the South and sapped its will to resist. He conceived of no positive contribution made by the African transplant, thought the South was better off without slavery, and saw the enduring legacy of emancipation to be an antagonism of race that would not abate. He hated blacks not because of their assumed racial inferiority, but because they killed his personal dreams of glory and adventure. They were not active agents in killing the dream, but, like the proverbial millstone, they dragged down the better instincts of the dominant race. Even their despised insolence was attributed to the encouragements and blandishments of the Yankee rather than an active resentment born of racial subordination. The Negro was a zero, a dead weight on society, and a blight on the body politic.

By the time Dawson was heard from again, he had moved from Richmond to Charleston, but far from imbibing that city's elixir of rebellion, the young Englishman had seemingly sobered on the subject of race relations and began arguing for a more accommodating spirit. Having joined the staff of the Charleston *Mercury*, Dawson surprised his employers, the Rhetts, by suggesting "that they should advise the South to swallow the Fourteenth Amendment, to avoid worse trouble." Dawson believed the *Mercury* was in a unique position to counsel moderation "because no one would suspect it of cowardice or disloyalty to the South." He further told the Rhetts that "it would insure the prosperity of *The Mercury*, make it the paper of the South and save the people from frightful misery."[9] To the Rhetts it must have been at least mildly amusing to hear a

---

7. Ibid., December 25, 1864.

8. Dawson to his father, June 13, 1865, ibid.

9. Dawson to R. R. Hemphill, January 28, 1876, Hemphill Family Papers, Duke. Abbeville *Medium*, February 9, 1876.

young white man who had not yet gained his own citizenship arguing to accept the prerogatives of citizenship for a race of former slaves.

Dawson had not suddenly seen the light of racial harmony, but he was beginning to move in the direction of a racial accommodation which would provide some modus vivendi until white supremacy could be restored. In another year, after acquiring part-ownership of the *Daily News,* Dawson advocated a biracial ticket in the Charleston municipal elections and was moving toward a policy of fusion with reform-minded Republicans.[10] In 1876 he held out to the last against the "Mississippi plan" of taking the state straight-out, and in so doing jeopardized his personal influence to sustain the reform administration of Daniel Chamberlain. Such an alliance led Belton O'Neall Townsend to declare that "it seemed as if a political millenium were about to dawn."[11] So earnestly did Dawson work for a spirit of racial conciliation that he won the plaudits of early historians of the New South. "At a time when it was dangerous in South Carolina to counsel moderation and advocate compromise," wrote Broadus Mitchell, "he favored the placing of negroes on the Democratic ticket for municipal office in Charleston." Virginius Dabney in his chronicle of liberalism in the South could affirm that "the editor of the *News and Courier* was always a staunch ally of the Negroes."[12]

Mitchell, writing in the early twentieth century, no doubt exaggerated the danger in advocating compromise and counseling moderation, for Dawson was joined by a very distinguished company of South Carolinians. He could easily have taken his cue from the likes of Wade Hampton or James Lawrence Orr. These men realized that a new day had dawned, that the Fourteenth Amendment was a part of the organic law, and that armed with the ballot the freedman was a political fact of life. They too sought some black and white arrangement through which, it was hoped, antebellum authority might continue to be asserted for the common weal. In the end they were all surprised to discover that the Negro had a political mind of his own, that he preferred to be governed by members of his own race, and that efforts to restore white supremacy under whatever ruse—biracial tickets or fusion—would be met with suspicion if not determined resistance.[13]

---

10. In addition to ibid., see Dawson to his father, August 26, 1868, Dawson Papers, Duke.

11. Belton O'Neall Townsend, "The Political Condition of South Carolina," *The Atlantic Monthly* (February, 1877), p. 182.

12. Broadus Mitchell, "Francis Warrington Dawson," *Dictionary of American Biography,* ed. by Allen Johnson and Dumas Malone (New York: Charles Scribner's Sons, 1930), vol. V, pp. 1512-52. Virginius Dabney, *Liberalism in the South* (Chapel Hill: University of North Carolina Press, 1932), pp. 231–32.

13. See Joel Williamson, *After Slavery: The Negro in South Carolina During Reconstruction, 1861–1877* (Chapel Hill: University of North Carolina Press, 1965), pp. 349–56.

During the decade of Reconstruction in South Carolina blacks participated in corruption and reform, passed good and bad laws, and wrote a constitution under which whites lived for twenty years after Redemption. Blacks were for the most part a benevolent majority. They seemed to understand the political philosophy of égalité far better than did their Caucasian neighbors who inherited the paradox of slavery and freedom and who, like their fathers, created myths to rationalize the dilemma. When later faced with disfranchisement, men like Robert Smalls, Thomas Ezekiel Miller, and Henry McNeal Turner spoke with a critical realism about race relations that the nation would not appreciate until the Second Reconstruction dissolved the myths that sustained both slavery and Jim Crow.

But black leaders of the time had to contend with a society blind to recent perceptions of reality. The Negro's creditable record during Reconstruction was achieved in the midst of a world that had been made by slaveholders and which only reluctantly yielded to the "moral capital" a civil war had produced. They labored while white men tried to use their ignorance, threatened their lives and property, or at best resisted passively. What ultimately broke the back of Reconstruction in South Carolina was that white men, North and South, had no faith in the capacity of the black man to govern. The last governor elected by blacks deserted them, and the nation turned its back so that white men could rule. A young Charleston reporter observed better than he knew when shortly after passage of the Fourteenth Amendment he wrote, "nothing can save us but a complete revulsion of feeling in the North."[14]

As the blue-clad troops marched out of Columbia and the red-shirted legions marched in, blacks were to be confronted by a Democratic governor who spoke remarkably like the last Republican. Even while many Democrats were rewriting the record book on election fraud and violence, Wade Hampton spoke of conciliation. He promised that under his administration the Negro would not be deprived of a single right he then exercised. Moreover, Hampton seemed sincere. So temperate was his manner and so moderate his words that contemporaries and historians have quarreled over whether it was Hampton's policy of conciliation or Martin Gary's ideas on white terror that won the election of 1876. Perhaps the best guess was that violence was essential in transforming the black majority into a minority, but that "it probably would have been impossible to carry a campaign of intimidation without serious interference from the national authorities had not the campaign been tempered by the moderation of Hampton."[15]

---

14. Dawson to his mother, September 2, 1865, Dawson Papers, Duke.

15. George Brown Tindall, *South Carolina Negroes, 1877-1900* (Columbia: University of South Carolina Press, 1952), p.13.

Although threat and appeasement were born twins in the campaign of '76, those who espoused moderation were not necessarily duplicitous. One observer of the schizophrenic mind induced by the tension of race in a free society remarked that "hypocrisy requires a rare clarity of mind combined with an unscrupulous intention to deceive."[16] Most of the Conservatives who stood with Hampton possessed neither the clarity of mind nor the intent to deceive that would have branded them as hypocrites. When Dawson proclaimed that "the South . . . is bound more strongly than by hooks of steel to a faithful and generous regard for the rights of every class of citizen," he was in earnest.[17] That a dual personality existed among South Carolina Democrats, born of divergent emotional and philosophical approaches to the problem of race, cannot be denied. Neither can it be denied that men like Hampton and Dawson represented a more accommodating spirit. One has only to turn to the correspondence of their antagonists within the party.

Hampton's enemies regarded him "as the exponent of extreme conservatism and niggerism," while they looked upon Martin Gary as "the unflinching advocate of White Supremacy."[18] Those who supported Hampton came under the same fire. One Gary journal condemned "Mr. Dawson and his followers" for their "leading ideas of moderation, toleration and liberality."[19] In fact it was much easier for the Garyites to attack a man like Dawson because of his alien birth. "He is an Englishman by birth," declared one paper, "and, as such, is not acquainted with the . . . history of the State." Another paper, concerned that a foreigner should be "the guide to public opinion and the mould of public expediency in South Carolina," asserted, "Why it takes a generation or two of training for foreigners to divest themselves of todyism." Still another journal complained, "The very idea of this paper, owned and controlled by a foreigner, saying it had made Gary 'show his hand' . . . is absurd."[20] It was often difficult to tell which the supporters of Gary despised more, Hampton's race policy or the "foreign" editor who espoused it.

The dualism which characterized the campaign of 1876 spilled over into Charleston's municipal elections of 1877. The city's business community, which sustained Hampton's stand on race just as they had formed the nucleus for the policy of fusion, was, for once, caught napping. The Trojan horse was Major William W. Sale. Organizing his forces in the late summer

---

16. Edmund Sears Morgan, "Slavery and Freedom: The American Paradox," *Journal of American History,* LIX (June, 1972), p. 7.

17. *News and Courier,* September 27, 1877.

18. Ellis G. Graydon to M. W. Gary, August 19, 1878, M. W. Gary Papers, South Caroliniana Library, University of South Carolina, cited hereafter as SCL.

19. Greenville *News,* September 8, 1878.

20. Ibid. Beaufort *Crescent,* May 13, 1880. Georgetown *Times and Comet,* May 20, 1880.

of 1877, Sale took the ward meetings by storm, gained the nomination of the city convention, and went on to win the election over an Independent in December. Sale was persona non grata among Charleston's Conservative elite. Reared in the seedbed of South Carolina extremism, "bloody Edgefield," Sale had been a resident of Charleston for "only" twenty years. His previous experience in public service consisted of one term as intendant of the infamous little town of Hamburg. The *News and Courier* voiced the opposition to Sale in blunt words. It was not that the ex-intendant was dishonest, but "that he has not proved his ability to deal with complicated administrative questions, and it is feared that he might be controlled by influences unfavorable to the security of property . . . and the maintenance of good feeling between the different classes of people."[21] In roundabout fashion Dawson was charging Sale with being too close to Gary, and there was good reason, for Gary's followers were looking confidently to the establishment of a rival newspaper in Charleston should Sale be elected.[22]

To counteract Sale's capture of the ward meetings, the business community formed an eleventh-hour committee of Conservative Democrats to interject some common sense into the city convention, but the Sale forces were too well organized and the effort failed. Conservatives viewed with particular alarm the absence of a sufficient representation of blacks on the aldermanic ticket. Speaking for the Conservatives, Dawson lamented the fact that at least "two or three more colored men" had not been nominated, but he hastened to reassure the colored population that the Democrats were still committed to the Hampton platform of 1876. These assurances became even more earnest when an Independent candidate emerged on a platform that criticized the regular Democrats for failing to live up to Hampton's promises.[23]

There were other critics of Dawson and his associates, men and women of an entirely different persuasion. Negroes and Republicans were justified in believing that Hampton's words merely served to mask the truth of white intentions. From their point of view, moderation was nothing more than a palliative prescribed by white men, while the malignancy of white supremacy was allowed to run its deadly course. Robert Smalls, Negro congressman, told a crowd of blacks in Beaufort that he would rather support Martin Gary than any other Democrat because "you know exactly where to find him and what to expect."[24] Laura Towne reflected this same suspicion when she wrote, "As for politics; they say Hampton is having a

---

21. *News and Courier,* October 27, 1877.

22. Thomas G. White to M. W. Gary, September 25, 1877, Gary Papers, scl.

23. The best information on the election is in the *News and Courier,* November 17, 20, 21, and 24; December 1, 5, 10, 12, and 14, 1877.

24. Quoted in Thomas G. White to M. W. Gary, September 25, 1877, Gary Papers, scl.

hard time restraining the fire-eaters, and that they are worrying him well. One paper says 'he knows how it is himself' now. He will never be able to keep his pledges about equal justice and all that, and he might have known it—probably he did before he made them."[25]

Laura Towne and Robert Smalls knew that despite Hampton's effort to appoint blacks to numerous lesser offices or Dawson's efforts to get black representation on an aldermanic ticket, both Hampton and Dawson were advocates of white supremacy no matter how tempered. For people like Smalls and Towne, people who had accomplished so much during Reconstruction, there could be no step back that did not ultimately seem like the beginning of a long journey back into a world foreshadowed by the Black Codes.

Yet the judgment of a routed band of courageous Republicans, while more nearly approximating an historical truth, may not serve the contemporary verdict as well as the judgment reached by men who vied with Dawson and Hampton for the allegiance of the white community, for it was in this context that a white man's mettle was most severely tested in post-Reconstruction South Carolina. Evidence of this judgment is found in a letter written by Gary and signed "White Supremacy." In the letter Gary launched into a rambling diatribe against Hampton's policy, at one point calling it "conciliation and kindness," but then striking through the phrase as if realizing the implication of his words.[26] Even more to the point was a stinging rebuke to Dawson, administered by a Gary journal, for having the temerity to defend Hampton's views. The trouble with Dawson, charged the paper, was that Dawson had accepted the hackneyed maxim "that the negro is 'a man and a brother;' that he was born free and equal with the white man." Such a view, it was argued, led inexorably to "miscegenation and a mongrel race, and a mongrel government." On reading this repudiation of the Dawson position, Gary wrote his confidant, Hugh Farley, saying, "Henry [Hugh's brother] . . . has written a good reply to Dawson's editorial, all I wish is for you to get it republished in Speight's paper or your own. The logic of Henry's position cannot be assailed."[27]

---

25. Rupert Sargent Holland, ed., *Letters and Diary of Laura M. Towne Written from the Sea Islands of South Carolina, 1862–1884* (Cambridge: Riverside Press, 1912), p. 264.

26. MS letter in Gary's hand to "Mr. Editor," ca. September 1878, Gary Papers, SCL. Henry Farley urged Gary not to publish the letter, which focused on an incident in which Hampton dined with two Negroes while being entertained by the president of Claflin College. The incident was one which Hampton could not have avoided without being discourteous in the extreme, and Farley correctly sensed that Gary's letter would simply backfire. Henry Farley to Gary, September 23 and October 11, 1878, Gary Papers, SCL.

27. The rebuke was provoked by a *News and Courier* editorial of August 29, 1878. The editorial which Gary wished circulated was first drafted by Henry Farley of the Columbia *Straightout* and was reprinted in A. M. Speight's Greenville *News,* September 8, 1878. Gary's letter was to Hugh Farley of the Spartanburg *Carolina Spartan,* September 8, 1878.

The Gary people had in fact stumbled on the key for interpreting Dawson's place in the evolution of race history in the South. As charged, Dawson believed that the Negro was "a man and a brother"; a fellow sojourner on the planet who, if not born equal, should at the very least be accorded the rights of a free man and guaranteed the equal protection of the laws. As a reform-minded liberal Dawson accepted the general outline of the American Creed, and with that acceptance, no matter his visceral adherence to white supremacy, he became vulnerable to those who argued from the premise of man's essential equality. This American Creed, or that "great national suggestion" as Gunnar Myrdal called it, inevitably pulled Dawson into the continuing national discourse on how best to fulfill the commitment to equality as expressed in the first American Revolution. Having given away the principle of the argument before engaging the debate, Dawson and like-thinkers on white supremacy would forever be vulnerable to outside criticism.[28]

It was in this spirit that Dawson, in the wake of Redemption, urged his fellow whites not to regard the black population "as a conquered race, or a subjugated people, but as citizens who have a deep personal interest in the welfare of the State, and who, under the law, have precisely the same rights that the white people have."[29] It was in this spirit that Dawson argued for the retention of a Negro fire company in Charleston even if it meant the exclusion of another white company. Such action he contended would be in "consonance with Democratic policy and promise in Charleston."[30] And it was in this same spirit that Dawson consistently opposed repeal of the state's civil rights law even though the federal law of 1875 had been overturned by the Supreme Court. He argued that if segregation were to be desired it should be achieved through price discrimination and not race separation, concluding as did most elite whites of his persuasion that "only the better class of colored people would care to pay for reserved seats, and to such colored people little or no objection is made."[31]

---

28. My reading of Dawson's position on race relations is influenced by the thesis advanced in George Brown Tindall's essay, "The Central Theme Revisited," in Charles Grier Sellers, Jr., ed., *The Southerner as American* (Chapel Hill: University of North Carolina Press, 1960). Tindall's thesis was in turn influenced by Gunnar Myrdal, *An American Dilemma: The Negro Problem and Modern Democracy* (New York: Harper and Brothers, 1944), the relevant sections being ch. 1, sec. 13; ch. 21; and Append. 2, sec. 3 and 4.

29. *News and Courier*, April 11, 1877.

30. Ibid., January 7, 1881.

31. Ibid., October 5, 1883, and November 5, 1884. This does not mean that Dawson found social mingling acceptable. In all probability he had not changed his views from a January 11, 1870, editorial in the *News* in which he declared, "All the laws that ever disgraced the statute book cannot compel the white man to seat his wife and children by the side of the negro. . . . The Supreme Court may kill profitable branches of trade, and violate private rights, but it cannot make the negro the social equal of the white man."

There was also a darker side to the tortured mind of South Carolina's moderate Redeemers. The most careful study of South Carolina Negroes in this period correctly observed that the liberal nature of the Hampton program "was largely negative in approach, merely promising that certain rights already gained by the Negroes would not be taken away . . . and it was also . . . basically a program of white supremacy."[32] Dawson underscored this point in an editorial designed to reassure President Hayes that the administration's southern policy had not been a failure. The editor told the president that nothing could have been done to alter the results. The recent elections were an evidence "that the colored people, even when they have a numerical majority, cannot hold their own against superior intelligence, means and courage of the whites." It was axiomatic, Dawson declared, that "when the two races come in conflict, whether in politics or in industrial life, the weaker race goes to the wall. This is the philosophy of the overthrow of negro domination in the South. Mr. Hayes cannot mend or change it, unless he plant in the body of every negro the heart and brain and soul of the white man." Dawson concluded with a promise that "the South will watch over them with solicitous care."[33]

A blood inheritance was not the only reason for the Negroes' subordination. Dawson also believed that the Negro had not earned the right to a full measure of equality. He consistently maintained that the Fourth of July was not properly the black man's day, though blacks had been the conspicuous celebrants since the end of the war. "The plain truth is," Dawson complained, "that emancipation and the suffrage cost the colored man nothing, and he will not make, for the maintenance of his rights and privileges, the sacrifices cheerfully made by the white race, to whom the ballot and the right of self-government represent the struggling of liberty for centuries."[34] Moreover, Dawson equated the maintenance of white rule with the revolutionary impulses that drove Englishmen to seek liberty all the way from the primeval forests of Saxon England to the American wilderness. "For peace, for security, for the conservation of their civil and political rights," he wrote, "the white people of South Carolina have fought before, and they will not abandon the fight now that the ballot is more effective than the bullet." On another occasion he justified the irregularities at election time "just as revolution or rebellion is permissible when there is no other escape from tyrannical government, under which neither life nor property is safe."[35]

---

32. Tindall, *South Carolina Negroes*, pp. 20–21.

33. *News and Courier*, November 16, 1878.

34. Ibid. See also the July 4 editions for 1876, 1877, and 1879.

35. Ibid., January 31, 1879, and April 23, 1881.

To subordinate the Negro it was necessary for Dawson to rob him of the attributes of the participatory citizen. The black man was a pawn, to be used for good or ill by the white men who controlled him. When D. H. Chamberlain declared the South Carolina Negro to be "mild, peaceful, order-loving, teachable, patient and religious," Dawson agreed, but from this warrant the editor drew entirely different conclusions. The Negro was docile, tractable, and a cully. Whatever successes Chamberlain claimed for the Constitution of 1868 were attributable to the Negroes' white overlords, just as the evils of Reconstruction resulted from black acquiescence in white plunder. In neither success nor venality was Dawson willing to accord the black man more than a passive role. As he later declared, "Until they acquire something of the knowledge and self-control which make the white race fit for self-government, the colored people . . . will be blind instruments for good or evil, in the hands of either Democrats or Republicans."[36]

Without apparent regard for consistency, Dawson flashed another image of the Negro before his readers. From the pages of the *News and Courier* South Carolinians saw the docile "Cuffee" transformed into the advance guard of "Voodooism" who conspired with sinister whites to "Africanize" the state. They read of "black savages," "ignorant Africans," or "Black Sheep," who were "insolent and aggressive," "ignorant and passionate," "lustful," "savage and relentless." The black man was at once an "ignorant dupe" and a "ravening wolf or blood-thirsty tiger." Dawson could no more shake the confusion and fear which haunted the master race since slavery began, than he could shake his abiding faith in English liberties. Wanting to believe the freedman numb to the full meaning of freedom, still servile and childlike, Dawson nonetheless harbored a suspicion that beneath his African skin the Negro was a seething cauldron of sentient, primal humanity, capable of erupting in a bestial fury against his civilized captors.

With such a confused and distorted conception of the Negro as citizen it is not surprising that Hampton Democrats had such difficulty in formulating policy consistent with the general's proclamation that no rights won during Reconstruction would be denied the Negro. Dawson ultimately resolved the difficulty by emphasizing the promise of equal protection under law, while seeking to circumscribe the Negro's right to that due process through which laws were made and applied. He felt that the Negro should look upon government as a trust, established to protect his interest until such time as he came of age. In turn he felt that the trustees had an obligation to permit their wards some measure of participation as a show of good faith. To that end, Dawson fought those in his party who argued for a

---

36. D. H. Chamberlain, "Reconstruction and the Negro," *North American Review* (February, 1879), p. 167. Dawson's reply appears in the *News and Courier*, February 14 and 17, 1879. Quoted material in the *News and Courier*, August 5, 1880.

complete proscription of the Negro, while at the same time carefully drawing the parameters within which blacks could participate.

In the courts, Dawson never argued that Negroes should be excluded from the witness stand or the jury box, though he frequently impeached their testimony and character. This was invariably true when blacks testified against whites in political cases. In the hearings which followed the Hamburg massacre, the *News and Courier* boldly asserted that the words of two young white men "would outweigh the words of excited and alarmed negroes" in any court of justice.[37] During the Ellenton trials, Chief Justice Waite complained bitterly about the manner in which black witnesses were abused and misrepresented by the Charleston press.[38] The tendency to call Negroes liars, despite overwhelming evidence to the contrary, was part of a larger pattern of suppressing the truth about the maltreatment of blacks. As B. O. Townsend observed, "When a political crime is committed, they palliate it, smooth over everything, charge the blame on the murdered victims, and indulge in loud generalities about their good feeling toward the negro, their desire for peace, their willingness to accept the situation."[39] The suppression of truth, no doubt, worked as powerfully as did Martin Gary's intemperate language to create a climate in which violence could flourish.

In the matter of representation, Dawson was equally intent on circumscribing the Negro, while not completely proscribing him. On numerous occasions he sought to defend their appointments to minor offices, or to block efforts to leave them off elective tickets. When it was rumored that the Charleston County Convention of 1884 was indisposed to grant any Negro representation, Dawson warned, "The white people are in the minority in South Carolina. It is the colored Democratic vote—coupled with that acquiescence in Democratic rule which expresses itself in abstinence from voting—that converts the Democratic minority into a majority." To the white delegates Dawson posed the question, "Will the colored people stay at home on election day, or continue to vote the Democratic ticket, if the Charleston Convention, reversing the policy of the party, present to the people, white and colored, an exclusively white ticket?"[40]

Suffrage was the most difficult problem for solution. The Fifteenth Amendment was a political fact of life, and the Democrats had promised to uphold all rights guaranteed by the Constitution. If honored, that commitment would have meant Negro domination of every free and fair election.

---

37. *News and Courier*, August 14, 1876.

38. M. R. Waite to his wife, May 20, 1877, Morrison Remick Waite Papers, Library of Congress, cited hereafter as LC.

39. Belton O'Neall Townsend, "South Carolina Morals," *Atlantic Monthly* (April, 1877), p. 471.

40. *News and Courier*, October 13, 1884.

The black majority was the central feature in Dawson's argument for a fusionist strategy prior to the nomination of Hampton. So constantly did the *News and Courier* emphasize the Negroes' majority that the straight-out press began referring to the Charleston paper as the "30,000 organ." But, promised the Edgefield *Advertiser*, "If the 30,000 organ will do its duty in Charleston, even the ruined City by the Sea will roll up a vote that will make the heart of the good citizens of that city beat free once more, and then we will send you down a majority from the up-country that will roll over your 30,000 majority and wipe it out forever!"[41]

The cock-crowing of the *Advertiser* represented the bloodier side of the Democratic campaign in 1876 which threatened to undo the promises of Hampton, so Dawson quickly set about to find words that might reconcile the Edgefield intent with the Hampton promise. He believed that any flagrant attempt to proscribe the 30,000 majority would bring down the wrath of the nation and would only prolong the agonies of Reconstruction. Finding one of those polite euphemisms which delude only those who wish to be deluded, Dawson called on the Democracy to pursue "the policy of Preference not Proscription." By this Dawson meant that whites were to make it unmistakably clear that the black man's job depended on his vote. He warned Charlestonians that thirty million dollars worth of their property was at stake. "Eight thousand Democrats, with thirty million dollars, to influence four thousand votes. Is that impossible or even difficult?" he asked.[42]

Dawson knew that euphemisms for intimidation were at best only a temporary expedient, and he labored tirelessly for a formula that would restrict the Negro suffrage legally. He knew that the Democrats would continue to use whatever means necessary to preserve their hegemony, and he believed that the "poisons" of political intimidation were effective. No person or people, however, could "feed on poison, year after year, and be vigorous and strong."[43] To find an antidote, Dawson and men like Colonel Edward McCrady turned to literacy qualifications as the surest way of guaranteeing preference for the white race while avoiding the odium of proscription. Though the South Carolina legislature eventually returned the infamous eight-box law as against the literacy test Dawson sought, the *News and Courier* bowed to the legislative will in the belief that the restriction of Negro suffrage would at least be legal. *The Nation*, an early advocate of the return to home rule in the South, saw better:

> These ingenious methods of fraud and falsification which in South Carolina have been developed to so high a degree of perfection, will only serve to

---

41. Edgefield *Advertiser,* August 10, 1876.
42. *News and Courier,* November 1, 1876.
43. Ibid., December 15, 1879.

corrupt and demoralize all classes that take any part in the politics of the State. It is a nursery of political crime teeming with the seed of future disaster. The advocates of the system do not know how soon its present victims will use it to plague its present beneficiaries. South Carolina is evidently in the hands of very shortsighted and dangerous friends.[44]

Closely related to the eight-box law was the effort to gerrymander the state so that the majority Negro population would have only one of South Carolina's seven congressional seats. By July 5, 1882, this political weapon had also become a part of South Carolina's arsenal in the fight to restrict the Negro's influence at the ballot box. When the New York *Tribune* called it a "monstrous crime against suffrage," Dawson fired back with what was becoming a refined southern strategy, the argument *tu quoque:*

> Is it, we ask, a crime to persuade the colored people to abstain from voting, or to induce them to vote the Democratic ticket, in order that a representative who is capable, honest and faithful should be elected, when the *Tribune* holds that it is a virtue for Protectionist manufacturers in the North to threaten their white workers with discharge and loss of employment if they vote against the interests of those who hire them? Is it wrong, we ask, to use in the interest of decency, justice and integrity . . . the means which are used everywhere in the North to secure the personal advantage of the pets of the Republicans?[45]

While seeking to protect the Negro vote within prescribed limits, Dawson and his friends also gave currency to a belief that would ultimately doom Negro voting altogether. They reasoned that the black man posed no threat as long as white men remained solid for the Democratic party. "The independent, not the colored Democrat," warned Dawson, "is the rock ahead in South Carolina."[46] Such a position doomed the Negro ballot because Conservatives knew that the alliance with the more radical elements of their party was not natural. Some, like William Mauldin, even looked forward to the day when the "ultra-Bourbons and Yankee haters in our own party" could be jettisoned in favor of a conservative union party "founded upon the issues of the day."[47] If splinter groups were inevitable, then the Negro vote, no matter how small, would remain as a constant

---

44. "Blundering in the South," *The Nation* (May 25, 1882), p. 438. The eight-box law required that votes for various classifications of office be placed in designated boxes. The clear intent of the law was to prey on the ignorance of the black voter.

45. *News and Courier,* July 21, 1882. Dawson's comparison between white domination of the black vote and business control of the labor vote is sustained by George M. Frederickson, *The Black Image in the White Mind: The Debate on Afro-American Character and Destiny, 1817–1914* (New York: Harper and Row, 1971), p. 212.

46. *News and Courier,* June 4, 1878.

47. William Lawrence Mauldin Diary, November 2, 1880, Southern Historical Collection, University of North Carolina.

threat to arbitrate disputes among whites. Worse still, whites might even wage campaigns promising full participation to blacks in an effort to curry favor.

Caught in this dilemma, Conservatives of the Dawson stripe seemed unable to suggest a way out and contented themselves with raising the specter of Negro rule any time independents had the audacity to speak up. It remained for "Pitchfork Ben" Tillman to seize the horns of the dilemma and to suggest its solution. In his debate with Dawson, Tillman charged that the people must no longer be held down by this threat of the Negro as "balance of power," and after his own rise to power, the Edgefield farmer proceeded to end that threat by calling a constitutional convention which successfully eviscerated the Fifteenth Amendment in South Carolina.[48] Disfranchisement was but the logical consequence of the Conservative premise that whites could not afford an honest difference of opinion as long as the Negro was in a position to arbitrate the dispute.

As if literacy tests, eight-box gauntlets, gerrymandered districts, and white solidarity were insufficient, Dawson also proved willing to buy the Negro's vote and his politicians. In the campaign of 1884, Dawson used money from the Democratic National Committee for that purpose and recommended similar action when his friend, Fitzhugh Lee, ran for governor of Virginia a year later.[49] A letter to General Matt Whitaker Ransom of North Carolina revealed the kind of callous insensitivity which accompanied the purchase of black politicians. Dawson wrote:

> I can place in your command, if you want him, a colored canvasser who ought to be of considerable service to you in your Colored districts.
> The man I speak of is named Byas [Benjamin Byas, an undistinguished Reconstruction legislator who had prior to his election served as an employee of the General Assembly]. Some years ago he had a little difficulty with one of our reporters, and, as the local paper said at the time, 'was shot in that portion of his person which is described by the second syllable of his name.' I do not think that he is a man of high moral character, and he probably shared in the plunder of the Radical House. His value lies in the fact that he was educated at Oberlin College, Ohio, where your colored Congressman O'Hara was educated, and is a capital speaker—aggressive, fluent, and putting in his points well. Congressman Dibble, who knows O'Hara's capacity, recommends Byas warmly.

---

48. *News and Courier,* August 29, 1888. For an excellent discussion of the 1895 Constitutional Convention see Tindall, *South Carolina Negroes,* pp. 81–91. See also William A. Mabry, "Ben Tillman Disfranchised the Negro," *South Atlantic Quarterly,* XXXVII (April, 1938), pp. 170–83; and George B. Tindall, "The Campaign for the Disfranchisement of Negroes in South Carolina," *Journal of Southern History,* XV (May, 1949), 212–34.

49. Letters from Dawson to M. P. Howell, W. H. Cuttino, Thomas M. Gilland, A. J. Hydricks, and Thomas Talbird, October 25, 1884; and Dawson to Fitzhugh Lee, August 14, 1885, Dawson Papers, Duke.

Dawson advised that Byas was "of course a Democrat for the campaign at least—and I presume for revenue only." The price would be cheap, "probably $100.00 a month, or less, paying his own expenses."[50]

There can be no doubt that Dawson wanted to protect the Negro from the harsher discriminations visited upon second-class citizens, but there was, of course, one crime that placed the black man completely beyond the pale, and like his Irish counterpart of the sixteenth century, he could be hunted down for it and shot like an animal. The offense was the rape of a white woman. While Dawson has been justly credited with strongly urging the demise of lynch-law, his countenancing summary executions for rape was an untended spillway through which poured all those passions which the rule of law supposedly held in check. "Seldom before the nineties," observed one student of this violence, "was it ever recognized by the press that most lynchings were for crimes other than rape."[51] Few incidents were fully investigated, but the *News and Courier* invariably claimed that "the provocation was the most awful that man can know; the guilt was certain; the doom just!" When a mob took the law into its own hands at Spartanburg, the paper could not condemn the action, "whatever its abstract impropriety and manifest unlawfulness." Again, "There was no doubt about the guilt of the suspected person. His character was bad, and a chain of circumstantial evidence was woven around him."[52]

Though the Conservative press eventually came to recognize the indiscriminate application of lynch-law and sought to end it, the social consequences of mob murder were already manifest. One study concluded that "the significance of lynching was broader than its ghastly effects upon the mob and its victim. Lynching became, willy-nilly, a factor in the establishment of a white terror that transformed the fluid situation created by Reconstruction back into a rigid caste system of white supremacy."[53]

Each step in the subordination of the Negro brutalized that part of the Redeemer conscience which was committed to the fundamental tenets of the American Creed. Perhaps for fear of becoming totally desensitized, Dawson seemed almost passionately committed to the causes of other minority and ethnic groups. He complained that the history of broken treaties with the Indians resulted in a situation in which "the National conscience has been cheated as well as the Indians." On another occasion the *News and Courier* scored the Democrats for truckling to the likes of Dennis Kearney, the California labor leader who himself was truckling "to the prejudices of base and ignorant persons in that State." This same issue

50. Dawson to M. W. Ransom, August 13, 1884, ibid.

51. Tindall, *South Carolina Negroes*, p. 245.

52. *News and Courier*, February 10, 1876, and June 19, 1879.

53. Tindall, *South Carolina Negroes*, p. 239.

which sought to defend the yellow man from Kearney's version of the white peril also produced an editorial proclaiming that more white blood made the Negro more educable.[54]

Of all freedom-seeking minorities, none received more attention from Dawson than did the Irish. As a good Gladstonian liberal and a veteran of the lost cause, Dawson saw in the Irish strike for home rule that great prejudice for freedom which was the heritage of all English-speaking people. The Irish were not asking for something that did not already belong to them through the Great Charter, the Petition of Right, and the Bill of Rights. To the Negro Dawson counseled patience, but to the Irishman he said, "No Sir! Never. As well use the somewhat hackneyed joke that they shall not go into the water until they learn to swim." If Dawson sensed a contradiction with his counsel to the Negro, he quickly resolved it with the confident assertion that the men urged to action were "white men & Irishmen & that is enough."[55]

The tension between freedom and caste not only forced Dawson to seek out surrogate commitments, it also helped fashion a deeper appreciation for the plight of the Negro. At times this appreciation bordered on genuine understanding. In attempting to account for the blacks' migratory urge following Reconstruction, Dawson came to some remarkable conclusions in one of his best editorial efforts. He began somewhat defensively by declaring that the Negro had not been generally mistreated at the hands of the white man, but he conceded that blacks knew "that they are no better off than they were when 'freedom came in.'" Under such circumstances any physical movement, great or small, was an exhibition of freedom. "The slave was a fixture," observed Dawson, "and fixity is, therefore, a badge of servitude." In the final analysis freedom was nothing unless they asserted it through mobility. "Even domestic servants," concluded the editorial, "do not care to remain long in one family, lest it appear that they cannot change employers."[56]

Argument was considered of no avail in attempting to dissuade the black man from the desire to emigrate. Dawson forewarned his readers that Negroes would pass over the bodies of fallen comrades in their effort to reach "Canaan." In slavery it had been "the Gospel Train" or "the Old Ship of Zion," today it was the molasses-tree of Liberia or the golden grain of Kansas. The *News and Courier* believed that it would take a long time to overcome such an ingrained faith in the promised land of the Old Testament. One thing was for sure, Democrats were in no position to do the

---

54. *News and Courier,* January 29 and February 3, 1879.

55. MS notes on a speech delivered by Dawson before the Grattan League, Charleston, ca. 1888, Dawson Papers, Duke.

56. *News and Courier,* April 29, 1879. For an extended analysis of the Negro's association of freedom with mobility see Williamson, *After Slavery,* pp. 32–44.

persuading, "for to the negroes the supremacy of the Democrats . . . is a cause of uneasiness, if not alarm." No better evidence of distrust could be found than the "steady flow of colored people from other counties to Beaufort county, the only County in this State which the Democrats did not carry in the last election."[57]

Dawson's editorial position on emigration was generally mixed. With the end of Reconstruction, South Carolina Negroes turned a hopeful eye toward Liberia and with the assistance of the American Colonization Society made a concerted effort to reach that distant shore. When confronted with such determination, Dawson responded by declaring that, to be sure, the Negro was free to leave, but that the whites in South Carolina would "look with regret upon any general emigration of the colored people." He candidly admitted that the Negro was most admirably suited as a common laborer, but he advised them that under a wise and just Democratic administration they would "earn more, and make greater progress, than in Liberia." Most of his editorials ended with the caveat that the black population should "look before they leap, lest the new movement prove to be another of the gigantic swindles of which they have been the victims during the past twelve years."[58]

By April, 1878, it was clear that South Carolina blacks were intent on sending some of their number to ancestral Africa, and the *News and Courier* was forced to acknowledge that "the migration of the colored people from the Southern States has begun." Dawson took the occasion for a philosophical look at the Negro's progress in America. He granted that they had done their part in making the country what it was. "Building better than they knew," he wrote, "their hands achieved the work that a higher race could not have performed." When the time was right and their work done, the black man's condition was changed with the stroke of a pen. But they were unprepared for new duties and responsibilities, and a period of riot and debauchery followed. With the restoration of good government, a thoughtful few came to "the sad conviction that, in the struggle for life, the fittest must survive, and that there is no place for the freedman on the vast continent of America." The result was a natural desire on the part of blacks to emigrate to Africa where they could establish a civilization, learned from whites, in which they would make up the superior element, "as here they must always remain the lowest in the social scale." Though doubting their success, Dawson wished them well, choosing to remember not their recent oppressiveness but their faithful simplicity and natural good-heartedness during slavery.[59]

Dawson's interest in the Liberian project led him to dispatch A. B. Williams to accompany the pilgrims on their voyage and to file a complete

---

57. *News and Courier,* April 29, 1879.

58. Ibid., July 5, 1877.

59. Ibid., April 18, 1878.

report on his findings. Before their departure on Easter Sunday, 1878, Dawson surveyed the motley crew and found them "not the stuff of which pioneers are made." They were "quiet, patient, docile people," but nowhere could he find "the young, stalwart, intelligent laborers and mechanics whom one would expect to lead the van of the migration of a whole race." And when the brave and desperate emigrants at last set sail, the *News and Courier* could sense a measure of "poetical justice" at the sight of "an old slaver, for such is the *Azor,* sailing from Charleston, with emigrants to Africa, and towed out by the *Wade Hampton!*"[60]

The reports which Williams sent back were generally fair but emphasized the suffering and mismanagement that accompanied the expedition— both of which were true. But even with the glaring problems held constantly in view, the blacks who remained behind would not be daunted. The *News and Courier* admitted that "Liberia, with all its drawbacks, is a more promising land than we had supposed, and while we believe that the mass of colored people had better avail themselves of the civilization that now surrounds and upholds them . . . we shall not be surprised if the letters of Mr. Williams give a marked impetus to emigration."[61] There was good reason for this assessment of the blacks' probable reaction to Williams's report, for the black community of Charleston had just greeted the news of the *Azor*'s landing with great enthusiasm. Dawson knew in the midst of such rejoicing that "the sad history of the suffering of the emigrants attracted less attention than the broad fact that Africa had at last been reached, and that the first voyage of the first Colonization vessel owned and directed by colored people had been successfully accomplished."[62]

Whites in South Carolina were by no means of one mind on the issue of black emigration. Some, notably Senator M. C. Butler, favored an expeditious removal of blacks from the state. Others were so convinced that general emigration would destroy the agricultural labor force that they proposed laws amounting to virtual peonage. In 1879 Senator Butler was reported as favoring the deportation of at least 100,000 of the state's Negro inhabitants, and by 1883 he had upped that figure to 200,000. Dawson could not agree with his friend in the Senate and in blunt language reminded the senator that there was no way to replace blacks with whites at the going wage. It took precious little forethought to realize that "white laborers will not be satisfied with the wages, shelter and rations given to the colored people; and white laborers in this country are the equals of their employers and cannot be treated as 'free negroes.'"[63]

---

60. Ibid., April 20 and 22, 1878.

61. Williams's material is summarized in ibid., August 6, 1878.

62. Ibid., June 17, 1878. See also Tindall, *South Carolina Negroes,* pp. 153–68.

63. *News and Courier,* January 13, 1881.

Dawson was convinced that the Negro must remain. He was after all "king of the cotton field." But he opposed yoking the Negro to the white man's plow through "labor contracts." This ingenious method of reducing the blacks to peonage became a part of South Carolina law in 1880. Dawson cautioned that such legislation could be turned just as easily against poor whites. He conceded that as Negroes gained their own farms labor would become scarce and wages would rise, but to prevent laborers from striving to improve their position on that account was unthinkable. Dawson warned "that the shafts now aimed at the poor negro will, if they hit the mark, be aimed at poor whites also. There is no escape. The idea of 'controlling labor,' by making it next to impossible for laborers to be anything but workers for wages, will have to be abandoned sooner or later." Realizing that the contagion of slavery was no less infectious than its opposite, liberty, Dawson proclaimed that "the tyranny of class is only a degree less odious than the tyranny of race."[64]

There is great danger in trying to read any man's thinking from the pages of a newspaper, yet Dawson's private correspondence was remarkably silent on the subject of race. The newspaper is a hazard because of the necessity of responding instantly and continuously to ever changing situations which evoke constantly shifting passions. The racial slur of one day becomes a cry of fraternity the next. But through it all there does run a thread which holds the fabric together and provides a clue for interpreting Dawson's position on race.

Such an understanding begins with the obvious fact that Dawson was a white supremacist who alternately despised and pitied the Negro, but it quickly proceeds to a second characteristic, equally strong, which served to confuse the first. The Jeffersonian heritage which infused late-nineteenth-century thought convinced men like Dawson that freedom could not be conferred by governments, that it was an attribute of the individual and could only spring from the independence afforded by wealth or property. Like Jefferson, Dawson distrusted "men who were free in name while their empty bellies made them thieves, threatening the property of honest men, or else made them slaves in fact to anyone who would feed them."[65] Such distrust made for a kind of racial egalitarianism, for the servitude of want and privation was no respecter of race. It led Dawson to doubt that there could be found among the "hard-fisted Democracy," the working poor of Charleston, men sufficiently free and independent to hold positions of public trust. It led him to conclude that price discrimination in public transportation would lead to a mingling with only the "better class of colored people . . . and to such people little or no objection is made."

---

64. Ibid., September 7, 1881.

65. Edmund S. Morgan, "Slavery and Freedom: The American Paradox," *Journal of American History*, LIX (June, 1972), p. 11.

Moreover, the Jeffersonian link between property and the free man had achieved a new importance by the late nineteenth century. Property was no longer an essential link; its "acquisition" came to represent the quintessential expression of democratic virtue. True equality was to be found in the market place, out of which emerged, through the rough and tumble of competition, a natural elite. Nothing could be more indiscriminate or democratic. Spencerian Darwinism, Malthusian calculus, and classical economics came to be identified with the virtues of the early republic—a process which one historian called a "materialization of social values." The hands-off philosophy which was a natural corollary marked a triumph for conservative thought, for the equation of democratic process with economic law preempted the egalitarian premise from which social criticism sprang. With social criticism paralyzed, the sympathetic impulses of the period—those which might have brought aid and succor to the less fortunate—were limited to "a great flowering of 'anti-cruelty' movements and limited-objective private charities."[66]

The overall impact of these influences operating together—white supremacy, Jeffersonian liberalism, and the "materialization of social values"—was not entirely negative. They may have reduced the editorial page to a mass of inconsistencies and paralyzed positive social thinking, but after that is said, these forces also produced in Dawson a flexible mental state. Unlike the supporters of Martin Gary and Ben Tillman, Dawson's mind was not set. He was still very much susceptible to suggestions emanating from whatever quarter that the Negro was a man and that just as no government by the stroke of a pen could set him free, no government should deprive him of an equal chance in the worldly struggle for survival.

Dawson and his friends may then be viewed as a great neutral force for good, depending critically on the amount of pressure applied from outside their own circle. A special correspondent to *The Nation* sensed this condition when he wrote, "[Hampton] occupies a peculiar position, in which through the force of circumstances and the pressure of outside opinion, he has hitherto been able to act upon his better judgement and yet to avoid entanglement." A later edition of the same magazine viewed with alarm the strength of the Gary-type prejudice but concluded that "so long as there is a nucleus of a party who are convinced that the political difficulty of the negro vote is to be faced by directing rather than destroying it . . . the course of events is their best ally, and all the multiform forces involved in renewed prosperity work with them, gain them adherents, and keep them in power."[67] While the latter article represented an all-too-sanguine reliance on the natural forces of prosperity, its objective

---

66. Robert Green McCloskey, *American Conservatism in the Age of Enterprise, 1865–1910* (Cambridge: Harvard University Press, 1951), pp. 18–21.

67. *The Nation*, special correspondent, May 24, 1877, and September 5, 1878.

point was that men like Dawson formed a nucleus capable of being activated for good by forces penetrating from outside. In the final count those outside forces, Republican party professionals or social agitators, abandoned their Negro friends at the South, and in so doing, abandoned also those southern whites whose mind-sets were susceptible to appeals from the American Creed.[68]

The reference to "Dawson and his friends" denotes a larger community sharing similar views, but it should be noted that Dawson's background resulted in a different commitment, at least at the visceral level, to the shared value system. The Greenville *News* was on the mark in its view that Dawson did "not understand the unwritten political law, which is made up of the customs, habits of thought, modes of reasoning, of certain repugnances and attractions of the inhabitants of the commonwealth." The up-country journal was particularly impressed with the fact that Dawson had never owned slaves and did not grow up among them.[69] While Dawson and Hampton could agree that "Negro degradation was not [and should not be] a necessary corollary of white supremacy,"[70] their routes to this spirit of paternalism and noblesse oblige were paved with a different mix of emotion and intellect, Dawson's being much more a matter of the mind.

By the end of the eighties Dawson and other Conservatives were looking for some grand scheme to resolve the dilemma of white over black in a nonslave society. Part of the exigence arose from a fear that the mudsills of white society were at work fulfilling Gary's prophecy that the central issue was ultimately "an antagonism of race." Under this circumstance and with no clear vision of the future, Dawson grabbed at whatever straws were offered, and the most available appeared to be Bishop Henry McNeal Turner's African dream.[71] Turner, a bishop in the African Methodist Episcopal Church, first attracted Dawson's attention with an article in the Nashville *Christian Advocate*. Turner contended that there had been a providential aspect to slavery. Though inhuman and cruel, slavery offered "the most rapid transition from barbarism to Christian civilization for the

---

68. See Tindall's "The Central Theme Revisited," p. 117.

69. Greenville *News,* September 8, 1878.

70. C. Vann Woodward, *The Strange Career of Jim Crow* (New York: Oxford University Press, 1966), p. 48. I agree with William J. Cooper, Jr., that the difference between Williamson (*After Slavery*) and Tindall (*South Carolina Negroes*), as to the onset of Jim Crow is largely a semantic quarrel, *The Conservative Regime: South Carolina, 1877–1890,* Johns Hopkins University Studies in Historical and Political Science, ser. LXXXVI, no. 1 (Baltimore: Johns Hopkins Press, 1968), pp. 111–12. All agree that the intent to guarantee racial dominance for whites was there from the beginning, but the progress of implementing that intent was marked by uncertainty and many discarded alternatives.

71. See Edwin S. Redkey, "Bishop Turner's African Dream," *Journal of American History,* LIV (September, 1967), pp. 271–90.

negro." But, Turner urged, the transition must not be allowed to stop. The Negro's destiny would not be fulfilled until some place were found where the Negro might commence the Christian work for which he had been schooled in slavery. In Africa the southern black could bring "millions to Christ and heaven."[72]

For those whites who had difficulty in responding to sentiment alone, Turner suggested a more practical consideration. Southern ports would vie with Europe for the African trade, always with the singular advantage of the Negro as a natural agent in the exploitation of the dark continent. "If the negro is a burden, a problem, or menace, and a source of vexation to our white friends," Turner wrote, "let them open up a highway to the land of his ancestry . . . and the dark negro problem will solve itself in a few years." To Dawson such a proposal offered one of those "sudden leaps from hell into heaven," and he agreed that the white man could aid in this noble work, not by reviling the Negro and treating him as an inferior, but only through a conscientious program of "uplift."[73]

The year after Dawson's death his friend, Senator Matthew Butler, introduced a bill in Congress to provide for the return of Afro-Americans to their ancestral home. Bishop Turner took the occasion to write Butler saying that the senator was "a successor in the negro's cause . . . of Jefferson, Henry, Garrison, Sumner, and Lincoln" (noble company for the man on the spot at bloody Hamburg) and that Butler would "go down in history as the pioneer of the grandest measure in the closing days of the nineteenth century." A few months earlier, Wade Hampton, who had shared Dawson's previous misgivings about emigration, wrote a northern friend saying, "I claim to be a good friend of the colored people, & it is in their interest as well as in those of my own race that I advocate their removal from this country." As an evidence of its practicability, Hampton enclosed a pamphlet, written by one of Dawson's staffers, entitled an "Appeal to Pharoah."[74]

It was never a possible dream, but for men who had promised in 1876 that Democratic hegemony would usher in an era of good feeling among the races, it was a last desperate effort to prove their own charity for the

---

72. *News and Courier*, November 11, 1888.

73. Ibid. Dawson's use of the term "uplift" was a conscious borrowing from the writings of men like Atticus G. Haygood. On July 11, 1881, Dawson gave a strong editorial endorsement to Bishop Haygood's *Our Brother in Black: His Freedom and His Future* (New York: Phillips and Hunt, 1881). At that time Dawson agreed with Haygood that a mass deportation of blacks would be impractical.

74. H. M. Turner to M. C. Butler, April 10, 1890, M. C. Butler Papers, SCL; Wade Hampton to a northern friend, November 12, 1889, Wade Hampton Collection, LC. The pamphlet referred to is Carlyle McKinley, *An Appeal to Pharoah: The Negro Problem and Its Radical Solution* (New York, 1890).

Negro. The hour was late and the advent of Jim Crow was close at hand. Dawson and company were the patrician descendants of Thomas Jefferson and could not shake their spiritual father's paradox. One historian explained:

> Jefferson's derogation of the Negro revealed the latent possibilities inherent in an accumulated popular tradition of Negro inferiority; it constituted, for all its qualifications, the most intense, extensive, and extreme formulation of anti-Negro "thought" offered by any American in the thirty years after the Revolution. Yet Thomas Jefferson left to Americans something else which may in the long run have been of greater importance—his prejudice for freedom and his larger equalitarian faith. It was this faith which must have caused him to fall gradually more silent on a subject which many of his fellow intellectuals were taking up with interest. For Jefferson more than for any of his known contemporaries, the subject was not an easy or a happy one.[75]

The same could be said for Dawson; the agony was real. The dual commitment to white supremacy and that "larger equalitarian faith" created an astigmatic view of the Negro. He was "our loving friend, our mortal enemy, two worlds together—a tiger and a child."[76]

---

75. Winthrop D. Jordan, *White Over Black: American Attitudes Toward the Negro, 1550-1812* (Chapel Hill: University of North Carolina Press, 1968), p. 481.

76. Thomas Wolfe, *The Wed and the Rock* (New York: Harper and Brothers, 1937), p. 181.

Chapter X
A Great Loss

Tuesday, March 12, 1889, was a pleasant day in Charleston. Winds were mild and easterly, and the sky was overcast but not threatening. Early morning temperatures were in the brisk forties but rose to a comfortable sixty degrees by midafternoon. The news of the day was rather dull, so the city continued to buzz with gossip about the sensational Saturday night murder in which a young white man was found with his throat slit from ear to ear, and about the Pickens case in which the father of a young black girl and his two accomplices were acquitted for their part in the lynching of the young girl's white slayer. Recent editorials in the *News and Courier* had drawn particular attention to the unusual twist taken by lynch law at Pickens.

As Charlestonians picked up their morning *News and Courier* they might have expected to find more discussion of the Pickens affair, but instead they read about two Richmond editors who had been prevented from engaging in a duel; an anti-Chinese riot in Milwaukee; and a story about the continued protest against high freight rates by Charleston truck growers. There was nothing to disturb a morning yawn as readers moved through the editorials to the back pages. The Academy of Music was featuring an animal act, and there was some hopeful talk about the prospects for a southern baseball league. Even the city council agenda for that evening promised little excitement, no valuation fights or anything likely to cause controversy. Like most eventful days, Tuesday, March 12, 1889, gave no hint of the tragic news a messenger would bring Mayor George Dwight Bryan as he presided at the city council meeting that evening.

Mayor Bryan was a Dawson Democrat. A close personal friend of the *News and Courier*'s editor, Bryan had represented Dawson in Washington during the difficult negotiations which surrounded Jimmie Morgan's appointment to the consular post at Melbourne. Bryan was thoroughly conservative, and his administration promised to continue the policy of cutting budgets to the bone and holding the line on new taxes. Dawson also had a sentimental attachment to the Bryan family, for it had been the mayor's father who swore Dawson in as a citizen of the United States. In many respects, Bryan's position at the helm of Charleston affairs was a testament to Dawson's own success in the old City by the Sea.

If Mayor Bryan were a symbol of the editor's success in Charleston, the man Bryan succeeded symbolized Dawson's increasing difficulties in the later years of the eighties. William Ashmead Courtenay was first elected mayor of Charleston in 1879 when he wrested the office from William W. Sale, a Garyite who embarrassed the city's conservative elite. At that time

Courtenay was all the conservative Democrats could have wished, and more. The fact that he served as Charleston's mayor for eight years, winning four elections, was proof of the satisfactory manner in which he conducted the city's business. A letter from Dawson in 1886 expressed the community's appreciation. "You have given to affairs an impetus in the right direction that will be felt for years to come," Dawson wrote, "& men will not be wanting, in case of need, to take up your work and continue it."[1]

By the fall of 1887 Dawson had soured on Mayor Courtenay, and the mayor had soured on Charleston's ruling establishment. In a letter to Patrick Walsh of the Augusta *Chronicle,* Dawson expressed confidence that George Bryan would be nominated and that Bryan would be "especially welcome after the fret and worry that our friend, Courtenay, so often causes us."[2] Just what caused Courtenay's growing alienation from Dawson and Charleston's conservative leadership was never clear, but it likely started when Courtenay's son was expelled from the conservative-dominated Citadel in September, 1885. Rumors quickly spread that the mayor was so angered at the failure of the academy's board of visitors to redress the felt injustice that he was prepared to join Ben Tillman's mounting protest against Charleston's "Dude Factory."[3] From that time on, Courtenay grew increasingly resentful of public criticism, particularly that of the *News and Courier,* and on at least one occasion threatened to resign.[4]

After leaving the mayor's office in December, 1887, Courtenay became a principal backer of the Charleston *World,* the latest in a long line of journals that had risen in response to complaints of ring rule in Charleston

---

1. Dawson to W. A. Courtenay, March 5, 1886, William Ashmead Courtenay Papers, South Caroliniana Library, University of South Carolina, cited hereafter as scl.

2. Dawson to Patrick Walsh, September 22, 1887, Hemphill Family Papers, Duke University Library, cited hereafter as Duke.

3. *News and Courier,* September 4, 1885.

4. In December, 1886, Courtenay and Dawson got into a scrap over Dawson's criticism of city tax valuation proposals, Courtenay to Dawson, December 29, 1886, Dawson Papers, Duke. In June and July, 1887, the *News and Courier* published advertised criticism of the mayor and council. Though Dawson refused to print the more scurrilous attacks, he explained to Courtenay that the "other side" had a right to be heard in that manner if they wished. See John McElree to Dawson, June 25, 1887; and a series of three undated letters ca. June, 1887, from Courtenay to Dawson, all in Dawson Papers, Duke. See also an editorial on the advertised criticism in the *News and Courier,* August 9, 1887.

Other information on the differences between the two men comes from three undated letters, ca. July, 1887, from Courtenay to Dawson concerning the editor's criticism of police affairs; and another series of three notes from Courtenay to Dawson, ca. January, 1888, concerning Dawson's failure to support one of Courtenay's favorite charities, Dawson Papers, Duke. In the Courtenay Papers, scl, see two undated letters from Dawson to Courtenay, ca. January, 1888, and letters from Dawson to Courtenay, May 7, and July 16, 1888.

and that promised to offer an alternative to the dictatorial voice of the *News and Courier*. In 1890 the *World* was the only daily in the state to endorse Tillman's nomination for governor, and the farmers who wished to overthrow conservative domination of the statehouse even considered making Courtenay their candidate in the unlikely event that Tillman should not receive the nod of the farmers' convention.[5] Courtenay's alienation from the Conservative regime was but the most conspicuous defection to a movement in Charleston which hoped to infuse the party structure with new blood. The "Belgian Block Farmers," as they were derisively called by party regulars,[6] sent a delegation to the farmers' convention of March, 1890, and played a decisive role in the decision to nominate Tillman in advance of the state Democratic convention.

While many of the dissenters eventually made common cause with Tillman, the movement in its early stages lacked a central focus. The first signs of an impending crisis in the old order came with the municipal elections of 1887. In October about two hundred working men, evenly divided between white and black, met to form the United Labor Party of Charleston. They cheered the name of Henry George and adopted a platform calling for many of the reforms urged by the single-taxer. They declared that both major political parties were no longer in touch with the vital issues of the day and urged cooperation with the national organization of the United Labor Party. At the conclusion of their meeting, a resolution was offered, requesting that the *News and Courier* not ridicule their efforts and declaring that they were "not a ring" and that "every citizen, regardless of social position, race or color, who signs our platform and cuts loose from the Democratic and Republican parties, will have an equal right in our deliberations."[7]

Dawson at first treated the movement with patronizing advice and later with contempt. He reached into his bag of editorial analysis and pulled out the old warnings about Negro rule should whites divide into warring factions. But the laborites were prepared for the hackneyed maxim and hurled it back with the declaration that times had changed. They reasoned that "just as many white men are disgusted with the Democratic party, so are many colored men ready to cut away from the Republican party and to join hands with the whites in the formation of a new organization that shall

---

5. William J. Cooper, Jr., *The Conservative Regime: South Carolina, 1877–1890*, Johns Hopkins Studies in Historical and Political Science, ser. LXXXVI, no. 1 (Baltimore: Johns Hopkins Press, 1968), pp. 187–88, 190.

6. William Watts Ball, *The State that Forgot: South Carolina's Surrender to Democracy* (Indianapolis: Bobbs-Merrill, 1932), p. 220. Belgian blocks are street-paving material.

7. *News and Courier,* October 14, 1887.

ignore 'dead issues' and guarantee equal rights for all."[8] Though the laborites were soundly defeated in the elections that December, they would later prove a force to be reckoned with.

The following February, 1888, the *News and Courier* began experiencing difficulty with disgruntled readers in the upper wards of Charleston, and Dawson moved to reverse the paper's declining circulation in that region of the city. He announced the establishment of an "Up-Town office" and promised that there would be no more grounds for complaints about insufficient coverage of happenings in the upper wards.[9] Simultaneously, Dawson took the occasion of the demise of the Augusta *Gazette* to lecture the public on the resources needed to run a first-class newspaper. He noted that the *Gazette* had been established out of personal animosity for Patrick Walsh (no doubt drawing the parallel to his own situation) and a mistaken belief that Augusta should have two morning papers. He made it clear that neither motive was sufficient to raise capital necessary for a successful venture.[10] The establishment of the up-town office and the gratuitous lecture on newspaper management were not simply coincidental, for on the seventh of February the first issue of the Charleston *World* hit the streets promising an outlet for up-towners and other dissidents.

Opposition to the *News and Courier* continued to fester. In June the "Up-Town clans" expressed irritation at not being invited by Dawson's paper to participate in the mass meeting which had been called to drum up support for a new hotel in Charleston.[11] Minor irritations soon became an open sore. In August dissidents circulated a petition calling for Ben Tillman to come to Charleston and address the issue of ring domination. Dawson taunted those responsible for bringing the Edgefield agitator to Charleston and challenged them to show their faces. He sneered that "even if we could trace those petitions and discover whose names they bear, it is more than probable that the names of the real engineers of the movement would not be found among them."[12] Dawson was convinced that the conspiracy had been hatched in the World-Budget Company offices at 39 Hayne Street, and his claim that "they are the cowards, liars and defamers" stung the *World*'s editor, Octavus Cohen, into a reply. Cohen addressed a personal note to Dawson, saying, "If you were correctly reported, I desire, as the responsible head of The World's-Budget Co., to brand your statement as a gratuitous slander, premeditatedly false,

8. Ibid., October 15, 18, November 10, and December 8, 1887. The laborites withdrew in favor of an Independent ticket in the December elections.

9. Ibid., February 2, 1888.

10. Ibid., February 3, 1888.

11. Ibid., June 10, 1888.

12. Ibid., August 31, 1888.

and known by you to have been false when you uttered it, and I hurl the base and wanton lie back in your teeth."[13]

The pervasiveness of the opposition was revealed a month later when dissidents in Dawson's own ward assembled at the German Artillery Hall to nominate a rival slate for the county convention. These disgruntled Democrats were for the most part young men who complained that four-fifths of the constituency of Ward 4 went virtually unrepresented. Dawson at first welcomed the dissenters as sure to increase interest and Democratic registration. He could not attack them openly and immediately because they were contesting his own nomination, and to bring them under the *News and Courier*'s withering fire would have brought charges of personal aggrandizement. Moreover it was Dawson's policy never to mention his own name in the *News and Courier* when it could be avoided. But once the dissidents had published their slate and Dawson had a chance to assess their relative strength, he opened on them as ingrates who had never bothered to use the party machinery which was available to them. The balloting went heavily in Dawson's favor, with the regular ticket picking up 628 votes to 369 for the Reform Democratic ticket.[14] Again Dawson and the party regulars had beaten back their challengers, but the very audacity shown by the dissenters did not augur well for men who had exercised undisputed sway for over a decade.

More than party solidarity was at stake in these rumblings of 1887 and 1888. The increasing factionalism was fueling the hopes of the rival *World,* and the heightened competition spelled trouble for the Old Lady of Broad Street. The feud between the *News and Courier* and the *World* was not simply a matter of name-calling or maneuvering to catch the right political winds. Dawson was too experienced a journalist not to know that at the heart of the fight would be the issue of who could produce the best newspaper. While political factionalism might give birth to a newspaper, he knew that only good journalism would sustain it. As a result, Dawson spent enormous energy making sure his paper got the best news and got it first. The *News and Courier* had from its beginning held exclusive rights to the Associated Press dispatches for Charleston, and Dawson continued to pay handsomely to maintain that monpoly.[15] Dawson also moved to buy up the services of the United Press as well, demanding that should the *World* drop its rights to the Sunday dispatches or the *Sun,* an evening paper, its

---

13. Octavus Cohen to Dawson, August 31, 1888, Dawson Papers, Duke.

14. *News and Courier,* September 28, 29, October 4 and 6, 1888.

15. On December 31, 1887, Dawson wrote Patrick Walsh of the Augusta *Chronicle* asking Walsh to join in a protest against the A.P. concerning the Greenville *News*'s receiving A.P. dispatches for $35.00 a week when the *News and Courier* paid $150 a week and the *Chronicle* a similar amount. That same day a formal complaint went to William Henry Smith, agent for the A.P., Dawson Papers, Duke.

rights to the daily service, the *News and Courier* would have exclusive rights to the forfeited franchises.[16]

Getting the news became an obsession. When the Associated Press failed to get their dispatches through on March 12, 1888, Dawson fired off an angry letter. He charged that the confidence of the Charleston public had been shaken in the ability of the *News and Courier* to get the news, while the *World*, with its poor news service, was able to scoop them. "The faith in *The News and Courier* and in the Associated Press has been unbounded," he declared, "and our appearance today, without telegraphic news, will give the opposition newspaper . . . a start that it could not have obtained in any other way." The next day an even greater calamity struck when the *World* came out with identical press dispatches, indicating that the news was either leaked or stolen. Dawson demanded an immediate and urgent investigation, but the problem of pirating news continued until early in 1889 when the sources from which the news was stolen were discovered and closed.[17]

The most painful consequence of the war with the *World* was that it ultimately forced Dawson to cut back on the *News and Courier*'s services. In July, 1887, the *News and Courier* had proudly gone to sixteen pages and two editions, and in that year the paper returned a handsome profit of $30,000 on a capital value of $300,000. In the following year, profits were down by a third despite efforts by Dawson to make his paper more attractive through such features as the political cartoon. With revenues falling the ever practical Rudolph Siegling, president of the News and Courier Company, wanted to retrench, but Dawson struggled on until necessity finally forced his hand. In September, 1888, he wrote N. G. Gonzales, saying that financial difficulties made it impossible to have more than one man in Columbia, but he expressed the belief that Gonzales could still beat the competition since "their correspondents have other News Paper work to do, while you give your whole time to our work." Dawson also regretted having to let Gonzales's brother, William Elliott, go, but promised to give him good recommendations. On the same day, Dawson ordered cutbacks in service from Augusta and Greenville.[18] While these and other measures enabled the *News and Courier* to reduce expenses by $6,000 in 1888,[19] it marked the first time in Dawson's twenty years of

16. Dawson to W. P. Phillips, July 1, and December 12, 1887, January 30 and February 3, 1888; Dawson to W. H. Smith, December 1, 1887, and January 6, 1888; Dawson to C. T. Williams, November 26, 1887; all in Hemphill Family Papers, Duke.

17. Dawson to W. H. Smith, March 12 and 13, 1888; and Dawson to J. C. Hemphill, January 30, 1889, ibid.

18. Dawson to N. G. Gonzales; to T. R. Gibson; and to T. E. Horton, September 8, 1888, ibid.

19. Memo from Dawson to Clarence Cary, February 9, 1889, Dawson Papers, Duke.

journalism that he was forced to survive by offering less rather than more news.

The strained financial conditions led directly to strained relationships with the staff. In September the paper's cashier and assistant bookkeeper jumped to the *World,* and though Dawson wished them well, he confided to Sarah that the move bewildered him.[20] Of graver consequence, but unknown to Dawson, were the efforts made by J. C. Hemphill and Carlyle McKinley to find other employment or to establish a newspaper of their own.[21] Part of the staff problem was due to Dawson himself. Having a tendency to be overbearing under normal circumstances, the editor must have been unduly severe on more than one occasion during this time of mounting stress. When he snapped at Gonzales for allowing the *World* and the Columbia *Register* to scoop a story, Gonzales answered politely but firmly that such reproach was "not the way to encourage one man to compete successfully with two." "It is a course which disheartens and hurts cruelly," concluded the Columbia correspondent, "and I ask you, if you wish me to remain on the *News and Courier,* to rest upon the simple assurance that so long as I am paid by it to work, I will do my fullest duty to the paper without other incentive than my own sense of right."[22]

During the fall and winter of 1888–89 the newspaper war did not abate. Political contests around the state, particularly the contest in George D. Tillman's congressional district,[23] provided ammunition for a number of engagements. In October Dawson wrote Sarah saying that "the newspaper . . . fight waxes hotter; but there is no way of telling what the end will be. It does not follow here that the fittest will survive." From friends he received encouragement and advice. A. B. Williams of the Greenville *News* wrote to say that "you may be sure that the war against the N & C

---

20. The two who jumped were J. Swinton Baynard and Wilson G. Harvey, Jr. (*News and Courier,* September 24, 1888). Dawson to his wife, ca. September, 1888, Dawson Papers, Duke.

21. A. B. Williams to J. C. Hemphill, October 18, 1888; William H. Breese to J. C. Hemphill, December 21, 1888; and C. R. Hemphill to J. C. Hemphill, December 28, 1888. Hemphill Family Papers, Duke.

22. N. G. Gonzales to Dawson, January 9, 1889, Dawson Papers, Duke.

23. Dawson was opposed to Congressman Tillman's renomination. He particularly objected to Tillman's stand on the tariff and his alleged opposition to Grover Cleveland. In October and November, 1888, angry words flew between the *World* and the *News and Courier* over Dawson's strictures against Tillman. See Dawson to his wife, ca. November, 1888, ibid. As a consequence of this same controversy, Dawson got into hot water with the Aldrich clan of Barnwell when the *News and Courier* got into the dispute between Robert Aldrich and Daniel Sullivan Henderson of Aiken as to who should oppose Tillman. Such bickering virtually assured Tillman's reelection. Dawson eventually patched up his relationship with the Aldriches. Numerous letters in the Dawson Papers, Duke, between August 30 and September 27, 1888, involve the subject. See also Dawson to D. S. Henderson, May 23, 1888, and Dawson to Alfred Aldrich, September 21, 1888, Hemphill Family Papers, Duke.

will have no help from me. Simply as a question of fair play I disapprove its method and conduct." Another friend advised Dawson to lay off the *World* since all it wanted was notoriety and that was what the *News and Courier* was giving it. Patrick Walsh, who had just emerged victorious from his contest with the Augusta *Gazette,* offered his sympathy. "I am sorry that you have to fight so hard for your chosen field in Charleston," he wrote. "My best wishes are with you. I believe the *Chronicle* will make some money this year. I hope you will do likewise . . . but I know what opposition of any kind means."[24]

The struggle to maintain the *News and Courier*'s preeminent position bore heavily upon Dawson's personal finances. In April, 1888, the threat of a change in the state and municipal tax laws forced the News and Courier Company into a financial reorganization. To prevent being taxed for the entire capital stock of $300,000, the company authorized the issuance of $240,000 in first mortgage bonds, to run for thirty years at 5 percent interest. This action gave the company a book value of $60,000 in stocks and a nontaxable liability for the remainder.[25] While the move was a good one for tax purposes, it added a fixed interest cost which aggravated financial conditions in periods of declining revenue. By the end of 1888 Dawson had committed $4,800 of his own resources and another $2,500 of Siegling's money to sustain the operating costs of the paper.[26] It was something he had done on other occasions, and it always paid off. But this time he was clearly overextended.

With mounting debts Dawson turned to his old friends in New York, and on January 26, 1889, he left for his last visit to that city. He had high hopes of enlisting the aid of Clarence Cary, the man he taught French while on board the Confederate warship *Nashville* and who was now a prosperous attorney, and B. R. Riordan, his old partner, who was then a cotton commission merchant. On arriving in New York, Dawson was invited to dinner by Cary and spent a pleasant evening in the company of Cary's sister, Mrs. Burton Harrison, her husband, and a rising young politico named Theodore Roosevelt. Earlier in the day he had a long discussion with Cary in a vain effort to find a buyer for $30,000 of *News and Courier* first mortgage bonds. By selling these bonds he hoped to pay off his personal debt amounting to "over thirty thousand, which represents purchases of stock in the company, and on which I am paying an interest of at least seven per cent." That evening, before retiring, he wrote Sarah telling

24. A. B. Williams to Dawson, November 23, 1888; E. A. Scott to Dawson, November 29, 1888; and Patrick Walsh to Dawson, January 15, 1889, Dawson Papers, Duke.

25. Dawson to stockholders, April 14, 1888, Hemphill Family Papers, Duke.

26. A Dawson memorandum of January 16, 1889, setting forth his involvement in the financial affairs of the News and Courier Company, Dawson Papers, Duke.

her that there was nothing certain but that Cary had placed him in contact with some men who might be able to help.[27]

Dawson spent the next two days in difficult negotiations, all of which proved "fruitless." On the third day, he wrote Sarah with the encouraging news that he had "struck a new trail, & it is hot enough to justify me in remaining until Monday night." He cautioned against raising her hopes too high, for "if it succeed it will merely be a transfer of my indebtedness from Chn to N.Y. which will save something in interest & take me out of the hands of the Charleston people." He explained that in Charleston "any sudden squeeze in the market for money wd be very dangerous, despite S's [Siegling's] good will and firm support." Dawson knew that while Siegling would stand by him, as president of the Bank of Charleston, Siegling would have "to do his duty by the Bank." Obviously exhausted from the tedious work of the day, Dawson concluded the letter on a more sentimental note. He told Sarah that his pleasantest hours were the moments after dinner when he could indulge his reverie in the rooms they occupied when she last returned from Europe. He also asked her to "tell the children there seems to be a conspiracy to give me pennies for their benefit"—a happy reference to the desire of their old friends to send the children presents of various sorts.[28] Dawson returned to Charleston on the fifth of February and continued his negotiations from there. Despite a willingness to make large concessions for a loan, he got no relief.[29]

Dawson had one other reason for being in New York that January. He was beginning to feel the onset of age and wanted to purchase a good life insurance policy, but even here, he could not get the amount sought. The agent wrote that he appreciated "the inconvenience that would be occasioned . . . by our absolutely declining your case," and therefore proposed that "we accept you for $2,500, which will probably enable you to get insurance elsewhere."[30] Dawson was not proving to be a good risk on any count. Indeed his health had not been good over the past two years. The strain and stress of work left him little time for the exercise and recreation to which he had been accustomed. Sailing, sparring with gloves, and visits to the cottage on Sullivan's Island, all of which he enjoyed immensely, were becoming less and less frequent activities. He began to suffer from a painfully ulcerated stomach and made a special trip to New York for treatment. In the absence of exercise his muscular body became more portly, though beneath his well-tailored clothes he bore his two-hundred-pound frame with the grace of the athlete he once was.

---

27. Dawson to his wife, January 30, 1889, ibid.

28. Ibid., January 31, February 1 and 2, 1889.

29. Memo from Dawson to Clarence Cary, February 9, 1889. See also Dawson to Cary, January 30, 1888, ibid.

30. G. W. Phillips to Dawson, January 30, 1889, ibid.

Such was the political, financial, emotional, and physical condition of Francis Warrington Dawson on that seemingly uneventful day in March, 1889. Though beleaguered, he was still the "colossus" of Broad Street. He had weathered many crises before and was likely to see this one through. If he had difficulties, those who opposed him were in little better shape, being cast more in the nature of raw recruits before the veteran. It was under these circumstances and at this time that a messenger appeared at the city council meeting on Tuesday night and asked to speak privately with Mayor Bryan. When Bryan came back into the council room, his face was ashen, and he asked to speak. "Gentlemen," he said in a voice that sounded strained and distant, "I am always loath to interfere with the conduct of public business, but I have an announcement to make about one who has been foremost in public service in this city and State and who is a personal friend to all of us here. A great public calamity has come to us; Capt. F. W. Dawson now lies dead in this city."[31] In an effort to hold back emotion, Mayor Bryan's words were official and restrained, but then, overcome by the moment, he sank into his seat and sobbed unashamedly.

The mayor was expecting some trouble that afternoon, for the chief of police had earlier asked for a warrant to search the premises of Dr. Thomas Ballard McDow on suspicion of foul play. But the mayor never thought the trouble would be this grievous. The police chief, Captain Joseph Golden, knew from the very beginning that trouble was brewing but was powerless to stop it. Golden was brought into the case on the Friday before when he received a message from the *News and Courier* offices requesting that he drop by to see Captain Dawson. Dawson told Golden about an anonymous report which alleged that the Dawsons' Swiss governess had been seen in disreputable company, and the editor asked that a special detective be assigned to investigate the matter. Golden agreed and assigned Sergeant John P. Dunn to shadow the suspects.[32]

Accordingly Dunn set up a watch on the following Monday and filed two reports. The first indicated that the governess, Hélène Marie Burdayron, showed no unusual behavior though she did "attract a great deal of attention on account of her dress." More likely it was her striking beauty that did the attracting. At the very eligible age of twenty-two, Burdayron was the kind of woman who could provide material for endless rounds of gossip in an age which, justified or not, believed that most heads of

---

31. *News and Courier*, March 14, 1889.

32. Unless otherwise indicated, the details of the murder are taken from the *News and Courier*, March 13–17 and June 25–30, 1889. These numbers of the *News and Courier* contain minutely detailed reports of all the testimony from the coroner's inquest of March 12 through the trial which ran from June 24–29. The transcript, as published by the paper, was taken from notes of the court stenographer. For a digest of these reports see Thomas K. Peck, "The Killing of Captain Dawson, 1889," in *Charleston Murders*, ed. Beatrice St. J. Ravenel (New York: Duell, Sloan and Pearce, 1947), pp. 71–110.

households indulged the Victorian double standard.[33] Later that same day, Dunn filed a second report, having discovered what it was suspected he might find. He saw Hélène take the red car at Meeting Street near Broad. She was soon joined by Dr. McDow, a young physician who lived a few doors from the Dawsons. McDow got on the car at Wentworth Street, and the two suspects proceeded to the upper terminus where they alighted and strolled about the unfrequented streets in the northwest section of the city. Dunn temporarily lost sight of the pair until he saw them step from the gate of a Negro shanty, though Dunn was positive they did not enter the house. Dunn again lost sight of them, but on returning to the corner of Rutledge and Bull, he saw McDow go into his house unaccompanied by the woman. With this information, Dunn went back to the central station house and filed his report.

The next morning, Tuesday, March 12, Chief Golden took the reports and delivered them to Captain Dawson. Dawson read the documents carefully and announced that he would attend to the matter on his way home to dinner. Chief Golden apparently sensed some agitation on Dawson's part, for he warned the editor against any direct or precipitate action, saying that McDow's reputation was not the best and that it would be better to take no notice of him. Golden also detailed a special duty policeman to the area. The chief later claimed that the policeman was there to investigate suspicious characters who were reportedly operating in the neighborhood. Counsel for the defendant charged that the more likely explanation was that Golden feared Dawson's going to McDow's office and causing trouble.

For the remainder of the morning and early afternoon, Dawson went about his regular routine, meeting with the staff at noon to make assignments and writing an editorial on profitable farming. Shortly after three o'clock, a little earlier than usual, Dawson said goodbye to his staff and headed for home. In his pocket were the two reports filed by Dunn. Stepping up on the blue car which ran down Broad and up Rutledge, Dawson encountered several friends, including his longtime associate, Major Julien Mitchell. The men engaged in amiable, light conversation, and Dawson appeared to be in very good spirits. When the car reached the corner of Bull Street, Captain Dawson pulled the check rein, bid his friends a good afternoon, and stepped off. Rather than going the fifty steps or so to his home, Dawson angled across Rutledge Street to McDow's residence, the doctor's house being two doors down from the corner of Bull and Rutledge and easily visible from the back piazzas of the Dawson house.

---

33. After Dawson was shot, his enemies circulated rumors alleging an unhappy marriage and Dawson's likely involvement with the Swiss governess. N. G. Gonzales to J. C. Hemphill, March 23, 1889, Narciso Gener Gonzales Papers, SCL.

McDow's office was on the bottom floor of his residence and opened from the side of the house onto Rutledge Steet. The house itself was typical of antebellum Charleston architecture, with three long piazzas opening from each floor and extending along the entire front. The house ran at a right angle from the street and faced a handsome garden. The main structure was an unpretentious solid brick, though the eaves were supported by slightly fancy brickwork and the heavy over-window "eyebrows" were cast in three different styles.[34] Dawson stepped up to the door at 75 Rutledge and pulled the leather strap leading to the door bell.

Dawson was not expecting to stay long. He did not even bother to take off his overcoat or his gloves, and continued to hold his cane. McDow's was the only testimony as to what happened next. Addressing the doctor in an abrupt manner, Dawson said, "I have just been informed of your ungentlemanly conduct towards one of my servants." When McDow denied the accusation, Dawson brushed it aside with an order that the doctor was not to see her again. McDow then asked by what authority Dawson forbade his seeing the girl, and Captain Dawson, no doubt angered by the doctor's resistance, swore, "I give you to understand that she is under my protection, and if you speak to her again I shall publish you in the papers."[35] By this time McDow's own temper had flared, and gathering his courage, he retorted, "And if you do, you infernal scoundrel, I will hold you personally responsible. Get out of my office!" At that point, McDow claimed, Dawson raised his cane and came down with a sharp blow to the doctor's head, almost simultaneously shoving his fist into McDow's chest, thereby throwing the doctor back onto a sofa in the office. When Dawson approached to strike again, McDow whipped a pistol out of his pocket and fired one shot. Dawson straightened up, staggered back, and gasped, "You have killed me."

Across the street a black carriage driver, George W. Harper, sat in the carriage box waiting for his passengers. He saw Captain Dawson enter the

---

34. The house is now numbered 101 Rutledge Avenue. For a description of the house see the Charleston *Evening Post,* July 3, 1968.

35. It has been argued that the threat to "publish" may have referred to an investigation the *News and Courier* was conducting for a New York insurance firm, involving the signing of false death certificates in the black community. It is suggested that McDow was the physician responsible and that publication would have ruined his practice. See S. Frank Logan, "Francis W. Dawson, 1840–1889: South Carolina Editor" (M.A. thesis, Duke University, 1947), p. 301.

This theory seems improbable since the *News and Courier* never mentioned any of these facts subsequent to the murder and since no effort was made by the prosecution to suggest it as motive for the killing. If Dawson had this information, he apparently never confided it to members of his staff. The origin of the theory is Warrington Dawson, who received his information "at second hand from declarations made to me by my mother" (*News and Courier,* August 24, 1958, p. C-1).

doctor's office but thought nothing of it. About four to five minutes later Harper heard a shot, then "two struggling kinds of groans," and then a voice pitched with tension saying, "You would take my life and now I have taken yours." Harper next saw a gentleman close the basement windows, and an old groundnut cake woman, who had peeped in to see what the commotion was, hurried over to Harper's carriage and with an anxious voice said, "Great God, somebody is murdered in there." Harper, knowing better than to get mixed up in white folks' trouble, did not move. Minutes later he saw McDow on the second floor piazza looking up and down the street—he seemed "cool as a cucumber." Harper's eyes next caught the butler running out to hitch McDow's carriage, followed by Mrs. McDow and her daughter who got in and rode off. About that time Harper's passengers finally came out, and clicking at his horse, he started up the street a little faster than usual. It was then that Harper saw the special duty policeman and, leaning over without coming to a full stop, said there had been "some murdering" going on down there.

The patrolman seemed to know exactly where to go. Pulling the gong at 75 Rutledge, Private Gordon waited until the door was pulled open slightly, and McDow peeped around the edge. Gordon asked if there were any trouble, and when McDow said no, he set out to find Chief Golden, who was riding the rounds. Golden went directly to the doctor's office and was also told that nothing was wrong. Highly suspicious by this time, Golden went to the *News and Courier* offices where he was informed that the Captain had left some time ago. A phone call to the already anxious Dawson household revealed that the editor was not there either. It was then that Chief Golden went to the mayor and asked for a warrant, but before the warrant could be served McDow surrendered himself to patrolman Gordon, saying he had shot and killed Captain Dawson. Almost three hours had passed from the time Dawson was shot at 3:40 P.M. until McDow surrendered himself. Detective John Hogan, who escorted McDow to jail, later testified that McDow confessed that he had shot to kill, that his profession had "learned him how to shoot to kill."

It was unlike the Captain not to call if he were going to be late for dinner, and Sarah grew increasingly fearful, especially after the call from the *News and Courier* office, that the worst had finally happened. Each time she heard footsteps she tried to convince herself it was Frank. On one occasion she opened the door to a slightly built man with dark complexion and black hair, a nice looking man, but one who had an extremely agitated look about him. When she asked what he wanted, he said, "Nothing," then turned and left hurriedly. McDow, hoping to warn Hélène Burdayron, confronted instead the woman he had just made a widow.

A little later Sarah heard steps again. This time it was Henry Baynard, a member of the *News and Courier* staff. Baynard looked ghastly. Ironically, Sarah's first thought was that Frank might have killed Baynard's brother

Swinton, who had just gone over to the *World* and who "deserved death" for continually exacerbating the differences between her husband and ex-Mayor Courtenay. But she could get nothing out of Baynard, who simply slumped into a chair in the hallway, a useless lump of weeping humanity. Sarah now knew, and when the door next opened to reveal Major Hemphill there could no longer be any doubt. Hemphill immediately strode over to where Baynard sat weeping and escorted him to the library. On his return, Sarah looked at him and firmly but quietly asked if Captain Dawson were dead. Hemphill, Dawson's handpicked successor and closest friend on the paper, answered, "Yes." Sarah thought she was about to die. The blood rushed from her face, and she grabbed the arm of a chair. But summoning the strength of duty, she gathered herself and told the butler to take the children to a neighbor's house. Ethel and Warrington would not be told of their father's death until morning.[36]

Hemphill did the thing he knew Captain Dawson would have liked best. He returned to the *News and Courier* and prepared the Old Lady of Broad Street for one of the biggest stories she would ever cover. Assigning his best reporter to collect the facts, he sat down to express the paper's grief. "Dead! Dead!" cried the *News and Courier*. "The man who moved among us yesterday in the flush of health, in the full vigor of manhood, performing with rare ability and conscientious devotion all the private and public duties of a citizen, is dead."

The weather itself captured the bewildering spirit of the day after. To a reporter it seemed as if "the very heavens wept." As the Captain lay in state at 43 Bull Street, the rain dashed drearily against the windowpanes thrown there by baleful gusts of wind. Young and old, high and low, bereft and curious filed past the bier from morning until midafternoon, bringing wreaths and sprays of flowers until the room could hold no more. A few moments before the coffin was closed, a hush fell over the room as Sarah entered for a last look at his face. As the casket was borne down the marble steps to begin its journey to the Pro-Cathedral, the crowd outside lined both sides of the street despite the inclement weather. At the cathedral Dawson's body was placed at the chancel in front of the assembled prelates who had come to pay their tributes to a Knight of St. Gregory. The crowd overflowed the church and spilled out into Queen Street. When the clergy had had their say, the men of the *News and Courier* bore their captain to the waiting hearse for the last ride through Charleston.

The rain continued to descend as the funeral cortège made its way up King Street. The usually busy shops and stores were closed and wore the

---

36. Sarah described the events of that day in a notebook recorded for Ethel and Warrington so that they might "better understand some things which will perplex you when you are older." Pages 1–87 were written in 1890 and pages 88–93 in 1893. The notebook is titled "Notebook on the Death of F. W. Dawson" and may be found in the Dawson Papers, Duke.

black bunting of death. Again the streets were lined as all Charleston united to pay its last respects. Moving slowly toward the Catholic cemetery of St. Lawrence, the procession passed the theatre where Dawson had reserved a box to take Ethel to the matinee. The box was closed and lined in black. Charlestonians could not remember such an outpouring of grief. The *News and Courier* expressed it publicly, "The death of Captain F. W. Dawson, soldier, scholar, and patriot, was one of those events which rise eminently above the common place of the history of Charleston and South Carolina." But one Carolinian put the sentiments of Dawson's friends best and privately. William Porcher Miles, who was then living in Louisiana, made a simple notation in his diary on hearing the news. "Horrible! Dawson will be a great loss to Charleston & South Carolina & the entire South. A man of brilliant talents—fearless & energetic."[37]

---

37. William Porcher Miles Diary, March 13, 1889, Southern Historical Collection, University of North Carolina.

Chapter XI
A Trial and a Cross

Even as Charleston mourned the passing of a leader and friends from across the nation sent their messages of condolence, the city was buzzing with talk of Dawson's assassin and the circumstances surrounding the murder. The coroner's inquest, which had been hastily summoned on the evening of the tragedy, told a tale of cruel murder and clumsy efforts to conceal the crime.[1] The story that leaked from the inquest and spread like fire contradicted McDow's own statement to a reporter from the *World.* In the interview McDow maintained that his failure to report the incident was caused by excitement, and indirectly by a quarrel earlier in the day with his wife.[2] The inquest, however, found traces of a calculated and grim effort to hide the evidence. They discovered that McDow had used his time to prepare a grave underneath the stairwell leading from his office, drag the body to that ignoble tomb, attempt to stuff it in, and failing in that, wrestle the corpse back into his office and try to clean up the messy attempt at concealment. Corroborating evidence was found when it was discovered that McDow's and Dawson's clothing were smudged with the whitewash and dirt from the stairwell diggings. As if these circumstances were not ignominious enough, the investigators had to fish Dawson's hat and cane from the bottom of an outdoor privy.

Further evidence seemed to indicate that the claim of self-defense was specious at best. McDow showed no marks from the caning he claimed to have received at the hands of Captain Dawson, and the bullet wound itself revealed that the editor had been shot from the side and behind. All this evidence led the grand jury to hand down a true bill for murder in the first degree and a charge of accessory after the fact against McDow's butler.

As many expected, the details that leaked from the Tuesday night inquest served to raise a lynch mob. A party of men soon started toward Magazine Street, where McDow was jailed. It was not certain whether the jailers would or could protect the doctor's life. As the lynchers drew near, a young Irishman suddenly shouted for the mob to stop. With pistols and

---

1. Unless otherwise indicated, the details surrounding Dawson's murder and the trial of McDow are taken from the *News and Courier,* March 13–17 and June 25–30, 1889. For a digest of these reports see Thomas K. Peck, "The Killing of Captain Dawson, 1889," in *Charleston Murders,* ed. Beatrice St. J. Ravenel (New York: Duell, Sloan and Pearce, 1947), pp. 71–110.

2. Clippings in the scrapbook made by Sarah Dawson, for Hélène Burdayron, to help clear Burdayron's name. Dawson Papers, Duke.

rope dangling at their sides, the men listened as the rough young man remonstrated with them saying, "Boys I believe we had better not do this. I've been thinking as we walked along about what the Captain said about lynching in the *News and Courier* and I don't think he would like it if he were here."[3] These words prevented another killing in Charleston, and the good citizens settled back to wait the due process of law.

Few doubted the outcome. McDow's story contained all the transparent contradictions of a liar. The *News and Courier* and other papers around the state and nation talked as if the fact of cold-blooded murder had been established. The presumption of innocence was further diminished by rumors about the doctor's bad character. Chief Golden laid the groundwork for that kind of talk when he told of warning Dawson about McDow's reputation for violence. It was said that the young doctor had been involved in a shooting scrape somewhere in Mississippi before coming to Charleston. His other credentials before setting up practice, however, were not those of a rough character. He was born in Camden, Kershaw County, and at the time of the trial was thirty-six years old. He established a commendable record at Cumberland University in Lebanon, Tennessee, and graduated valedictorian of his class in the Medical College at Charleston. Despite his record of accomplishment, McDow was rumored to be an abortionist, a drug-user, and a man the medical society wished to blackball. His family life was also much discussed. His marriage to a German girl was said to have been for money, and as the trial revealed, he soon tired of her rather bovine appearance and behavior.

McDow's unsavory reputation was frequently contrasted with Dawson's courtly demeanor and chivalric intent on the day of his death. People looked favorably upon a man whose mission was to rescue the governess of his children from the clutches of an evil man. When Mrs. Dawson brought Hélène Burdayron to America, the Dawsons assumed an obligation to see that her introduction to society was proper and morally sound. While McDow used her innocence, so the story went, Captain Dawson, acting as a father would, sought to save the girl from certain ruin at the hands of the disreputable and shameless doctor. Under these circumstances, civilization itself demanded that McDow be punished.

The case of Thomas Ballard McDow came up for trial at the June term of the court of General Sessions for Charleston County. The presiding judge was General Joseph Brevard Kershaw of the Fifth Judicial Circuit. When the court convened at 10:00 A.M. on the twenty-fourth of June, the courthouse was packed. The defendant was brought from jail, where he had been held without bail since the night of the murder. The defendant's father, Dr. R. S. McDow of Lancaster, took a seat near his son. The

---

3. Quoted in William Watts Ball, *The State that Forgot: South Carolina's Surrender to Democracy* (Indianapolis: Bobbs-Merrill, 1932), p. 173.

attorneys for the trial were among the best in South Carolina: the vener-
able Judge Andrew Gordon Magrath, a Civil War governor of the state
and a not infrequent collaborator with Dawson, was joined by Mr. Asher
D. Cohen, a brilliant cross-examiner, in the unenviable and difficult task of
representing the defendant. On the other side sat the solicitor of the First
Circuit, Mr. William St. Julien Jervey, who was ably assisted by Dawson's
good friend and personal attorney, Mr. Henry Augustus Middleton Smith.
Mr. Julien Mitchell, whose services McDow tried to secure because of his
brilliant reputation as a defense lawyer, later joined the prosecution in
summation. The younger members of the Charleston bar joined the throng
in hopes of learning from the clash of these legal minds.

At five minutes past ten o'clock, Judge Kershaw's gavel came down and
brought the assembled multitude to order. Fortunately, the rain outside
kept the temperature inside at a tolerable level. After McDow entered his
plea of not guilty by reason of self-defense, the court proceeded to select a
jury. Considerable time was spent in challenging prospective jurors, and as
finally impaneled the list read: Arthur Middleton, white; A. McCobb, Jr.,
white; George G. Butler, white; C. C. Leslie, colored; P. H. Alston,
colored; Alex McKenzie, colored; Julius M. Bing, colored; Robert Scan-
lon, colored; P. McG. McInnes, white; Alexander Sims, colored; W. H.
Burgess, colored; and A. H. Prince, white. The stage was set for one of the
most extraordinary trials in Charleston's history.

The first important witness was Dr. William Middleton Michel, an older
member of the medical profession and the man who performed the autopsy
on Captain Dawson. His testimony became critical in the six-day trial, for
the prosecution relied on it as scientific proof that the deceased had been
shot from behind. The medical terminology of Dr. Michel's official report
established that Captain Dawson "came to his death from a pistol shot,
which entered the right side of the abdomen, below the floating ribs,
penetrated the abdominal cavity, ranged horizontally, grooved the lower
border of [the] right kidney, opened the vena cava—large vein of the whole
body—and caused death from internal hemorrhage almost immediately."[4]
Dr. Michel also established that he found no powder burns on the
deceased's clothes, indicating that the gun was not fired at close range. Dr.
Michel left an opening for the defense, however, when he disclosed that he
had not traced the bullet to its final lodgement in the tissue.

On the second day the state called its most spectacular witness, the
beautiful Hélène Marie Burdayron. There followed what all agreed was an
astonishing performance by a young woman who had difficulty in understanding English, her mother tongue being French. After pleas to allow her
to testify through an interpreter were rejected, the witness proceeded

---

4. "Examination of the Body of Capt. F. W. Dawson," Middleton Michel, M.D., March
14, 1889. South Carolina Historical Society, Charleston, South Carolina.

through two and a half hours of direct and cross examination without budging an inch from the outline of her open and frank story. She explained that she and McDow met in early February, and that the doctor importuned her to run away with him from the very beginning. She told of how McDow visited her in the Dawson's own home while Sarah was away in Washington, how she had accepted a watch from him, and how they had exchanged books. She even conceded giving the doctor a book titled *Twixt Love and Law* which concerned an unmarried girl falling in love with a married man. When the defense tried to suggest that such behavior was provocative, her innocent denials gained the sympathy of the court.

Even the Nestor of the Charleston bar, Judge Magrath, could do nothing with the witness. The impression she left was that of a confused, innocent girl, who had been unscrupulously used by McDow. Even her failure to flatly refuse his advances seemed more the result of his exciting her sympathy with tales of his unhappy marriage than any seduction on her part. The defense was absolutely correct in charging that her testimony had no bearing on the guilt or innocence of their client, but they knew that Burdayron's performance added to the weight of evidence suggesting that Dawson's mission that afternoon was in the name of chivalry and civilized behavior. Burdayron added one other element to the drama. She gave the case a sexual dimension which caused tongues to wag and people to declare that there was stuff for a novel in the case of *South Carolina* v. *McDow*. [5]

The interest excited by Burdayron's appearance did not divert the defense from its careful strategy. Their plan was to discredit Dr. Michel's testimony and to develop McDow's claim of self-defense. Cohen was assigned the task of examining Dr. Michel, and a better laywer could not have been found for the job. Cohen was an acknowledged master of the *suaviter in modo* art of cross-examination. Events played into Cohen's hand. First, the defense called its own expert, who testified from an examination of the decedent's clothing that it was possible for the bullet to have entered from the side and front. To counter his testimony, the state called a second expert, a distinguished member of the faculty of the medical college, who supported Dr. Michel's analysis. But he also sug-

---

5. A novel has been written by Robert Molloy, *An Afternoon in March* (New York: Doubleday, 1958). The book is based on a close examination of the newspaper accounts, and the dialogue is frequently verbatim. Molloy offers some extremely valuable insights into the nuances behind the observable facts. He creates a genuine sympathy for McDow (Harold Thatcher Fairchild in the novel) without detracting from Dawson (Colonel Nowell Molyneux Ponsonby Devere). Molloy's exploration of the sexual motive is plausible. He suggests that Devere (Dawson) was never guilty of an impropriety but that his agitation over Fairchild's (McDow's) advances was triggered by his own subliminal but definite feelings for Burdayron. Molloy also creates a reasonable theory for self-defense. He assumes that Dawson in fact caned McDow, hitting him on the shoulder instead of the head, and that a missed blow could well have exposed Dawson's right side to McDow's pistol. Molloy does not, however, account for the absence of powder burns.

gested under cross-examination that it would have been better had Dr. Michel traced the bullet to its final lodgement, and he also suggested that Michel's theory, that a bullet could be deflected by other than a bony substance, was dated.

Cohen saw his opening. Dr. Michel had not been present for the testimony of the state's second expert, and so Cohen put Michel on the stand again. The canny attorney started by going over the same old ground and seemed to be getting nowhere. Then he turned to Dr. Michel and asked, "Well, Doctor, would you have any respect for the opinion of a man who stated that a ball could not be deflected from a straight course by anything but a hard, bony substance?" As the doctor asked Cohen to repeat the question, the audience, seeing what Cohen was up to, leaned forward in eager anticipation. Michel pondered the question a moment and replied, "I should say that such a man had no knowledge of physiology, anatomy, surgery, or medical science." A roar of laughter shook the hall. Dr. Michel had just impeached, notwithstanding the merits of his own view, the testimony of the professor of clinical surgery in the Medical College of South Carolina. Cohen did not even turn to the jury with the triumphant smile he usually employed. He knew that, at last, an element of doubt had been thrust into the prosecution's expert testimony.

The remainder of the defense was devoted to buttressing the claim of self-defense. They called the Negro carriage driver, George Harper, who stuck to his story of hearing McDow shout, "You would take my life and now I have taken yours." They sought to prove that McDow had been caned by calling the doctor who examined McDow the day after and found a slight contusion on his scalp. (The prosecution countered that testimony by suggesting that the bruise was likely caused by McDow's striking his head on the stairwell as he tried to bury the body.) To add to their theory of self-defense, Cohen and Magrath contrasted the physical attributes of the two men, declaring McDow a mere "pygmy" when compared to Dawson. They strongly implied that the police, knowing of Dawson's violent intentions, were in the neighborhood that afternoon to protect the influential editor should he run into trouble. Counsel for the defense also sought to establish that Dawson had a reputation for violence and aggressiveness. They called one of the editor's old enemies, ex-Mayor Sale, who described Dawson as "more on the bulldog order than anything else I can think of." This strategy, however, backfired when they next selected a witness at random who testified just the opposite. Momentarily flustered by this hostile witness, Cohen turned to the court and explained that the witness had been selected "promiscuously, and, as your Honor will see, we have had no conference with him." Judge Kershaw provoked a round of laughter with the comment, "It is unfortunate that you have not had one."

The summaries were lengthy. The defense adroitly went to the emotional appeals of self-defense, which in South Carolina traditionally spelled acquittal. They talked about a man's home being his castle and drew vivid pictures of McDow's being thrashed by an enraged man and, having no exit of escape, defending himself with the weapon he carried in his hip pocket. The whole affair was unfortunate and tragic, McDow was full of remorse, but any man would have done the same. The defense was at its dramatic best when finally turning to the subject of Miss Burdayron. Her testimony given four days before was not remembered with great clarity, but her charming beauty was. No man could resist her, particularly if she encouraged the advances. And then Magrath lifted high a copy of *Twixt Love and Law* and shouted, "Here, here is the book which she gave him to read. She knew what was in it. I have no hesitation in saying it is one of the vilest and most indecent books of the class of immoral literature of the day."

After reviewing all the facts, Judge Magrath reminded the jurors of the law and their responsibility under it. He sympathized with them. "You have been left to grope in the dark," he said, "in a condition of things out of which the grossest injustice might have been done to the accused. If it hadn't occurred accidentally, nay providentially, that the coachmen (Harper) had been on Rutledge Street that afternoon, no power on earth could have saved the accused." The defense rested its case.

Major Julien Mitchell summed up for the state. He began by noting that there existed one undisputed fact: McDow took the life of Captain F. W. Dawson. He then described the amiable, jovial mood Dawson had been in on the afternoon of his murder. He recalled all the evidence which disputed the claim of self-defense. McDow did not show the marks of a man who had been caned. Worse still, McDow admitted that he lied when he first told reporters that he had taken the gun from his desk drawer, and that he lied because a reporter told him the story would sound better that way. Now McDow claimed to have drawn the gun from his person, because to have retrieved it from the desk would have denied the claim of self-defense. Could the jury believe a man who would perjure himself and who had every reason to do so? Moreover, if McDow shot at close range in self-defense, why were there no powder burns? How could a man at close range fire with his right hand and strike his victim in the right side and slightly to the back? An extreme act of contortion would have been required. Julien reviewed all the efforts at concealment and asked if these were the actions of an innocent man. He then reminded the jury that, while the learned doctors may have disagreed over the deflection of bullets, there was no disagreement over the direction and entry of the deadly missle.

Mitchell had no ready response for Harper's testimony, other than to doubt that a man's hearing could be so keen at such a distance, and as to Miss Burdayron, he took the high road. "Well, now," he said, "my observations on life have taught me this: I have never seen a man seduced by a woman yet. The initiative always begins with him. Why? Because his passions are the strongest." Some poetry seemed fitting, so he quoted:

> Woman is the lesser man, and all her passions matched with mine
> Are as moonlight unto sunlight, or as water unto wine.

That bit of eloquence done, the state was now ready to leave the matter of retribution for injustice done in the hands of the jury.

All agreed that the defense had done a masterful job. Some thought the prosecution a bit lame.[6] Where McDow's conviction had been a foregone conclusion, there was now some doubt. Much would depend on the jury's predisposition. The jury retired for their deliberations a little after noon on Saturday, June 29. They made one more request for evidence, a diagram of the doctor's office. Then at three o'clock the phone rang to alert Judge Kershaw that the jury had reached a verdict. The courtroom was quickly packed again. In particular, a large number of blacks who had been following the trial intently from the back half of the hall seemed curiously eager to hear the verdict. McDow was brought forward, and though appearing a bit nervous, he smiled to friends. Judge Kershaw then inquired of the foreman if the jury had agreed on a verdict and the foreman nodded that they had. The jury maintained an inscrutable silence. Taking the sheet of paper from the foreman, the clerk turned and announced, "The State against Thomas Ballard McDow. We find the defendant not guilty." A cheer welled up from the densely packed courtroom and continued until the embarrassed judge gaveled several times for order, threatening to jail the entire crowd for contempt if they did not refrain from such a public display. As McDow left for his carriage, he was greeted by another ovation from a large crowd of Negroes who had gathered to see him off.

The reaction underscored some suspicions entertained by Captain Dawson's more ardent supporters. These suspicions do not explain the verdict (for it was a simple fact that South Carolinians typically were not disposed to convict a man who could make a case for self-defense in a crime of passion), but they do offer some clue to the mind-set of the jurors as they received the facts. Dawson's friends were convinced that the jury had been packed for acquittal from the very beginning. Patrick Walsh, who came in person to report for the Augusta *Chronicle,* interviewed Solicitor Jervey immediately following the trial. When asked to account for the verdict, Jervey declared that "it is the subjection of reason to a preconceived judgement." When asked to be more specific, Jervey began by noting that it was "the first time on record that a white man has been tried by a jury on which there were colored men in any trial of note." The solicitor then declared that it was his carefully documented judgment that the behavior

---

6. Unsigned letter to Sarah Dawson, July 2, 1889, Dawson Papers, Duke.

of the Negroes grew out of editorials Dawson had written on the Pickens lynch trial. (It will be recalled that this case involved blacks lynching a white man for the killing of a young black girl.) In these editorials Dawson favored clemency but also drew "a contrast between the races unfavorable to the chastity of the colored race." Jervey said that these editorials were "worked up to show that he was an enemy to the colored race."[7]

A reporter for the New York *Herald* came to the same conclusion, finding that "the race prejudice was adroitly managed." He overheard one Negro "to say . . . that after this he wasn't going to allow any white man to call him a nigger."[8] There was good reason for this outpouring of sentiment among the blacks. On the eve of his death, Captain Dawson had written a highly inflammatory editorial which underscored the race prejudice that blacks believed to be the hallmark of white rule, conservative or otherwise. The subject of the editorial was the Pickens trial, in which three of the six defendants were convicted of murder, while the father, a friend, and a white accomplice were acquitted. The Greenville *News* argued that the entire party should have been acquitted on the grounds that there should be no distinction between the assault of a white girl by blacks and the assault of a Negro girl by whites. The *News and Courier,* though objecting to all lynchings, white or black, mildly reproached its up-state rival saying:

> It is on account of the horror which attaches to the crime when a white person is assaulted by a negro that lynching has been condoned by worthy and worthless people. It cannot be professed for a moment that any such horror attaches to the crime when an aggressor is a white man, and the object is a colored woman. It seems harsh and cruel to say this: but it is the truth. . . . The distinction is drawn, and properly drawn, between the white victim and the colored victim, or there is no difference between the personal purity of the one race and the other.[9]

Though the editorial went on to express the hope that the conviction of the three blacks would have a deterent on whites as well, the black community was justified in the disgust and indignation that these sentiments no doubt excited.

It was more difficult to account for the five white men on the jury. After asking around, the reporter for the New York *Herald* felt that it was the bitterness "toward Captain Dawson on account of his course in party

---

7. Reprint from the Augusta *Chronicle* in the *News and Courier,* July 2, 1889. Jervey may have overstated the significance of blacks serving on the jury which tried McDow. Though the evidence is admittedly negative in nature, the author could find no concerted effort to systematically exclude blacks from a venire before 1889. The full effects of Jim Crow apparently awaited the constitutional convention of 1895.

8. Clipping in the scrapbook prepared by Sarah Dawson for Hélène Burdayron, Dawson Papers, Duke.

9. *News and Courier,* March 11, 1889.

factional fights."[10] Indeed one of the jurors, A. McCobb, Jr., had been a ringleader among the Ward 4 dissenters and, as Sarah alleged, was foiled by Captain Dawson in his effort to benefit from federal patronage.[11] The Charleston *Daily Sun* minced no words in coming to the conclusion that "the world will not be deceived and it is folly to disguise from ourselves that this case between the state and a citizen . . . degenerated into a contest between factions and was finally decided upon extrinsic issues and not upon its legal merits."[12] Similar sentiment was voiced around the state. N. G. Gonzales wrote from Columbia that "in Columbia, I suppose, Capt. Dawson had fewer enemies than elsewhere, but even here there are some 'fellows of the baser sort' who still slander in corners." In a letter to former Mayor Courtenay, a prominent citizen of Greenville said, "Our wisest citizens are disposed to hear all the facts which have ended in so shocking a tragedy—before reaching a conclusion. The history of Mr. Dawson is too well known, in State matters, to the majority of the *up country* democracy to be rewritten in the gush of sentimental sympathy."[13]

These were the voices of men who had been on the wrong side of Dawson's editorial pen, and they by no means represented the majority sentiment. Dawson's funeral was the closest thing to a state occasion that Charlestonians could remember. Flags were flown at half mast. Presidents, senators, congressmen, editors, governors, all rushed their letters of sympathy and tribute to Charleston and the aggrieved family. People with names of little consequence expressed their sense of outrage in other ways, as the man who offered to serve as Sarah's personal body guard against the acquitted manslayer, McDow, or the illiterate scrawl, signed by "the Big (5) of Jersey City, N.J.," which promised to "put this McDow out of the way" and in a manner "Worse than *Jack the Riper Dose his Worke.*"[14]

This outpouring of sympathy was little consolation to the widow. Sarah's bitterness was intense, and she came to detest the hypocrisy of a society with pretensions to chivalry and the civil virtues—a hypocrisy she believed to be more exaggerated in Charleston and South Carolina than in any other place in the South.[15] She consistently refused to do biographical sketches of

---

10. Clipping, Sarah Dawson scrapbook for Hélène Burdayron, Dawson Papers, Duke.

11. *News and Courier,* September 28, 1888; and marginal note in Sarah Dawson scrapbook for Hélène Burdayron, Dawson Papers, Duke.

12. Clipping, Sarah Dawson scrapbook for Hélène Burdayron, Dawson Papers, Duke.

13. N. G. Gonzales to J. C. Hemphill, March 23, 1889, N. G. Gonzales Papers, SCL; and Henry D. Capers to W. A. Courtenay, March 20, 1889, W. A. Courtenay Papers, SCL.

14. "The Big (5) of Jersey City" to Sarah Dawson, July 15, 1889, Dawson Papers, Duke.

15. An M.A. thesis written at the University of North Carolina treats the subject of Sarah's critique of southern society, beginning with her famous diary and continuing through the transforming experience of Captain Dawson's death. See Mary Katherine Davis, "Sarah Morgan Dawson: A Renunciation of Southern Society" (1970).

her late husband, and when finally prevailed upon to write such an article, the manuscript was so vindictive it could not be published. The acid dripping from her pen, she wrote, "He served the State with the devotion, the ability, the power, and the unselfishness never given to a son of South Carolina. For there is nothing more conspicuous in her history than the Selfishness that breathes in every leader and Statesman she has ever produced. Selfishness is the impalpable something that makes the peculiar atmosphere of the State."[16]

Her bitterness was aggravated by the poor financial condition of the estate she inherited. She became convinced that Dawson's partner, Rudolph Siegling, was ruthlessly and criminally taking advantage of her and the children. She wrote extravagant denunciations of Siegling to the stockholders of the *News and Courier,* and she implored editors from over the state to come to her aid. Sarah's brother in New York tried to temper her anger by explaining that her position, while "uncomfortable," was "not an unusual one." He patiently advised her that the estate, though not as valuable as she and Frank had hoped, would still enable her to "live comfortably and independently . . . for the rest of her life." And he tried to make her understand that Siegling was acting within his legal rights, even if he did not show the leniency that might be expected.[17] Her personal attorney and friend, Henry A. M. Smith, was even reduced to warning that he would have to step down as counsellor if she did not stop her denunciations. "It simply . . . tends to weaken and impair my power of doing anything for you. I think I have a right to ask as little as this. You shd keep your thoughts to yourself if I am to have the duty of protecting your interests."[18]

Sarah and the children continued to live in Charleston after the murder, but when Ethel married in 1898, Warrington convinced his mother to come and live with him in Paris. Through these years her spirits gradually improved, though she spent part of her time leaving records to indicate Siegling's perfidy and recording dreams, premonitions, and other reflections concerning her husband's murder. Hélène Burdayron stayed with the family for another year, until a quarrel resulted in her dismissal in April, 1890. This dispute left Sarah and her son convinced that Burdayron knew that McDow had actually plotted to murder Captain Dawson.[19] The later

---

16. MS biographical sketch of F. W. Dawson written in 1894 by his wife at the request of J. T. White for the *National Cyclopedia of Biography,* Dawson Papers, Duke.

17. See a series of letters from Philip Hickey Morgan to Sarah, November 9, 20, and 25, 1889, April 19, June 29, July 10 and 22, 1890. Quoted material comes from the letter of November 25. See also Sarah Dawson to Stockholders and Bondholders of the News and Courier Company, 1890, ibid.

18. H. A. M. Smith to Sarah, January 23, 1890, ibid.

19. See Sarah Dawson, "Notebook on the Death of F. W. Dawson," and a memorandum by Warrington Dawson, "Murder with Premeditation and an Accessory before the Fact," ibid.

years in Paris were happier. She spent her time writing and admiring the accomplishments of her son, who showed some promise as a writer and who served frequently as an agent for the United States government in France. Sarah died on the fifth of May, 1909, in Paris. Warrington was in East Africa with Teddy Roosevelt's expedition, and Ethel was busy looking after her growing family in West Orange, New Jersey.

Though alone, Sarah died content. Her son was becoming the success she had always known he would be, and her daughter was happily married to a New York attorney. Moreover, she had put time and distance between herself and the southern society she both loved and hated, in the manner of the southern writers and intellectuals who "can't go home again," but who never get away. Her body was brought back to Charleston, and she was buried alongside the man she believed to be the most perfect human being she had ever known. Three years before her death, Sarah returned to her Confederate diary and added a postscript. The entry was dated January 27, 1906, and read, "Saturday. Thirty-two years ago today—only it was a Tuesday—1874, Jan. 27th—we were married. Nearly seventeen years I have been alone. My beloved is Mine, and I am His, and Love is stronger than Death."[20]

The other principal on that disastrous afternoon in March came to what many felt to be a fitting end. Though barred from the medical society, McDow continued to practice medicine among a clientele drawn chiefly from the black community. Not surprisingly, his wife and daughter left him shortly after the trial, and it was said that Sarah Dawson haunted him in the streets, "following him silently, pointing, until he committed suicide."[21] Though this tale of the doctor's end was not precise to fact, he did die under circumstances which suggested painful loneliness. On a Saturday evening in July, 1904, McDow retired to his room, placed a glass of water by his bed, and lay back to rest a moment. His body was not discovered until the following Tuesday when the foul odor of death had permeated the residence at 75 Rutledge Street.[22]

In the years which followed Captain Dawson's death there were more calls to raise a monument to his memory. N. G. Gonzales, by then founding editor of the Columbia *State*, became particularly insistent when Atlanta remembered Henry Grady with a statue in the very center of that busy metropolis. As late as 1951, William Watts Ball nominated four people whose lives and labors for South Carolina deserved monuments to their memory. Among the select four, Captain Francis Warrington Daw-

---

20. Sarah Morgan Dawson, *A Confederate Girl's Diary*, intro. Warrington Dawson, ed. James Irving Robertson, Jr., Civil War Centennial Series (Bloomington: Indiana University Press, 1960), p. 473.

21. Letter from Stuyvesant Barry to the author, February 12, 1974.

22. *News and Courier*, July 27, 1904.

son's name again appeared.[23] Despite all these calls to memorialize the founder and editor of the Charleston *News and Courier,* the only monument in Charleston today is an inconspicuous black granite cross in St. Lawrence cemetery. On this marker is the hero's name and a simple reminder that life is embraced by two dates.

---

23. Columbia *State,* October 26, 1891; and *News and Courier,* March 6, 1951.

Bibliography

I. Primary Sources

A. *Manuscripts*

Clemson University Library, Clemson, South Carolina.
  Clemson History File
Duke University Library, Durham, North Carolina.
  William Watts Ball Papers
  Ellison Capers Papers
  Daniel Henry Chamberlain Papers
  Francis Warrington Dawson, I and II, Papers
  Samuel Dibble Papers
  Wade Hampton Papers
  Hemphill Family Papers
  Louis Manigault Papers
  Thomas C. Perrin Papers
  William Dunlap Simpson Papers
  Josephus Woodruff Diary (copy)
Library of Congress, Washington, D.C.
  Thomas Francis Bayard Papers
  Benjamin Franklin Butler Papers
  Stephen Grover Cleveland Papers
  Wade Hampton Papers (Personal Miscellaneous File)
  Daniel S. Lamont Papers
  Morrison Remick Waite Papers
  William Collins Whitney Papers
South Carolina Department of Archives, Columbia, South Carolina.
  Executive Files: Letterbooks of Governors Wade Hampton, William Dunlap
  Simpson, Thomas B. Jeter, Johnson Hagood, Hugh Smith Thompson, John C.
  Sheppard, and John Peter Richardson
South Carolina Historical Society, Charleston, South Carolina.
  Joseph Walker Barnwell typescript reminiscence
  James Conner Papers
  Report of the Examination of the Body of Francis Warrington Dawson, by Dr.
  William Middleton Michel (Miscellaneous File)
South Caroliniana Library, University of South Carolina, Columbia, South Carolina.
  Milledge Luke Bonham Papers
  Matthew Calbraith Butler Papers
  William Ashmead Courtenay Papers
  Robert Means Davis Papers
  Francis Warrington Dawson Papers

Martin Witherspoon Gary Papers
Narciso Gener Gonzales Papers
Wade Hampton Papers
John Cheves Haskell Letter Book
Ellison Summerfield Keitt Papers
Charles Spencer McCall Papers
Benjamin Franklin Perry Papers
John S. Richardson Papers
William Dunlap Simpson Papers
Yates Snowden Papers
Hugh Smith Thompson Papers
Williams-Chesnut-Manning Papers
Southern Historical Collection, University of North Carolina, Chapel Hill, North
Carolina.
Raleigh Edward Colston Papers
Francis Warrington Dawson Papers
Elliott-Gonzales Papers
William Lawrence Mauldin Diary
William Porcher Miles Diary
James Lawrence Orr–William C. Patterson Papers
Francis Butler Simkins, notes on Benjamin Ryan Tillman
William Dunlap Simpson Papers
Daniel Augustus Tompkins Papers
Trenholm Family Papers

B. *Official Records and Documents*

Biographical Directory of the American Congress, 1774–1927. Washington: Gov-
ernment Printing Office, 1928.
Official Records of the Union and Confederate Navies in the War of the Rebellion.
Series I, vol. 1. Washington: 1884.
*Journal of the House of Representatives of the General Assembly of the State of
South Carolina,* 1874–1890.
Journal of the Senate of the General Assembly of the State of South Carolina,
1874–1890.
Reports and Resolutions of the General Assembly of the State of South Carolina,
1877–1878.
City of Charleston. *Year Book,* 1883, 1884, 1886, and 1887. Charleston: The News
and Courier Book Presses.
Records of Wills. Office of Judge of Probate, Charleston, South Carolina.

C. *Newspapers and Periodicals*

Abbeville *Medium,* 1876–1889 (broken)
Abbeville *Press and Banner,* 1876–1877
Atlanta *Constitution,* 1880–1889
Augusta *Chronicle and Constitutionalist,* 1876, 1886, and 1889
Camden *Journal,* September 17, 1868, and March 27, 1873

Camden *Kershaw Gazette*, 1874, 1876, 1879, and 1881 (broken)
Charleston *Courier*, 1867–1873
Charleston *Daily Republican*, 1870–1871 (broken)
Charleston *Journal of Commerce*, 1876–1878 (broken)
Charleston *Mercury*, 1868, and August 27, 1880
Charleston *News*, 1867–1873
Charleston *News and Courier*, 1873–1890
Charleston *New Era*, March 20, 1880
Cheraw *Carolina Sun*, August 11, 1881
Chester *Reporter*, August 5, 1881
Columbia *Daily Register*, 1876–1888 (broken)
Columbia *Daily Union*, January 10 and September 30, 1872, and March 13, 1874
Columbia *Palmetto Yeoman*, October 7, 1879, and April 2, 1883
Columbia *Phoenix*, 1867–1878 (broken)
Columbia *Reform Signal*, May 18, 1882
Darlington *News*, July 28, 1881, and August 16, 1883
Darlington *Democrat*, November 18, 1868
Edgefield *Advertiser*, 1872–1879 (broken)
Florence *Pioneer*, March 29, 1876
Greenville *Cotton Plant*, September, 1877
Greenville *Daily News*, February 21, 1878
Greenville and New York *Southern Herald and Working Man*, January 1, 1876
Laurensville *Herald*, March 5, 1869, May 4, 1877, May 27, 1881
Lexington *Dispatch*, August 3, 1881
Marion *Crescent*, December 16, 1868
The Nation (New York), 1876–1890
New York *Times*, 1874–1890
North American Review, 1876–1890
Orangeburg *Times*, 1872 (broken), and August 7, 1873
Spartanburg *Carolina Spartan*, 1876 (broken)
Yorkville *Enquirer*, 1864–1877 (broken)

D. Travel Accounts, Memoirs, Reports, and Miscellaneous Writings

Address of W. H. Wallace before the Wallace House Association, 1886.
   [University of North Carolina Library.]
*An Address to the People of the United States, Adopted at a Conference of Citizens
   Held at Columbia, South Carolina, July 20 and 21st, 1876.* Columbia: Republican
   Printing Company, 1876.
Allen, Walter. *Governor Chamberlain's Administration in South Carolina: A
   Chapter of Reconstruction in the Southern States.* New York: G. P. Putnam's
   Sons, 1888.
Bagby, George W. *The Old Virginia Gentlemen and Other Sketches.* Edited with an
   introduction by Thomas Nelson Page. New York: Charles Scribner's Sons, 1911.
Barry, Ethel Dawson. "Reminiscences." [Typescript copy in the possession of the
   author.]
Campbell, George. *White and Black: The Outcome of a Visit to the United States.*
   London: Chatto and Windus, 1879.

Capers, Henry Dickson. *The Life and Times of C. G. Memminger*. Richmond: Everett Waddey Company, 1893.

Cash, Ellerbe Bogan Crawford. *The Cash-Shannon Duel*. Appendix by Bessie Cash Irby. Boykin, South Carolina: 1930. First printed Greenville: The Daily News Job Printing Office, 1881.

The Centennial of Incorporation, 1783–1883. Charleston: The City of Charleston, 1883.

Chamberlain, Daniel Henry. "The Race Problem at the South." *New Englander* 52 (June, 1890), 507–27.

———. "Reconstruction and the Negro." *North American Review* (February, 1879), pp. 161–73.

Charleston Directory, 1866. Compiled by Burke and Roinest. New York: M. B. Brown and Company, 1866.

Charleston City Directory for 1867–68. Charleston: Jno Orrin Lea and Company, 1867.

Dawson, Francis Warrington. *Reminiscences of Confederate Service, 1861–1865*. Charleston: The News and Courier Book Presses, 1882.

Dawson, Sarah Morgan. *A Confederate Girl's Diary*. Introduction by Warrington Dawson. Boston: Houghton Mifflin Company, 1913.

———. *Idem*. Edited by James I. Robertson, Jr. Civil War Centennial Series. Bloomington: Indiana University Press, 1960.

De Forest, John William. *A Union Officer in the Reconstruction*. Edited with an introduction by James H. Croushore and David Morris Potter. New Haven: Yale University Press, 1948.

Delany, Martin Robison. *The Condition, Elevation, Emigration, and Destiny of the Colored People of the United States*. New York: Arno Press and *The New York Times*, 1968.

Dixon, William Hepworth. *White Conquest*. London: Chatto and Windus, 1876.

The Earthquake, 1886: The City Council of Charleston, South Carolina, to the Executive Relief Committee. Charleston, 1887. [University of North Carolina Library.]

1886: The Earthquake: Report of Executive Relief Committee 1887. Charleston: Lucas, Richardson and Company, 1887.

Gayarré, Charles. "The Southern Question." *North American Review* (November–December, 1877), pp. 472–98.

Hampton, Wade. *Free Men! Free Ballots!! Free Schools!!! The Pledges of General Wade Hampton, Democratic Candidate for Governor of the Colored People of South Carolina, 1865–1876*. Charleston: Charleston County Democratic Executive Committee, 1876. [Dawson pamphlets, University of North Carolina Library.]

———. "Negro Suffrage." *North American Review* (March, 1879), pp. 239–44.

———. "The Race Problem in the South." Extract from *Forum Extra*, 1 (March, 1890). [Dawson pamphlets, University of North Carolina Library.]

———. "What Negro Supremacy Means." *Forum*, 5 (June, 1888), 383–95.

Haygood, Atticus G. *Our Brother in Black: His Freedom and His Future*. New York: Phillips and Hunt, 1881.

Henley, S. W. *The Cash Family of South Carolina*. Wadesboro, North Carolina: Intelligencer Print, 1884.

Hogan, Edward. "South Carolina To-Day." *International Review* 8 (February, 1880), 105–19.

Holcombe, John W. and Hubert M. Skinner. *Life and Public Services of Thomas A. Hendricks with Selected Speeches and Writings*. Indianapolis: Carlon and Hollenbeck, 1886.

McClure, Alexander Kelly. *The South: Its Industrial, Financial, and Political Condition*. Philadelphia: Lippincott, 1886.

McKinley, Carlyle. *An Appeal to Pharaoh: The Negro Problem and Its Radical Solution*. New York: Fords, Howard, and Hulbert, 1890.

The Massacre of Six Colored Citizens of the United States at Hamburg, S. C., on July 4, 1876. Debate in the 44th Congress, 1st Session, 1875–1876, House of Representatives [University of North Carolina Library.]

Molloy, Robert. *An Afternoon in March*. New York: Doubleday and Company, 1958.

Morgan, James Morris. *Recollections of a Rebel Reefer*. Boston: Houghton Mifflin Company, 1917.

"Our Women in the War": The Lives They Lived, the Deaths They Died. Compiled from *The Weekly News and Courier*. Charleston: The *News and Courier* Book Presses, 1885.

"Pamphlets." 70 vols. Compiled by Francis Warrington Dawson. [A collection of reports, addresses, resolutions, and miscellaneous writings on all aspects of South Carolina life in the University of North Carolina Library.]

Perry, Benjamin Franklin. *Biographical Sketches of Eminent American Statesmen with Speeches, Addresses and Letters by Ex-Governor B. F. Perry*. Introduction by Wade Hampton. Philadelphia: Ferre Press, 1887.

——. *Reminiscences of Public Men*. Preface by Hext M. Perry. Philadelphia: John D. Avil and Company, 1883.

Porter, Anthony Toomer. *Led On! Step by Step: Scenes from Clerical, Military, and Plantation Life in the South, 1828–1898*. New York: G. P. Putnam's Sons, 1898.

Reeks, Joseph William. "A Catholic Soldier." *The Month: A Catholic Magazine and Review* 66 (1889), 273–78.

Ross, Fitzgerald. *Cities and Camps of the Confederate States*. Edited by Richard Barksdale Harwell. Urbana: University of Illinois Press, 1958.

Sorrel, General G. Moxley. *Recollections of a Confederate Staff Officer*. Edited by Bell Irvin Wiley. Jackson, Tennessee: McCowat-Mercer Press, 1958.

South Carolina in 1884. Charleston: *News and Courier*, 1884.

South Carolina in 1888. Charleston: Walker, Evans, and Cogswell, 1888.

The South Carolina State Gazetteer and Business Directory for 1880–81. Compiled by R. A. Smith. Charleston: 1880.

A South Carolinian. [Belton O'Neall Townsend.] "The Political Condition of South Carolina." *Atlantic Monthly* (February, 1877), pp. 177–94.

——. "South Carolina Morals." *Atlantic Monthly* (February, 1877), pp. 467–75.

——. "South Carolina Society." *Atlantic Monthly* (June, 1877), pp. 670–84.

Towne, Laura Matilda. *Letters and Diary of Laura M. Towne, Written from the Sea Islands of South Carolina, 1862–1884*. Edited by Rupert Sargent Holland. Cambridge: Riverside Press, 1912.

Trescott, William Henry. "The Southern Question." *North American Review* (October, 1876), pp. 249–80.

Warner, Charles Dudley. *Studies in the South and West with Comments on Canada.*
New York: Harper and Brothers, 1889.

II. Secondary Sources

A. General Works and Special Studies

Abbott, Martin. *The Freedmen's Bureau in South Carolina, 1865–1872.* Chapel
Hill: University of North Carolina Press, 1967.
Alderman, Edwin Anderson and Joel Chandler Harris, ed. *Library of Southern
Literature,* vol. 3. Atlanta: Martin and Hoyt, 1909.
Ball, William Watts. *An Episode in South Carolina Politics,* 1915 [University of
North Carolina Library.]
———. *The State that Forgot: South Carolina's Surrender to Democrary.* Indianapo-
lis: Bobbs-Merrill Company, 1932.
Barnard, Harry. *Rutherford B. Hayes and His America.* Indianapolis: Bobbs-Mer-
rill Company, 1954.
Barry, Stuyvesant. "F. W. Dawson and The Charleston *News and Courier.* "
Senior thesis, Harvard University, 1931.
Bleser, Carol K. Rothrock. *The Promised Land: The History of the South Carolina
Land Commission, 1869–1890.* Columbia: University of South Carolina Press,
1969.
Blodgett, Geoffrey Thomas. *The Gentle Reformers: Massachusetts Democrats in
the Cleveland Era.* Cambridge: Harvard University Press, 1966.
Bond, O. J. *The Story of the Citadel.* Richmond: Garrett and Massie, 1936.
Brooks, U. R. *South Carolina Bench and Bar,* vol. 1. Columbia: The State Co.,
1908.
Clark, Ernest Culpepper. "The Response to Urbanism in Henry W. Grady's New
South." Master's thesis, Emory University, 1968.
Clark, Thomas Dionysius, ed. *Travels in the New South: A Bibliography.* vol. 1,
The Postwar South, 1865–1900: An Era of Reconstruction and Readjustment.
Norman: University of Oklahoma Press, 1962.
Clay, Howard Bunyan. "Daniel Augustus Tompkins: An American Bourbon."
Ph.D. dissertation, University of North Carolina, 1950.
Cooper, William James, Jr. *The Conservative Regime: South Carolina, 1877–1890.*
Johns Hopkins University Studies in Historical and Political Science, series 86,
no. 1. Baltimore: Johns Hopkins Press, 1968.
Dabney, Virginius. *Liberalism in the South.* Chapel Hill: University of North
Carolina Press, 1932.
Daly, Louise Porter Haskell. *Alexander Cheves Haskell: The Portrait of a Man.*
Norwood, Massachusetts: Plimpton Press, 1934.
Daniel, Robert Norman. *Furman University: A History.* Greenville: Furman
University, 1951.
Daniels, Jonathan. *They Will Be Heard: America's Crusading Newspaper Editors.*
New York: McGraw Hill Book Co., 1965.
Davis, Mary Katherine. "Sarah Morgan Dawson: A Renunciation of Southern
Society." Master's thesis, University of North Carolina, 1970.

Dawson, Francis Warrintgon, Jr., *Le Nègre Aux États-Unis*. Paris: E. Guilmoto, 1912.

De Leon, Thomas Cooper. *Belles, Beaux and Brains of the 60's*. New York: G. W. Dillingham Co., 1909.

Derrick, Samual Melancthon. *Centennial History of the South Carolina Railroad*. Columbia: The State Company, 1930.

Easterby, James Harold. *A History of the College of Charleston: Founded 1770*. The Scribner Press, 1935.

Frederickson, George M. *The Black Image in the White Mind: The Debate on Afro-American Character and Destiny, 1817–1914*. New York: Harper and Row, 1971.

Garlington, J. C. *Men of the Time: Sketches of Living Notables. A Biographical Encyclopedia of Contemporaneous South Carolina Leaders*. Spartanburg: Garlington Publishing Co., 1902.

Gaston, Paul Morton. *The New South Creed: A Study in Southern Mythmaking*. New York: Alfred A. Knopf, 1970.

Goldman, Eric Frederick. *Rendezvous with Destiny: A History of Modern American Reform*. New York: Alfred A. Knopf, 1952.

Goodrich, Carter. *Government Promotion of American Canals and Railroads, 1800–1890*. New York: Columbia University Press, 1960.

Green, Edwin L. *A History of the University of South Carolina*. Columbia: The State Co., 1916.

Harrigan, Anthony, ed. *The Editor and the Republic: Papers and Addresses of William Watts Ball*. Chapel Hill: University of North Carolina Press, 1954.

Hemphill, James C., ed. *Men of Mark in South Carolina*. 4 vols. Washington: Men of Mark Publishing Co., 1907.

Hendrick, Burton Jesse. *The Life and Letters of Walter H. Page*, vol. 1. New York: Doubleday, Page and Co., 1922.

Hesseltine, William Best. *Civil War Prisons: A Study in War Psychology*. New York: Frederick Ungar Publishing Co., 1958.

——. *Confederate Leaders in the New South*. Baton Rouge: Louisiana State University Press, 1950.

Hirsch, Mark David. *William C. Whitney: Modern Warwick*. New York: Dodd, Mead and Company, 1948.

Hirshson, Stanley P. *Farewell to the Bloody Shirt: Northern Republicans and the Southern Negro, 1877–1893*. Bloomington: Indiana University Press, 1962.

Hofstadter, Richard. *The Age of Reform: From Bryan to F.D.R.* New York: Alfred A. Knopf, 1955.

Hollis, Daniel Walker. *University of South Carolina*. vol. 2, *College to University*. Columbia: University of South Carolina Press, 1956.

Hollis, John Porter. *The Early Period of Reconstruction in South Carolina*. Johns Hopkins University Studies in Historical and Political Science, series 23, nos. 1–2. Baltimore: Johns Hopkins Press, 1905.

Holt, Thomas C. *Black over White: Negro Political Leadership in South Carolina during Reconstruction*. Blacks in the New World. Urbana: University of Illinois Press, 1977.

Hoole, W. Stanley. *Vizitelly Covers the Confederacy*. Confederate Centennial Studies, no. 4. Tuscaloosa: Confederate Publishing Co., 1957.

Jarrell, Hampton McNeely. *Wade Hampton and the Negro: The Road Not Taken.* Columbia: University of South Carolina Press, 1949.

Johnson, Guion Griffis. "The Ideology of White Supremacy, 1876–1910." In Fletcher Melvin Green, ed., *Essays in Southern History.* The James Sprunt Studies in History and Political Science, University of North Carolina, vol. 31. Chapel Hill: University of North Carolina Press, 1949.

Jones, Katherine M. *Heroines of Dixie.* New York: Bobbs-Merrill Company, 1955.

Jones, Lewis Pinckney. *Stormy Petrel: N. G. Gonzales and His State.* Columbia: University of South Carolina Press, 1973.

Jordan, Frank E., Jr. *The Primary State: A History of the Democratic Party in South Carolina, 1876–1962,* 1966.

Jordan, Winthrop Donaldson. *White Over Black: American Attitudes Toward the Negro, 1550–1812.* Chapel Hill: University of North Carolina Press, 1968.

Kelley, Robert Lloyd. *The Transatlantic Persuasion: The Liberal-Democratic Mind in the Age of Gladstone.* New York: Alfred A. Knopf, 1969.

Kelly, Barbara LaLance. "The Redemption of South Carolina: 1875–76." Master's thesis, University of North Carolina, 1972.

King, William L. *The Newspaper Press of Charleston, South Carolina.* Charleston: Edward Perry, 1872.

Klein, Maury. *The Great Richmond Terminal: A Study in Businessmen and Business Strategy.* Charlottesville: University Press of Virginia, 1970.

Lambert, John Ralph. *Arthur Pue Gorman.* Southern Biography Series, edited by Thomas Harry Williams. Baton Rouge: Louisiana State University Press, 1953.

Lamson, Peggy. *The Glorious Failure: Black Congressman Robert Brown Elliott and the Reconstruction in South Carolina.* New York: W. W. Norton and Company, 1973.

Latimer, S. L., Jr. *The Story of the State, 1891–1969, and The Gonzales Brothers.* Columbia: The State Printing Company, 1970.

Logan, Samuel Frank. "Francis W. Dawson. 1840–1889: South Carolina Editor." Master's thesis, Duke University, 1947.

Lonn, Ella. *Foreigners in the Confederacy.* Chapel Hill: University of North Carolina Press, 1940.

McCloskey, Robert Green. *American Conservatism in the Age of Enterprise, 1865–1910.* Cambridge: Harvard University Press, 1951.

McCrady, Edward, Jr., and Samuel A. Ashe. *Cyclopedia of Eminent and Representative Men of the Carolinas of the Nineteenth Century,* vol. 1. Madison, Wisconsin: Brant and Fuller, 1892.

Maddex, Jack Pendleton, Jr. *The Virginia Conservatives, 1867–1879: A Study in Reconstruction Politics.* Chapel Hill: University of North Carolina Press, 1970.

Magrath, C. Peter. *Morrison R. Waite: The Triumph of Character.* New York: Macmillan Company, 1963.

Matthews, Linda Hardy McCarter. "N. G. Gonzales: Southern Editor and Crusader, 1858–1903." Ph.D. dissertation, Duke University, 1971.

Miller, Perry Gilbert Eddy, ed. *American Thought: Civil War to World War I.* New York: Holt, Rinehart and Winston, 1954.

Mitchell, Broadus. *The Rise of the Cotton Mills in the South.* Baltimore: Johns Hopkins Press, 1921.

Molloy, Robert. *Charleston: A Gracious Heritage.* New York: Appleton-Century Co., 1947.

Morgan, H. Wayne. *From Hayes to McKinley: National Party Politics, 1877–1896.* Syracuse: Syracuse University Press, 1969.

Mullen, Harris H. *The Cash-Shannon Duel.* Tampa, Florida: Trend House, 1963.

Myrdal, Gunnar. *An American Dilemma: The Negro Problem and Modern Democracy.* New York: Harper and Brothers, 1944.

Neal, Diane. "Benjamin Ryan Tillman: The South Carolina Years, 1847–1894." Ph.D. dissertation, Kent State University, 1976.

Nevins, Allan. *Grover Cleveland: A Study in Courage.* New York: Dodd, Mead and Company, 1933.

Nixon, Raymond Blalock. *Henry W. Grady: Spokesman of the New South.* New York: Alfred A. Knopf, 1943.

Parks, Edd Winnfield, ed. *Southern Poets.* American Writers Series, ed. H. H. Clark. New York: American Book Company, 1936.

Patton, James Welch. "The Republican Party in South Carolina, 1876–1895." In Fletcher Melvin Green, ed., *Essays in Southern History.* The James Sprunt Studies in History and Political Science, University of North Carolina, vol. 31. Chapel Hill: University of North Carolina Press, 1949.

Peck, Thomas K. "The Killing of Captain Dawson—1889." In Beatrice St. Julien Ravenel, ed., *Charleston Murders.* New York: Duell, Sloan and Pearce, 1947.

Pike, James Shepherd. *The Prostrate State: South Carolina Under Negro Government.* Edited with an introduction by Robert F. Durden. New York: Harper and Row, 1968.

Randall, Dale Bertrand Jonas. *Joseph Conrad and Warrington Dawson: The Record of a Friendship.* Durham: Duke University Press, 1968.

Ravenel, Beatrice St. Julien. *Charleston: The Place and the People.* New York: Macmillan Company, 1906.

Rhett, Robert Goodwyn. *Charleston: An Epic of Carolina.* Richmond: Garrett and Massie, 1940.

Rogers, George Calvin, Jr. *Charleston in the Age of the Pinckneys.* The Centers of Civilization Series. Norman: University of Oklahoma Press, 1969.

Roper, John H. "The Radical Mission: The University of South Carolina in Reconstruction." Master's thesis, University of North Carolina, 1973.

Rose, Willie Lee. *Rehearsal for Reconstruction: The Port Royal Experiment.* Introduction by Comer Vann Woodward. Indianapolis: Bobbs-Merrill Company, 1964.

Ross, Earle Dudley. *The Liberal Republican Movement.* New York: Henry Holt and Company, 1919.

Sanders, Albert Neely. "The South Carolina Railroad Commission, 1878–1895." Master's thesis, University of North Carolina, 1948.

Sanger, Donald Bridgman and Thomas Robson Hay. *James Longstreet.* Baton Rouge: Louisiana State University Press, 1952.

Sass, Herbert Ravenel. *Outspoken: 150 Years of The News and Courier.* Columbia: University of South Carolina Press, 1953.

Scharf, J. Thomas. *History of the Confederate States Navy from Its Organization to the Surrender of Its Last Vessel.* New York: Rogers and Sherwood, 1887.

Scott, Anne Firor. *The Southern Lady: From Pedestal to Politics.* Chicago: University of Chicago Press, 1970.

Sheppard, William Arthur. *Red Shirts Remembered: Southern Brigadiers of the Reconstruction Period.* Atlanta: Ruralist Press, 1940.

Simkins, Francis Butler. *Pitchfork Ben Tillman: South Carolinian.* Southern Biography Series, edited by Fred C. Cole and Wendell Holmes Stephenson. Baton Rouge: Louisiana State University Press, 1944.

———. *The Tillman Movement in South Carolina.* Durham: Duke University Press, 1926.

———, and Robert Hilliard Woody. *South Carolina during Reconstruction.* Chapel Hill: University of North Carolina Press, 1932.

Snowden, Yates. *History of South Carolina.* 5 vols. Chicago: Lewis Publishing Company, 1920.

Sproat, John Gerald. *The Best Men: Liberal Reformers in the Gilded Age.* New York: Oxford University Press, 1968.

Stark, John D. *Damned Upcountryman: William Watts Ball. A Study in American Conservatism.* Durham: Duke University Press, 1968.

Stony, Samuel Gaillard. *This Is Charleston.* Charleston: Carolina Art Association, 1944.

Stover, John Ford. *The Railroads of the South, 1865–1900: A Study in Finance and Control.* Chapel Hill: University of North Carolina Press, 1955.

Tansill, Charles Callan. *The Congressional Career of Thomas Francis Bayard, 1869–1889.* Georgetown University Studies in History, no. 1. Washington: Georgetown University Press, 1946.

Taylor, Alrutheus Ambush. *The Negro in South Carolina During Reconstruction.* Washington: Association for the Study of Negro Life and History, 1924.

Thompson, Henry Tazewell. *Ousting the Carpetbagger from South Carolina.* Columbia: R. L. Bryan Company, 1926.

Tindall, George Brown. "The Central Theme Revisited." In Charles Grier Sellers, Jr., ed., *The Southerner As American.* Chapel Hill: University of North Carolina Press, 1960.

———. *South Carolina Negroes, 1877–1900.* Columbia: University of South Carolina Press, 1952.

Turnbull, Robert J. *Bibliography of South Carolina, 1563–1950.* 5 vols. Charlottesville: University Press of Virginia, 1956.

Wallace, David Duncan. *The History of South Carolina.* vol. 3. New York: The American Historical Society, 1934.

Wauchope, George Armstrong. *The Writers of South Carolina.* Columbia: The State Company, 1910.

Way, William. *History of the New England Society of Charleston, South Carolina, for One Hundred Years, 1819–1919.* Charleston: New England Society, 1920.

Webster, Laura Josephine. *The Operation of the Freedmen's Bureau in South Carolina.* Smith College Studies, vol. 1, no. 2. Northampton: Department of History of Smith College, 1916.

White, Laura Amanda. *Robert Barnwell Rhett: Father of Secession.* New York: Century Company, 1931.

Wiebe, Robert Huddleston. *The Search for Order, 1877–1920.* The Making of America, edited by David Donald. New York: Hill and Wang, 1967.

Williams, Alfred Brockenbrough. *Hampton and His Red Shirts: South Carolina's Deliverance in 1876.* Charleston: Walker, Evans and Cogswell, 1935.

Williams, Charles Braxton. "Francis Warrington Dawson: Editor, *The Charleston News and Courier.* " Master's thesis, University of South Carolina, 1926.

Williamson, Joel. *After Slavery: The Negro in South Carolina During Reconstruction, 1861–1877.* Chapel Hill: University of North Carolina Press, 1965.

Wilson, Edmund. *Patriotic Gore: Studies in the Literature of the American Civil War.* New York: Oxford University Press, 1962.

Wolff, Robert Paul, Barrington Moore, Jr., and Herbert Marcuse. *A Critique of Pure Tolerance.* Boston: Beacon Press, 1965.

Woodward, C. Vann. *Origins of the New South, 1877–1913.* vol. 9. A History of the South, edited by Wendell Holmes Stephenson and Ellis Merton Coulter. 10 vols. Baton Rouge: Louisiana State University Press, 1951.

——. *Reunion and Reaction: The Compromise of 1877 and the End of Reconstruction.* Boston: Little, Brown and Company, 1966.

——. *The Strange Career of Jim Crow.* New York: Oxford University Press, 1966.

Woody, Robert Hilliard. *Republican Newspapers of South Carolina.* Southern Sketches, edited by J. D. Eggleston. Series I, no. 10. Charlottesville: Historical Publishing Company, 1936.

B. Periodical Articles

Abbott, Martin. "The Freedman's Bureau and Negro Schooling in South Carolina." *South Carolina Historical Magazine* 57 (1956), 65–81.

——, ed. "James L. Orr on Congressional Reconstruction." *South Carolina Historical Magazine* 54 (1953), 141–55.

Clark, Ernest Culpepper. "Henry Grady's New South: A Rebuttal from Charleston." *The Southern Speech Communication Journal* 41 (Summer, 1976), 346–58.

——. "Sarah Morgan and Francis Dawson: Raising the Woman Question in Reconstruction South Carolina." *South Carolina Historical Magazine* 81 (January, 1980), 8–23.

Clark, Thomas Dionysius. "The Country Newspaper: A Factor in Southern Opinion, 1865–1930." *Journal of Southern History* 14 (February, 1948), 3–33.

Clendenen, Clarence C. "President Hayes' 'Withdrawal' of the Troops—An Enduring Myth." *South Carolina Historical Magazine* 70 (1969), 240–50.

De Santis, Vincent P. "President Hayes's Southern Policy." *Journal of Southern History* 21 (November, 1955), 476–94.

Douglas, W. Ernest. "Retreat from Conservatism." *Proceedings of the South Carolina Historical Association* 28 (1958), 3–11.

Dubose, William Porcher and B. J. Ramage. "Wade Hampton." *Sewanee Review Quarterly* 10 (July, 1902), 364–73.

Durden, Robert Franklin. "The Ambiguous Antislavery Crusade of James S. Pike." *South Carolina Historical Magazine* 56 (1955), 187–95.

Easterby, James Harold. "The Granger Movement in South Carolina." *Proceedings of the South Carolina Historical Association* 1 (1931), 21–32.

Goodrich, Carter. "American Development Policy: The Case of Internal Improvements." *Journal of Economic History* 16 (December, 1956), 449–60.

——. "Local Government Planning of Internal Improvements." *Political Science Quarterly* 66 (September, 1951), 411–45.

——. "Public Spirit and American Improvements." *Proceedings of the Philosophical Society* 92 (1948), 305–9.

——. "The Revulsion against Internal Improvements." *Journal of Economic History* 10 (November, 1950), 145–69.

Holmes, Henry Schulz, comp. "The Trenholm Family." *South Carolina Historical and Genealogical Magazine* 16 (1915), 151–63.

Hornon, Joseph M., Jr. "British Sympathies in the American Civil War: A Reconsideration." *Journal of Southern History* 33 (August, 1967), 356–67.

Jones, Lewis Pinckney. "Ambrosio José Gonzales, A Cuban Patriot in Carolina." *South Carolina Historical Magazine* 56 (1955), 67–84.

——. "Two Roads Tried—And One Detour." *South Carolina Historical Magazine* 79 (1978), 206–18.

Jones, Newton B. "The Washington Light Infantry at the Bunker Hill Centennial." *South Carolina Historical Magazine* 65 (1964), 195–204.

Lander, Ernest M., Jr. "Charleston: Manufacturing Center of the Old South." *Journal of Southern History* 26 (August, 1960), 330–51.

Logan, Samuel Frank. "Francis Warrington Dawson, 1840–1889: South Carolina Editor." *Proceedings of the South Carolina Historical Association* 22 (1952), 13–28.

Mabry, William Alexander. "Ben Tillman Disfranchised the Negro." *South Atlantic Quarterly* 37 (April, 1938), 170–83.

Macaulay, Neill Webster, Jr. "South Carolina Reconstruction Historiography." *South Carolina Historical Magazine* 65 (1964), 20–32.

McLaurin, Melton A. "Early Labor Union Organizational Efforts in South Carolina Cotton Mills, 1880–1905." *South Carolina Historical Magazine* 72 (1971), 44–80.

Marcus, Robert D. "Wendell Phillips and American Institutions." *Journal of American History* 56 (June, 1969), 41–58.

Morgan, Edmund Sears. "Slavery and Freedom: The American Paradox." *Journal of American History* 59 (June, 1972), 5–29.

Mouzon, Harold A. "The Carolina Art Association: Its First Hundred Years." *South Carolina Historical Magazine* 59 (1958), 125–38.

Mullen, Harris H. "Make . . . Arrangements for a Hostile Meeting." *South Carolina History Illustrated* 1 (May, 1970), 26–31, 62–63.

Nielsen, J. V., Jr. "Post-Confederate Finance in South Carolina." *South Carolina Historical Magazine* 56 (1955), 85–114.

Redkey, Edwin Storer. "Bishop Turner's African Dream." *Journal of American History* 54 (September, 1967), 271–90.

Sanders, Albert Neely. "Jim Crow Comes to South Carolina." *Proceedings of the South Carolina Historical Association* 36 (1966), 27–39.

Scroggs, Jack Benton. "Carpetbagger Constitutional Reform in the South Atlantic States, 1867–1868." *Journal of Southern History* 27 (November, 1961), 475–93.

——. "Southern Reconstruction: A Radical View." *Journal of Southern History* 24 (November, 1958), 407–29.

Simkins, Francis Butler. "Ben Tillman's View of the Negro." *Journal of Southern History* 3 (May, 1937), 161–74.

——. "The Election of 1876 in South Carolina." *South Atlantic Quarterly* 21 (October, 1922), 335–51.

———. "Race Legislation in South Carolina Since 1865. Part II, 1869 and After." *South Atlantic Quarterly* 20 (April, 1921), 165–77.

Tindall, George Brown. "The Campaign for the Disfranchisement of Negroes in South Carolina." *Journal of Southern History* 15 (May, 1949), 212–34.

———. "The Liberian Exodus of 1878." *South Carolina Historical and Genealogical Magazine* 53 (1952), 133–45.

Tischendorf, Alfred P. "A Note on British Enterprise in South Carolina, 1872–1886." *South Carolina Historical Magazine* 56 (1956), 196–99.

Williams, Jack Kenny. "The Code of Honor in Ante-Bellum South Carolina." *South Carolina Historical Magazine* 56 (1953), 113–28.

Woody, Robert Hilliard. "Behind the Scenes in the Reconstruction Legislature of South Carolina: Diary of Josephus Woodruff." *Journal of Southern History* 2 (February, 1936), 78–102, and 2 (May, 1936), 233–59.

Index

Francis Warrington Dawson
and the Politics of Restoration
was keyboarded for electronic scanner
by Connie Farr
and set on the Merganthaler Linotron 606
in Clarendon and Times Roman
by Akra Data, Inc., Birmingham, Alabama.
The printer was Thomson-Shore, Inc.,
Dexter, Michigan,
and the binder was John H. Dekker and Sons,
Grand Rapids, Michigan.

Book design: Anna F. Jacobs
Production: Paul R. Kennedy